Cold
Warriors

Cold Warriors

Manliness on Trial in the Rhetoric of the West

Suzanne Clark

Southern Illinois University Press
Carbondale and Edwardsville

Library of Congress Cataloging-in-Publication Data

Clark, Suzanne.
    Cold warriors : manliness on trial in the rhetoric of the West / Suzanne Clark.
        p. cm.
    Includes bibliographical references (p.) and index.
    1. American literature—20th century—History and criticism. 2. Men in lit-
erature. 3. Literature and society—United States—History—20th century. 4. National characteristics, American, in literature. 5. World War, 1939–1945—Literature and the war. 6. Rhetoric—Political aspects—United States. 7. Gender
identity in literature. 8. World politics in literature. 9. Masculinity in literature.
10. Cold War in literature. 11. Soldiers in literature. I. Title.
PS173.M36C57 2000
810.9'353—dc21   99-39120
ISBN 0-8093-2302-8 (cloth : alk. paper)   CIP

The paper used in this publication meets the minimum requirements of American National Standard for Information Sciences—Permanence of Paper for
Printed Library Materials, ANSI Z39.48-1992. ∞

For Opal R. and Robert D. Clark

Contents

Preface

Cold Warriors **began with my realization,** after I'd finished a book about the earlier gendering of literary history, *Sentimental Modernism,* that the invisibility of women writers during the Cold War was related to anti-communism. Its demonizing rhetoric made scapegoats but also supported a logic of rational exclusion that I call "national realism." Hemingway seemed at first to me, as to other feminists, the very avatar of a masculinist domination, but as I looked at his fate during the Cold War more closely, I came to see that male gendering as well was demonized by the critics. This complicated my story. During work on Bernard Malamud's *A New Life* and the banality of the Cold War academy, I came accidentally to discover the story of a faculty firing and the persecution of scientists that Malamud knew. It became ever clearer that Cold War policies linked literature, science, and national politics together with gender issues in ways that were complex and reverberating, that had much to do with how the demonized "other" could be represented. The reliance of Cold War ideology upon ideas of the West supported by the genres of the Western has recently been widely discussed by cultural historians. This led me to think about women writers who allied themselves with the Western's "other," with Native American cultures as a site of resistance to the cowboys in charge. Mari Sandoz wrote hybrid narratives of the frontier, especially of Native Americans. But even though she is a precursor to postmodern writing and perhaps to identity politics, she wrote under a regime of national realism so dominant that it enforced resistance to hybridity and mixed forms. Ursula Le Guin's writing marks the emergence from a pre-Vietnam Cold War culture that could impose modernist logic. She challenged the "Great Divide" into high culture and (feminized) mass culture with her science fiction and fantasy. I think her work has much to teach us about how that transition worked, about what can change in the way we think of gender and heroes, and even about how militarism could invent and enforce what may be called real.

My debts are many. My research has been supported by a Summer Research Grant from the University of Oregon to work on Bernard Malamud; another Summer Research Grant to write the chapter on Ernest Hemingway; a Research Fellowship from the Center for the Study of

Women and Society at the University of Oregon to write about Ursula Le Guin; and a sabbatical granted by the English department and the University of Oregon during which I was able to begin much of this project's work. The Oregon Council of the Humanities provided a fellowship for work on Bernard Malamud.

I have been able to benefit from the Special Collections of the Oregon State University Library's Malamud materials, and—most especially—their extraordinary collection of Linus Pauling's papers. I thank in particular Cliff Mead, Special Collections Librarian, for his extensive help with these, and Ramesh S. Krishnamurthy. The Oregon State University Archives were extremely helpful as well, providing me microfilm readers and well-organized access to President Strand's files on the Spitzer case. The University of Nebraska library was the source of materials in Mari Sandoz's archives, and they made my work easy and pleasant. I thank as well the Nebraska Historical Society for their assistance. I was fortunate to benefit, before he died recently, from the expertise of Charles Mann, Special Collections Librarian of the Pattee Library at Pennsylvania State University, who brought to my attention evidence the Cold War abrogated scholarship, such as that of Fred Pattee, that included women writers.

I am especially grateful to Ursula Le Guin, whose extensive responses to my chapter on her work manifested a truly generous spirit. Ann Malamud graciously spent hours with me answering questions about her husband and about her own experiences in the Corvallis, Oregon of the fifties; I cannot thank her enough for her kindness. The English department at Oregon State University has an enduring interest in Bernard Malamud and has helped me again and again. I thank in particular Chester Garrison (who first started me on the path of research on Malamud), James Groshong, Ed Smith, Bill Potts, Faith Norris, Nelson Sandgren, and all others who were willing to be interviewed by me. The encouragement of Oregon State University faculty David Robinson, Michael Oriard, Kerry Ahearn, Jon Lewis, and Robert Schwartz has made all the difference. Jon Lewis's careful reading of chapter 4 was enormously helpful. Thanks to Nancy Armstrong, both for giving me the courage to do a book on the fifties, and for her long-term support of my work.

Russell Reising invited me to present an early draft of the work on Hemingway at the Toledo Conference on the Cold War; the chance to interact with others working on this period was invaluable, and I thank them all, particularly Jamie Barlowe. I thank the English department of Pennsylvania State University for inviting me to give a talk about this project at an early stage. Their interested responses both gave me fortitude and shaped me up. Michael Reynolds generously shared ideas about the Cold War Hemingway. Richard Stein and Nathaniel Teich reviewed the manuscript and urged me on. My colleague, Shari Huhndorf, gave me an extremely valuable reading of the Mari Sandoz chapter after I imagined it was finished; I was able to rethink several points in it as a result. I hope these helpful readers will not think their time was ill spent.

Thanks to editors who have worked with me at Southern Illinois University Press: Tracy Sobol (who often encouraged me with her interest in the manuscript), John Gehner, Karl Kageff, and Carol Burns.

I have leaned on my friends again and again during this project. To Lisa Ede, who has not only had faith that this book was worth writing but also shown me how to get writing done, I owe more than I can record. To Cheryl Glenn, who has always welcomed my desires to have her listen, and furnished dinner on occasion besides, I owe reciprocal hospitality of mind and house. To Linda Kintz, who has with grace endured multiple panel presentations on the theory and practice of the Real, who has shown me how a news junkie can nevertheless be a productive scholar, who has steadfastly shared an interest in Julia Kristeva, I wish the one thing I know she lacks: more sun. To my family—Laurie, Gary, Ginny, Roger, Robert, Roxanne, Elizabeth, Margaret, Catherine, Darrell, and my father, Robert Clark—I owe much for the hours stolen away from duties and from family relationships and for their loving tolerance of neglect.

To Sandra Spanier, who has read and/or listened to all of this more than anyone should, who has helped me out in innumerable ways—including the help of putting me up in Nebraska and Pennsylvania alike, who has been the best of friends through each and every chapter, I must give much more than thanks—a promise to go on to new conversations.

For permission to quote certain material, I gratefully acknowledge the following:

From his unpublished letters to Linus Pauling (Apr. 22, 1945; Feb. 9, 1949), permission granted by Ralph Spitzer.

From an unpublished 1967 lecture by Bernard Malamud and a letter by Malamud to Theodore Solotaroff (Feb. 21, 1962), permission granted by Ann D. Malamud.

From letters by Linus B. Pauling to Ralph Spitzer (Sept. 26, 1945), Milton Burton (Feb. 28, 1949), and A. L. Strand (Mar. 1, 1949). Courtesy of the Ava Helen and Linus Pauling Papers, Oregon State University.

Cold Warriors

Introduction: The Frontier Rhetoric of the Cold War and the Crisis of Manliness

A cowboy will not submit tamely to an insult, and is ever ready to avenge his own wrongs; nor has he an overwrought fear of shedding blood. He possesses, in fact, few of the emasculated, milk-and-water moralities admired by the pseudo-philanthropists; but he does possess, to a very high degree, the stern, manly qualities that are invaluable to a nation. . . .

In our dealings with the Indians we have erred quite as often through sentimentality as through willful wrong-doing.

—Theodore Roosevelt, *Ranch Life and the Hunting Trail*

Under the double authority of political and moral realism, the Cold Warrior of the West was at once universal and yet specifically linked to the stories of the American frontier. The ideological extremity of the Cold Warrior, whose identity was purified of communism and totalitarianism— but also of gender, race, color, sexuality, or class—was invisible. What helped to keep it invisible was the visibility of a historical—Western—manliness recuperated from the American past, attacked by liberals, and yet undergirding the claims of American nationalism.

This study of the Cold Warrior returns to the strange combination of forces that conspired to suppress dissent and hybridity in the name of a nationalized West after World War II. Anticommunism diverted attention from a more widespread suppression. The Cold War silenced women writers on several levels, together with others excluded from the struggle over white male identity—men as well as women. Manliness itself, and the old warrior ethic it invoked, was on trial. The return from World War II plunged American men into a confusion about identities that literature as well as mass culture struggled to address.

Studies of Cold War cultural history have begun to consider these changing constructions of maleness. Frank Krutnik's *In a Lonely Street* studies the way hybrid crime films emerged into the "tough" thrillers of film noir after the war, in response to the tensions and the necessity of redefining masculine identity. Susan Jeffords's studies of the Vietnam war, in *The Remasculinization of America* and *Hard Bodies*, elucidate what happened later in the Cold War, after the shifting relationships to a changing patriarchal culture generated a new, overt connection between male gendering and ideas of the nation, a "remasculinization." David Savran's reading of Arthur Miller and Tennessee Williams, *Communists, Cowboys, and Queers,* opens up a critical perspective on the repressive and hegemonic gender culture that emerged with the Cold War, as well as the possibilities for change that can be located in Cold War writing. And Steven Cohan, in *Masked Men*, has argued that, since gender is always performative (in the Judith Butler sense), the movies of the fifties can reveal the struggle over differences in cultural masculinity even though the Cold War culture thought of gender as much more stable than it in fact was.[1] I too take Judith Butler's argument to heart, and I too seek to notice the struggles over male gender in texts that did not seem to challenge cultural manliness. Her idea is that representation enacts (through repetition) the apparent stabilities of gender and heterosexuality. Our understanding of sexuality and gender even at the level of the body can undergo historical challenge—and change. Nevertheless, studies of maleness during the Cold War such as these, with their emphasis on film and drama, interestingly suggest that the performativity of gender is less visible in genres that are less obviously theatrical. And I am especially interested in the Cold War moments when manliness performs both powerfully and invisibly.[2]

There is another problem with the study of manliness that I view as very important. During the Cold War, gender issues were not separate from issues of national identity and were intertwined with the virulence of anticommunism in ways that continue to influence our reading of male and female writers during the Cold War. This study aims to examine the intersection of the struggle over manliness with the claims—not just in literature, but in policy—that national identity was the only nonideology; a true/real (male) locus for power. The realism of the military West rested upon the gendered mythology of an American West at the site of the hero, the warrior—the one who is necessarily silent about his mastery.

At the same time that defining national/individual/American identity in the Cold War involved a brand new configuration of cultural history, it called upon the nostalgia for the old discourses of the West (the national manliness asserted by Theodore Roosevelt) to claim that there was and always had been only one real American identity. The strength of this unanimity depended not upon agreement but upon tension: American history became the singular force arrayed against the feminized threat of communism. Women were not silent and not in agreement, as we can see by the examples of women writers themselves, many of them successful in middlebrow nonfiction as well as fiction, and in mainstream but nonliterary genres, from children's writing to biography to science fiction—Mari Sandoz and Ursula Le Guin, for example. But male writers subverted the claims of national identity as well, at some risk of finding themselves outside the boundaries not only of public rhetoric, but also of the literary: men as different from one another as the determinedly masculine Ernest Hemingway and the antiheroic storyteller of the everyday, Bernard Malamud. These challenges existed without emerging into dominance, without becoming cultural knowledge. How could such an understanding operate? What produces such an epistemological politics?

I do not mean to argue that the military man provided the model subject for everyone in the Cold War, but that the apparent conflict over manliness covered over and enabled oppressive agreements about male power. Far from adopting the manly warrior as hero after the victories of World War II, intellectuals turned away from heroics and extremity to a more tragic sense of history and to a poetics of ambiguity. Nonetheless, the intellectuals shared the claim to a position of transcendent objectivity that characterized the hypermasculinity of national policy. By "hypermasculinity" I mean a male gendering elevated above all questions of marked gender. That is, far from advocating openly a manliness that might have been contested, they took their own whiteness and maleness, together with American authenticity, as unmarked, neutral positions of superior reason. They operated upon an unwarranted assumption about the referentiality of language and rhetoric. Critics from Lionel Trilling to Cleanth Brooks helped to police the division between history and literature that effectively contained the potential subversions of literature and eliminated diversity. A politics resistant to postmodern complexities of gender, sexuality, or race—or of representation—could threaten not only writing by women or by people of color, not only modernism's shocking experiments in style and content, but any text that aspired to show ambiguity as more than poetic. The politics of simplification threatened even Ernest Hemingway, whose representations of manliness were more complex than the Cold Warrior could allow.

Cold War literature with strong connections to genres of manliness— the Western, the adventure story, crime fiction—might be popular but transgressed the containment of poetic language and threatened to reveal the hypermasculine crisis. Writers who struggled across that constitutive separation made the crisis visible. They put their own writing in limit zones, violating the critical understanding that intellectuals were articulating. Writers who violated the containment of gender did not, as they otherwise might, successfully challenge it, since that understanding was grounded in the larger configurations of the Cold War. The struggle over manliness illustrates how a challenge to gender categories could seem unreadable without broader cultural change.

I undertake this study with the conviction that history constrains what we can say and what we can know, but that the constraints are, within severe but unknowable limits, open to revision. I am examining these various texts from the forties and fifties to see how they negotiated the situation of the Cold Warrior, how they both repeated and deviated from the consensus discourse and the history that constrained them. How could they be discarded with suspicion? How did they find a position from which to write?

In this book, I read inside the discursive history of a period when demonology clearly organized American thought in a central and centralizing form. But the question is: does the discourse that has come to be labeled McCarthyism operate only at the margins, as an epiphenomenon of a liberal, democratic, post-Enlightenment culture that has other redeeming (and central) features? Or does the political demonology occupy the center of political history, as Michael Paul Rogin argues? What about the apparently undivided center? The illusion of continuity and lack of division is what I want to dispute. To put this another way: the concept of ideology as dictatorial or totalitarian itself belongs to a logic of the Cold War. It is no surprise to find that writers who offer forms of resistance to a central national subject might suffer from critical dismissal. However, the accusations that locate difference on the sensational margins, as Senator McCarthy's notorious hearings did, may trick our attention like a magician's slight of hand. Might the *resistance* to demonology also inhabit the center, in plain view, as the widely read stories told by women such as Mari Sandoz and Ursula Le Guin suggest? Just as anticommunist persecutions had their first effects before McCarthy, even before Truman's loyalty programs and dismissals? The demonology of the center can be accompanied by another mode of political rhetoric; the history that wins can be accompanied by other stories—perhaps women's stories—and other traditions, such as the Native American, can provide resources for cultural renewal.

I am writing this book within the context of a widespread desire to broaden cultural history, a demand for multiculturalism, together with the critique of multiculturalism as inadequate to a more thoroughgoing and radical change. An outpouring of publications is recalling the forgotten literatures of women, people of color, proletarian writers, gay and lesbian writers. At the same time, this very multicultural desire often finds itself captured and turned to familiar ends. Without abandoning the joy of discovery and restoration, I am pausing to become self-conscious about the pressures that have worked before on literary critics as both readers and writers. Let us not be naïve about how thoroughly intertwined are political and economic forces with the representation of culture. Anticommunism moved liberals to support the project of a security state apparatus; anticommunism found as its object a feminized assortment of targets, most significantly labor unions and civil rights groups. What

Ellen Schrecker details, in *Many Are the Crimes,* is the way a network of "professional" anticommunists could mobilize, through institutional contacts, organizations such as the FBI, the Civil Service Commission, the American Legion, the A F of L, and the DAR, to effectively produce a "red scare" that would demonize those associated with Communist Party activism and those even distantly related to the Communist Party itself. Thus, issues of international politics could be translated into issues of class, race, and gender.

The story of the Americas includes what Patricia Limerick named the "legacy of conquest." Prolonging the national extremity of World War II, the Cold War relegitimated conquest and assumed a history of whiteness. Schools all over the country taught the next generation that the great victory of World War II continued the American history of innocent triumph and thus attempted to continue the "Victory Culture" that was, as Tom Engelhardt has argued, already crumbling. The genocide experienced by American Indians and the slavery of African Americans, like the Holocaust tormenting the history of Jews and the terrible purification of Hiroshima, would have made the victorious narrative of American postwar history appear both diminished and guilty. The resistance of Cold War critics to multicultural literature corresponds to the political denial that provided a motivation for Cold War policies of blame.

In the following chapters, I examine the complexities of a gendered struggle and a splitting that the rhetorical simplicities of the Cold War covered over. As both national and individual identities came under maximum explosive stress, the old realities threatened to dissolve. Even though a hypermasculine national mythology joined manhood, realism, and the frontier ethic—the sort of ethic that Theodore Roosevelt had once represented—the splitting and the arbitrariness were obvious all along. The spectacle supported the myth but also threatened at every moment to undermine it by its increasingly evident unreality. What might seem un-American, I will show, were threats to this myth of the real—and the manly.

It isn't obvious that the Cold War had anything to do with the American West (the atomic bomb might instead almost make one nostalgic about rifles and six-guns as weaponry), and yet it was punctuated by images of the cowboy and the soldier (both played by John Wayne). In the pages to follow, I trace how the idea of the real and the West and Theodore Roosevelt's arena of strenuous manliness were rearticulated in the Cold War arena and underwrote the new international politics of East and West. Neither international politics nor literature seemed necessarily connected to the old fables of manliness that the warriors of the frontier had represented, but the phrase "Cold Warriors" entered the language because those old fables supported the new order. The West became a euphemism that conjoined frontier myth to national behavior in a global context. The category of the West continues ambiguously to refer to the American West and to the international West. Returning to this complex of frontier ideology will, as I will show, make more evident the suppressed relationships between national politics and literature. The arena of the Cold Warrior was a new historical era, but it made heavy use of the discourses that came before.

In order to understand postwar modernity, we have to understand the way that all of Western civilization suddenly found itself *inside* American military/industrial history.[3] Europe was devastated; it provided no substantial mediation or barrier between the United States and the Soviet Union. If the meeting of the two powers at Berlin rapidly took on the character of a shoot-out at the O.K. Corral, that is because the entire West was governed by narratives of the Western. Though the foreign policy of "realism" and "containment" articulated by George F. Kennan seemed to advocate limits and restraint, it also functioned to transfer frontier narratives and their particular internalized colonialism into a postwar modernity that would also exercise a colonialism in the name of fatal necessity, or the Real. The United States, playing the role of the marshal or the cavalry, had to be *realistic* about the aggression threatened by the Reds. The most telling characteristic of the threat was the way (in the persons of spies, communists, and fellow travelers) it was located within. The widespread change of former Marxists to a new interest in Freud reflected the general movement of interiorization.

I will be working toward these questions in my conclusion: Where were women in this? Where were the others? What produced the invisibility of ethnic and racial identities? What accounts for the Cold War silencing of women and nonwhite peoples? How is the denial of gender I am associating with Cold War hypermasculinity related to the way that frontier history celebrated white conquest as if it were indeed colorless? I have become convinced that the way to respond to this question must include an examination of the cultural gendering of men and the ways that "manliness" and hypermasculinity functioned to foreclose other positions for male subjectivity.

As I will show, these difficulties in manhood affected not only mass culture, but also scientists and intellectuals. The voids appeared in the ways spokesmen could represent the culture. During the first decades of the Cold War, the American nation seemed unified, and the American individual seemed the universal . . . *man*. I do not mean that nationalist rhetoric prevailed—although it did—but that it seemed not like rhetoric, but a discourse of *realism*. Only the other side had an "ideology." Foreign-policy realism in its George Kennan form meant that the United States would practice a strategy of containment. This affected literary realism, of course: containment meant that literature governed the sphere of the imaginary and overextended when it became rhetorical. Lionel Trilling advocated moral realism as a stance for critics; moral realism limited and contained literary tendencies to utopian fantasy by acknowledging the tragic implications of ideological extremity.

However, far from ending a history of extremity, World War II finished off the threat from Hitler and Japan by opening a new place for the fascist imagination within the United States. There are terrible similarities between the rhetoric of anti-Semitism and the rhetoric of anticommunism. Since many of those persecuted as communists were Jewish, there was an anti-Semitic cast to the furor. Worse, the pretense of racial purity both covered over and relegitimated historical abuses. The nature of the threat came in part out of the means of victory. Nuclear weapons threatened the disintegration of American cities—if an enemy used them. But nuclear history threatened American self-righteousness, since we had been the only ones to use them. At the level of foreign policy, fascist propaganda against communism from the thirties and the war years provided a familiar and convenient rhetoric. Refugees from Europe brought their own histories on both Left and Right. At the level of the spectacle, displaced from the past to the future, the resonance of the nuclear fear we ourselves had instigated at Hiroshima made the arena a twilight struggle to dominate fear.[4] The Iron Curtain and the Berlin Wall underscored the extent to which borders were under siege.

The increasingly professionalized intellectual class saw the liberal imagination redefined not as the very agent of progress but in opposition to heroic extremity. Public intellectuals such as Lionel Trilling represented the withdrawal from heroism in literary thought.[5] The scientists, from Albert Einstein to Robert Oppenheimer, might have seemed the new heroes of nuclear victory, but they provided the strongest and most controversial voices for restraint. The Cold War required that the victorious United States practice the realism of containment.

But the old stories of manliness, strength, courage, and the strenuous life in the West that Theodore Roosevelt had connected to the national future at the beginning of the century, in the heyday of literary realism and naturalism, did not go away. They entered into the public sphere as a renewed appetite for Westerns and cowboy singers (Gene Autry, Roy Rogers), and into politics in the developing struggle between "hawks" and "doves." The American discourse of nationalism associated with Teddy Roosevelt's optimistic rhetoric changed so that progress itself might be connected not to reform or to improving people's lives or even to such colonialism as building the Panama Canal, but to being bold enough to use the bomb again. Aggressive attack against an enemy took on its most perverse form in the persecution of the Left that McCarthy came to represent. The Cold War arena combined nativism and bellicosity in an uncanny mimicry of the European fascist anticommunism of the thirties. The myths of the West came to operate according to a logic of scapegoating and the abjection of the feminine.

Women have been alert to the unmarked gender and to the increasingly troubled and troubling figure of the warrior hero in modern culture, where technology amplifies the destructive power of war and diminishes the significance of the fighter. During the Cold War, women writers such as Mari Sandoz and Ursula Le Guin wrote about warrior trouble from the standpoint of a white woman, and they saw the problem as one of both whiteness and gender. Their representations aimed to expose the hybrid subject of the Cold War, rather than to engage in opposition. Their ethical excess was, of course, "contained" at a number of levels, as I will show.

The violent reconfiguration of the Cold War into a shoot-out silenced a "middle" that was seen as banal, domestic, sentimental, and boring. It screened out the complex struggles for the allegiance of the middle class, and it denied openings in the consensus. This reconfiguration was signaled by Richard Chase's claim in *The American Novel and Its Traditions* that literature in the United States is governed not so much by realism as by myth—not characterized by the nineteenth-century realism of European fiction, but by the mythmaking capacities of romance. Chase specifically distinguishes American fiction from the "middlebrow" novel so successful in English fiction, and his condemnation of the middlebrow successfully condemns as well the mainstream of domestic fiction without admitting to gender's centrality. Only the literature of the extreme is properly American literature (that is, of quality) in Chase's astounding characterization: "Wherever American literature has pursued the middle way it has tended by a kind of native fatality not to reconcile but merely to deny or ignore the polarities of our culture" (10). Repeating the gesture of containment that separated literature from the political by emphasizing its mythical function, as the new critics emphasized the formal, aesthetic organicism, Chase demonstrated how the Cold War consensus shored up the claims of a national realism by segregating it from narratives of the imagination and assigning both to male subjects. Furthermore, Chase demonstrates how the elaborate career of ambivalence practiced by Cold War intellectuals such as Lionel Trilling could none the less fail to safeguard criticism from the polarities and extremity that undergirded Cold War narratives. Women writers could be neither realists (that belonged to history) nor romancers (for they were already too fanciful, and too lodged in the domestic middlebrow culture).

Cold War literary and cultural critics resisted the transition from the rationalism of the modern to the multiplicity and ambiguity of the postmodern and tried to maintain the divide that separated high culture from low. As the Cold War spread its influence into every aspect of society, one of its most startling effects was to segregate warrior stories from both "realism" (science, politics, history) and from highbrow literature. I say "startling" because the threats of force are nevertheless precisely what supported the powerful claims made by critics and public officials alike. A kind of supermasculinity obviously characterized the superheroes of Cold War popular culture in film, television, comic books, and sports. But critics who wrote about literature favored the antiheroic and denied, as Ursula Le Guin complains, the need of a culture for fables. That is, they opposed any writing/reading of literature as rhetoric or as moral or ideological allegory. In the wake of this containment of the literary, several important investigations of masculinity and the Cold War, such as Jeffords's, Cohan's, and Krutnik's, have focussed on the history of film. But failure to challenge literary history as well obscures the struggles of writers and critics and elides the problem of the division between elite culture and mass culture that was so characteristic of the Cold War consensus.

The already ambiguous conflation of nation-state (Soviet) and ideology (communist) in the portrayal of enemies abstracted and covered over a many-layered set of repressions that not only silenced women, but also others colonized by national projects, whose objections or affiliations might bring them fatally back into view.[6] The subject of the Cold War was military, although the war enlisted all of everyday life. This had the effect of making all other discourses seem not only internal, but also more subjective, more unreal as more distant from the military project. Even the struggle between science and the national interest was not won by science, and those scientists who insisted on sharing atomic secrets could be put to death as spies. Maximum objectivity and realism was not attributed to the scientists who advocated open international inquiry, but rather to the bureaucracy that took away their passports. In chapter 4 I will discuss in detail the case of Linus Pauling and his protégé, chemist Ralph Spitzer. Surely the Rosenberg executions enforced not just power but belief in the possibility of subversion through sharing of scientific knowledge, now conflated with the development of weaponry. The stakes were the highest: the arms race cost more than both world wars combined. "Verifiability" became a standard of proof and mark of suspicion shared by nuclear weapons negotiations and the philosophy of science. The quarrel over Lysenko's genetics preceded the discovery of DNA's double helix as scientific frontiers moved from physics (the external world) to the internal world of the gene.

What the Cold War imposed as a consensus was a set of claims about the reality represented by the national narrative that not only abjected gendered, racial, and working-class subjects, in the name of threatened manhood, but also put manhood itself in an impossible—splitting—position. The unusual, exaggerated constraints of Cold War discourse threatened other versions of manhood; in particular those formerly associated with progressive and liberal politics, with the popular front, and with anticapitalist ethics emanating from religious discourses. The Cold War polarization of East and West also set the pattern for containing such threats: purify the legitimate subject and displace the blame onto a gendered other. The scapegoating logic of anticommunism disguised and relieved the splitting in the hero of Western manliness.

Howard Hawks's classic Western film *Red River* (1948) shows two versions of a Western hero in conflict. John Wayne plays the role of a tough cattle baron; Montgomery Clift is Matthew Garth, an orphan rescued by Wayne years before he went off to fight. Wayne's character, Tom Dunson, tells the Texas Civil War vets, "You've come back from the war, your place stole by carpetbaggers—you've got nothing left." Even though he owns the biggest ranch in Texas, Dunson himself is short of cash. They set north on a cattle drive with a certain desperation. Along the way, Dunson violates the loyalty of his cowboys by his tyrannical willfulness, until Garth leads a rebellion and successfully delivers the cattle via the Chisholm Trail to the new Abilene railroad. As the townspeople and cowboys celebrate their financial success, Dunson/Wayne catches up and confronts Garth/Clift; he will kill the younger man for crossing him although he loves him like a son. They fight, but Dunson finally must relent when Garth refuses to shoot back and the woman who loves the younger man cries out against the struggle. He adds the younger man's initial to his brand.

The generational conflict in *Red River* foreshadows the conflicts that a rising youth culture would play out during the Cold War, even though the baby-boomers of the sixties were just being born in 1948. Clift/Garth is willing to take a chance on the future (head for Abilene) rather than staying on the already mapped road. His service in the Civil War on the losing side has made him and the cowboys more empathetic, not harder, like the older Wayne/Dunson. Steven Cohan in *Masked Men* argues that the "highly charged contest between the soft boy and the hard man in *Red River* dramatizes . . . a shift in the mainstream culture's demands upon masculinity" (208). An older paternalism is in conflict with a younger version of progress. *Red River* stages the splitting between two versions of manliness that would become more politicized but not resolved: the unrelenting patriarch represented by John Wayne and the more realistic (but perhaps weaker) liberal represented by Montgomery Clift.

The two actors would themselves become icons of the hard and the soft, gender exaggeration and gender ambiguity, although John Wayne would prevail in the new mythology of the Western. (Hawks had originally asked Hemingway's friend Gary Cooper to take the part, but Cooper declined because the character was too ruthless). Montgomery Clift, on the other hand, was among the new breed of Cold War stars who were sensitive and nonconformist, such as James Dean and Marlon Brando. As Vito Russo, in *The Celluloid Closet: Homosexuality in The Movies,* has pointed out, the sexual ambiguity of the new man opens up a homoerotic subtext in such films. In *Red River,* for example, there is not only the differentiated relationship between the older and younger heroes, but also a charged scene between Montgomery Clift and another man in which their admiration of their guns seems sexualized indeed. Marlon Brando's *The Men* presented the story of paraplegics after the war, the diminished body of manliness redeemed by the values of mind and personality. Paralysis in that film seems to represent the impossibility of a warrior manliness as viable cultural paradigm. Nevertheless, such characters did not mark the emergence of a revolutionary subject or of homosexual politics into plain view. Even Tennessee Williams, as David Savron argued in *Communists, Cowboys, and Queers,* could not escape the politics of masculinity that positioned him this side of utopia during the fifties and sixties.

The splitting subject of manliness and the appearance of a new, alienated hero did not make a place for women or the feminized, either. Literary critics might disdain the normal male hero of American nationalism, but they were nonetheless under the influence of the cultural hypermasculinity. Nina Baym's early, influential, and still oft-cited piece, "Melodramas of Beset Manhood," argued some time ago—in 1981—that "the theories controlling our reading of American literature have led to the exclusion of women authors from the canon" (123). She pointed out the nationalist orientation of American criticism, and its exclusivity. By emphasizing the (minimal) alienation of its favored writers from the mainstream, Cold War criticism contained all contradiction within a "consensus criticism of the consensus" (129). Baym was describing the basic modernist strategy, adopted by critics after World War II: to define literature against a feminized other, particularly against the sentimental writing by women, who were held to represent the mass consensus.

Cold War fables that defined the American individual in terms of a melodramatic encounter between man and society captured the American intellectual. Baym argued that the story was gendered even though its subject was supposed to represent human nature because it featured heroic man overcoming social obstacles and embracing seductive wilderness that were both feminized. She pointed out, however, that there were works not only by women, but also by men that did not fit this pattern—including Hemingway's *For Whom the Bell Tolls.* Baym proposed three explanations for the prominence of "beset manhood" in critical writing: sexist bias in the mindset of critics even when their standards are nonsexist; inferior work by women because of gendered social conditions; and gender-related bias that critical theories impose retroactively, anachronistically. She traced the way critics described an exclusive American romanticism that was based on the inferiority of the women writers, from F. O. Matthiessen, Lionel Trilling, and Leslie Fiedler, among others, to the influential group that included Henry Nash Smith, Charles Feidelson, R. W. B. Lewis, Richard Chase, and Daniel Hoffman.

I am arguing that the Cold War version of the American hero condensed political and cultural identities for this group of critics, displacing gender onto enemy spaces. The resulting version of American literary history imposed a massive retroactive censure upon a range of writing that included women's work. It also gendered and dismissed political radical writing, proletarian fiction, works by important African American writers including not only W. E. B. Du Bois (who was associated with Marxist thought), but also Zora Neale Hurston (who was not). Native Americans were again relegated to a vanishing past. Donald Pease has made the connection between this version of American exceptionalism and Cold War history.[7] Baym did not explicitly attribute this nationalistic critical gendering to Cold War politics. However, the critics she mentioned overlap with those Pease identified as the "Cold War consensus."

What made it especially difficult to critique the Cold War consensus was its apparent continuity with a selective past. Haven't we had wars repeatedly, and warriors; haven't we been living in a hypermasculine phallogocentrism since the Greeks; hasn't the frontier provided the dominant mythos of American culture from the beginning? But this illusion of seamless (fatally necessary) tradition is an effect of the Cold War, not a precedent. Writers who struggled against it had in fact, other traditions upon which to draw—however discredited—and that may also allow us to read differently. Women writers had a considerable heritage that was well known before World War II.[8] However, the woman's tradition was disparaged as sentimental and conjoined with the particular distortions of Cold War domesticity, so that by the sixties college professors were claiming that no women had ever written literature and Nina Baym could find no women in the canon in 1980. Reactionary periods are discontinuous, although they rely on appeals to fundamental continuity. Feminists in the seventies seemed to be inventing feminism for the first time in history—an effect of the Cold War that provides remarkable evidence of its power to obscure the past. Thus even though women writers have had a well-documented history and have been important to the writing of literary history in particular, it continues to be important to discover ancestors. But what I especially want to demonstrate about the Cold War is how it introduced *in the name of continuity* a radical break with traditions, a new and dramatically more limited literary history that has masqueraded as the "traditional canon" ever since. The 1998 Modern Library selection of the one hundred greatest books of the twentieth century was scandalous for its neglect of women writers: it simply reinscribed the understanding of the canon that had been so powerfully constituted by the early Cold War, even after thirty years of hard work on feminist recoveries.

The Cold War consensus distorted the history of radicalism in this country as well. In particular, it reconfigured identification with other workers as a class to identification with other workers as a gender. The progressive past has been more difficult to recover, in certain respects, than the past of feminism, because the very words used to represent it have been appropriated and outlawed. Before World War II, the Popular Front was destroyed, and during the Cold War the Communist Party was destroyed, together with the memory of union associations. The cultural history of the working-class Left has been restored largely outside the working class.[9] That is, academic allegiance to progressive politics, and academic Marxism, have not succeeded in attracting widespread allegiance from working-class and union members (while feminism is a mass movement).

The rise of progressive intellectuals during the sixties, of civil rights activism and of New Left social movements, together with feminism, transferred class struggle into identity politics without (notoriously) the support of the working class. This was in part because the masculinity of the national subject was articulated on two levels that then began to split along class lines. On the one hand, the subject of reason and American pluralism was transparent, universal, ungendered, and normalized—feminists identified this reasonable speaker as "white male" because it excluded as irrational all others marked by race or gender, most obviously women. On the other hand, the man in the arena of American superiority was visible, male, adventurous, and patriarchal. He appeared in the person of John Wayne and reappeared as Ronald Reagan at the intersection of Western and war drama. As the identifications of working-class males transferred (under threat of persecution for subversion) from the now un-American labor collectives to the gendered mythology of the individual and to the racialized versions of class, the symbolic and imaginary versions of the male subject of the American nation began to split along class lines, as a splitting of mind and body. Only the strength of denial that kept the consensus together prevented this splitting from becoming obvious—until Vietnam.

The representation of manhood as political power became especially visible during the eighties. As Susan Jeffords argued in *Hard Bodies*, Reagan's connections to Hollywood secured a masculinity that supported presidential credibility through the persuasiveness of the visible male body appearing in eighties films. One must be willing to prove through combat not only claims of personal identity, but, more significantly, claims about the real, represented as objective fact: the "hard bodies" that Jeffords has described as the male icons of the Reagan era represented not the apotheosis of heroic masculinity, but the increasingly difficult pressure of unreality on a manhood made hyperbolic by the Cold War. The hard bodies thus mark the twentieth-century crisis of militarism, with its nationalistic appeal to manly realism.

The Cold War is not over; it lives on in the imaginary where it was so firmly installed through nuclear trauma and phobia. Taking up competitive despair into advanced technology, the global economy at the end of the twentieth century wages virtual warfare. Bill Gates of Microsoft models the particular success of the brilliant strategist. The best participants—the denizens of cyberspace—may train on the most violent of computer games. The battle and the warrior give shape to the cultural narratives—to sports, to commercials, to bodybuilding. It is not difficult to see a continuity between the narratives of capitalism and the embodiment of warfare. I do not mean, however, to argue for the determinism of these continuities, but rather to trace how an illusion of agreement, imposed by what Alan Nadel has called the "containment culture" of the Cold War, reinscribes power. The illusion of agreement about gender that emerges from warrior definitions reiterates but also disperses cultural narratives and the selves they make possible. My focus is on the illusion, and on attempts to use the illusion of consensus and containment as a strategy of representation that depends upon fables of manliness.

When the Gulf War seemed to demonstrate an ahistorical American appetite for warfare, many critics of nationalism despaired of ever emerging from Cold War militarism. Barbara Ehrenreich wrote about the cultural dominance of identities allied with war in her 1990 *Time* magazine commentary:

> A leftist might blame "imperialism"; a right-winger would call our problem "internationalism." But an anthropologist, taking the long view, might say this is just what warriors do. Intoxicated by their own drumbeats and war songs, fascinated by the glint of steel and the prospect of blood, they will go forth, time and again, to war. (100)

Far from asserting that what warriors do may be associated with a manliness that transcends history, however, I am interested in the conditioning imposed not just by culture but by a specific cultural moment. If the United States may be seen as a "warrior culture," the intoxication is renewed—and challenged—at multiple levels as it is performed. Indeed, the very term "warrior" overlays a tribal context onto the dissociated and disembodied activities of a postmodern culture, revealing the desire for a communally defined ethos along with its lack. Ursula Le Guin has portrayed alternative cultures for the future in which, she imagines, a warrior might be just a stage in adolescence.[10] The American Cold War seemed to impose a militarism that exaggerated the masculinity and emphasized its aggressiveness at the same time that national policy defended itself against just such masculinity in the Soviet Union, disavowing the identification.

So what I mean by the manliness and hypermasculinity of the American Cold War is a function of a specific time and place. At the same time that manhood was everywhere invoked and women were largely silenced and—as Moms—vilified, manliness was also, especially for intellectuals, impossible. In *No Man's Land: Letters from the Front*, Sandra Gilbert and Susan Gubar note the "revulsion against outworn masculine roles" in writers such as Joseph Heller and Kurt Vonnegut, so that "hopeless, hapless masculine reinvention repeatedly propels the comic escapades of a host of antiheroes" (319). At the same time, popular culture featured excessively masculine heroes—and the comics featured, indeed, Superman. I agree with Susan Jeffords about the significance of male bodies in the history of the eighties, and that a form of identity politics that used masculine categories informed the way the culture dealt with the feminizing loss of Vietnam. Gendered representations of manhood reemerge in the operations of the American national subject, as Jeffords describes. In my view, this marks an aspect of the gender politics signaled by the emergence of feminism as well. However, what prevailed before the Vietnam war, both the manliness of the working-class man and the hypermasculine antiheroics of the intellectual, seemed not a politics of gender only because the politics of a gendered illusion kept it submerged. What appeared as a remasculinization after Vietnam was in some respects the emergence into middlebrow and highbrow culture of identifications with masculinity that had existed in popular culture superheroes all along. The distinctions maintained between high and mass culture in the first part of the Cold War masked the extent to which policy makers and literary critics were enlisted in the national myth. During the sixties, feminists inaugurated, in what might be described as a powerful backlash, a response to the overwhelming hypermasculinity of Cold War culture. With the proclaimed end of the Cold War, what is becoming increasingly evident is how the identity politics of manliness during the Cold War silenced not only women writers but men as well, and made, indeed, a certain ethics of manhood impossible to represent.[11] Since Vietnam, most of the American middle class have achieved a distance from bodies at risk: it may in fact be argued that keeping the middle class out of risky warfare was part of the scandal of that struggle. But the warrior theme has not diminished.

The gaps in experience between men and women helped split the field of modernist literature after World War I—the angry vilification of women's optimism during the progressive era as "sentimental," memories left airless by mustard gas condemning naïve celebrations of a natural world or a spiritual transcendence.[12] After World War II there were different kinds of silence: including denial that war wounds might forever damage the hopes for *The Best Years of Our Lives,* in spite of the film's representation of veterans' painful homecomings, and denial that the women sent home to the suburbs might themselves have ambitions and desires. Kaja Silverman examines representations of male trauma that violate the assumptions of phallic superiority from the perspective of psychoanalytic film criticism in *Male Subjectivity at the Margins.* Another split opened up between the fantasy ideology to assuage consumers, and a so-called realistic ideology, a tragic vision to satisfy international high culture: optimism for the mass market (and the rise of Disney); pessimism for the intelligentsia—John Wayne for the masses, but Meursault or Raskolnikov or Humbert Humbert for the critics.

At the same time that a certain narrative of disillusionment became, in literature, the only believable story, those who had more terrible stories to tell could, apparently, say nothing. Both the Holocaust and Hiroshima produced victims who could not talk about their experience, which came to be represented as the worst nightmares of the future.[13] The silence came not only from the writers; if Shoshana Felman and Dori Laub are right, indeed, it was most of all the lack of an audience that forbade disclosure, as they argue in *Testimony.* As the 1948 film *The Best Years of Our Lives* suggested, not even the celebrated heroes of World War II could come back home and speak the truth about their war experiences, and the adjustment to wounds was not only necessary for those like the young soldier who lost his hands. Stephen Spielberg's 1998 *Saving Private Ryan* claims to reveal for the first time, fifty-four years later, the horrors faced by World War II veterans of the Normandy invasion. John Wayne covered over, rather than representing, the body of the male warrior.

Twentieth-century literature has been inflected by warfare, but the victims may not be able to put the shock of their lives into messages others can hear: the very capacity of literature to respond to the cultural history of a people has been under duress. What is learned through pain resists what reason might offer, as Elaine Scarry discusses in *The Body in Pain.* Given the powerful separations inflicted by suffering, what kind of audience—what critical reader—might constitute itself to address the silence of denial and anger? American Jewish fiction did not have the unsettling effect of what Gilles Deleuze and Felix Guattari, writing about Kafka, called "minority literature," even though it was widely seen as "ethnic," because its assimilating trajectory reinforced majority inattention to the Holocaust.

In this book I read the figuring of masculinity during the Cold War as a preface to contemporary warfare, which is economic, racial, and ecological. I trace the gendered narratives of family and country to mark the violence and the denial. What cannot be heard—complications in the story of national unity—is abjected from the constructed narratives of culture.

After the first two chapters, which discuss the place of stories in relationship to Cold War narratives, I turn to specific examples of texts, which compel attention to these issues, in spite of the operation of denial. The writers I examine at some length in this study engage the fables of manliness in discourses that are particularly important to the joining of the West, nationalism, and reality: natural history (Ernest Hemingway and Mari Sandoz); Cold War science (Bernard Malamud and Ursula Le Guin); history (Hemingway, Malamud, Sandoz), anthropology (Sandoz and Le Guin); Native American culture (Hemingway, Sandoz, and Le Guin); the intellectual community (Malamud, Le Guin). Each of these writers threatens to expose the repressed hybridity of national culture. I have chosen Hemingway and Malamud to discuss for the very different ways they engage the problem of the manly heroic and its implications not only for literature, but also for science and for national policy. I have chosen Sandoz and Le Guin for their very different resolutions to the problem of critiquing warrior identities and finding a position for women's agency in writing. Hemingway and Sandoz show us the modification of an earlier writing career by the Cold War. Malamud and Le Guin anticipate the Cold War impact on postmodernism. Sandoz and Le Guin show how a writing under the sign of gender might by its very lack of purity make use of what Homi Bhabha calls, in "DissemiNation," the "displaced agency" of postcolonial subjects such as the Native American. The storytelling associated with immigrant Jews and Native Americans looked dangerously sentimental, a lapse both Malamud and Le Guin have risked.

In the context of such a history, it is a disabling mistake to think of the renewal of tradition as necessarily a reactionary nostalgia. Bhabha argues that the new internationalism associated with postcolonial hybridity offers a chance to reread tradition through the position of those on the margins, a chance for renewal that makes use of the very processes of identity:

> The "right" to signify from the periphery of authorized power and privilege . . . is resourced by the power of tradition to be reinscribed through the conditions of contingency and contradictoriness that attend upon the lives of those who are "in the minority". The recognition that tradition bestows is a partial form of identification. In restaging the past, it introduces other, incommensurable cultural temporalities into the invention of tradition. This process estranges any immediate access to an originary identity or a "received" tradition. (*Location of Culture* 2)

The processes of estrangement make ideology appear, that which once seemed simply true, real, and obvious.[14]

nated the femininized East in story after story: Owen Wister's *The Virginian* exemplified the plot.

But the Cold War put that manliness inherited from the Victorians and from Roosevelt on trial. The aftermath of World War II saw the skepticism of intellectuals enter widely into American culture, a new version of Enlightenment humanism. Just as the ethic of national manliness seemed most forcefully triumphant, with the dropping of atomic weapons on Hiroshima and Nagasaki, those very weapons made the extremity of warrior narratives seem more dangerous. In other words, manliness entered into an identity politics that put gendered men (together with women) on the margins.

The results would be paradoxical. As manliness came to appear more and more a symptom of excess, the always-gendered work of women appeared even more excessive and even more marginal—in need of a containment policy that would be domestic. *Woman's Day* taught Rosie the Riveter how to cook hamburger in her new suburban home (and happily leave the paying jobs for men) while Charles Atlas's advertisements appealed to skinny weaklings who needed to increase their strength to combat the bullies on the beach. The rearranging of gender roles was accompanied by a widespread denial of cultural identities: by the sixties, the famous photographic exhibit that aimed to show human multiplicity showed a unity instead: *The Family of Man,* it was designated. The denial of difference had consequences. The Cold War period from 1945 to 1970 eliminated the work of women, ethnic writers, and the proletarians from academic literature departments, and found the work of overly gendered men (Hemingway, for example) deeply problematic.

Manliness did not go away; manliness was put on trial. Rationality did not lose its hidden assumptions that the universal subject was male; but reasonable men denied with increased force that it was possible to be neutral and objective and be gendered. This had the repressive effects on those marked by race, class, sexuality, and gender that critics of identity politics have described so extensively for the last decades.

The conflation of a genderless liberalism with the antiliberal politics of manliness in these descriptions has been confusing. Why was Hemingway under attack by Cold War critics? Should feminists join the attack on Hemingway, and if we do, are we agreeing that a genderless position is possible? Does the critique of American frontier manhood written by Mari Sandoz serve to undermine a dominant manliness—or to shore up the liberal attack on gender that characterized the Cold War? In the atmosphere of public trial that came to be called McCarthyism, what does the persecution of scientists and artists as un-American do to the viability of a liberal individualism? Did sexual violations of propriety substitute for or cover over the radical challenge of political dissent, as Bernard

Malamud intimates? While the struggle between manliness and objectivity displaced male subjects, their trauma—what Nina Baym called "Melo-dramas of Beset Manhood"—served to repress attention to the trauma of others. But this obsessive cultural attention to a single issue of gender identification might look different from a perspective not shaped by the global binaries of East and West or the abstract masculinity that subtends it. Ursula Le Guin began in the Cold War sixties to write of a cure by perspective—the regional, the situated, and the homely—that would make it apparent that "The Warrior Is a Stage Adolescents Go Through." This book questions through these texts the identity politics of manliness in the Cold War context of persecution and trial. The involvement of men in identity politics was not obvious, but it set the stage for subsequent cultural history.

1

The Un-American and the Unreal: Modern Bodies and New Frontiers

> Thus, we have a choice between disavowing "historical" *reality* (the only radical one, that of death) which places us in the series of the signifier alone (paranoid delirium or its suturing, which is science), or disavowing *desire* (that is, the transference of one signifier to another), an action which makes our body into a symptom and/or a fight against death. In the first case, we have the 'truth' of the signifier, which eventually can be demonstrated (science), but only at the expense of disavowing reality; the psychotic and the scientist bear witness (tragically for the one, optimistically for the other) to an impossible reality; they fail to articulate reality *[le réel]*. In the second case, we have the truth of the symptom, expressed by a suffering body or by a kind of prompted language; the latter is always a semblance, plausible but never true, and only its accidents (slips, errors of reasoning, etc.) relate it to the first case, that is, to the impossibility of "truth."
>
> —Julia Kristeva, "The True-Real"

The logic of the Cold War is so extravagant that it may be easier to persuade us now, in postmodern, postcolonial, postcommunist, and post–Cold War contexts, that the Real itself is unrepresentable and not articulated with truth. In *The Imaginary War*, Mary Kaldor argues that the Cold War imposed a set of interpretations and assumptions upon our reading of contemporary history that now—since that Cold War era has ended—may be seen as discourse, the product of imagery as well as of events. I would extend this argument further. Not only did national policy rely on the figurative representation of un-American enemies for its power to convince, but more audaciously, some of the chief proponents of anticommunism—not just Joseph McCarthy but more notably the FBI—presented as "fact" evidence they knew to be invented, according to Ellen Schrecker's research in *Many Are the Crimes*. What I call "national realism" to designate the rhetorical formation of the Cold War was founded on the conviction that reality, like criminal guilt or innocence, is on trial. It was a discourse proceeding from the disorientation of profound shock—the trauma of the atomic bomb, the returning veterans, the post-Holocaust refugees, the new responsibility of the United States, the difficulty of assessing Soviet policies. Older narratives that had served to define historical reality were disrupted and reconstituted around national extremity. National realism claimed to be objective, factual, and realistic—nonpartisan, nonextreme, nonpolitical. Trauma anchored conviction.

In this chapter, I will examine the Cold War relationship between realism as a political or scientific appeal to authority and realism as mimesis in literature. I will show how national realism might have been formed out of the older discourses of frontier manliness. The very idea that national policy, science, and fiction might all be viewed as rhetorical and political violates a central tenet of Cold War discourse. It was, rather, characteristic of the Cold War academy to distinguish rigorously politics, science, and literature as entirely different uses of language—pragmatic, factual, and mythical—which ought not to be confused. Literary critics defined literature as belonging to the realm of myth, of imagination and romance. The best literature should be treated objectively, as a whole created by its maker (poesis) rather than something merely imitated from reality (mimesis). The Cold War critics (New York intellectuals, Americanists, and New Critics alike, in spite of substantial differences), successfully defined modernism in terms of its deviations from the real and the normal. Thus critics distracted attention from the close affiliation of literary modernism with the discourses of national policy and the practices of "containment."

What I will argue leads me in certain ways to be contradictory. On the one hand, I want to emphasize the complex and multiple historical play of narratives that defines and redefines manliness and the real. On the other hand, I am describing a historical moment characterized by its apparent simplicity, a single narrative frozen into ahistoricity. The freezing of time and change in the Cold War culture was an illusion, but when I talk about the Cold War configuration, I reproduce that illusion: of a simplicity that contains threat. In the chapters that follow, I will show how threats to simplicity were always in plain view, contained only by denial—a refusal to talk about the most banal and everyday commonalities. A kind of dream logic organized culture by a series of condensations and displacements that kept the old dream of frontier alive. Freedom and opportunity seemed to require defense—surveillance to guard against attack and a nuclear cavalry as an enforcer.

A second apparent contradiction will appear in the way I talk about realism. On the one hand, the Cold War maintained a careful distinction between discourses that spoke about facts truly and discourses that were imaginative or expressive or persuasive or just imitations. On the other hand, from my position writing after the poststructuralist critique of such assumptions about language, the sense of knowledgeable authority or *realism* that informed foreign policy or gave credibility to the FBI is no less an effect of rhetoric, figure, and style than the illusion of reality produced by literary *realism*. I am arguing that discourses of policy and science were literary in some respects, but I am even more interested in showing how the need to assert their truthfulness and reality resulted in producing a void for literary realism that interacted with the rupture of male subjectivity.

I begin with an important figure of thought in the Cold War dream logic, a condensation: although the conflict of East and West started with the alliances and hostilities of nation-states, it was not just the Soviet Union but rather international Communism as an ideology that provided an implacable, overdetermined "other" around which American culture might reorganize a whole series of discourses, from science to poetry. This condensation belongs to dream logic, but the United States foreign policy based on it claimed realism and objectivity. George F. Kennan's policy of containment, persuasively outlined in the "long telegram" that inaugurated the foreign policy of the United States during the Cold War, defined the arena of struggle. What would be contained was not only the Soviet Union, but also the threat of political thought. The United States was objective and truthful; the Soviet Union was rhetorical and ideological: "The very disrespect of Russians for objective truth—indeed, their disbelief in its existence—leads them to view all stated facts as instruments for furtherance of one ulterior purpose or another" (203).[1]

George Kennan's long telegram was persuasive because of its use of figurative language. It bases its analysis on metaphorical threats that evoke a political unconscious of abjection:

> Soviet leaders are driven necessities of their own past and present position to put forward a dogma which [views the] outside world as evil, hostile and menacing; but as bearing within itself germs of creeping disease and destined to be wracked with growing international convulsions until it is given final coup de grace by rising power of socialism and yields to new and better world. (qtd. in Bernstein and Matusow 202–3)

Later, it is communism itself that is "like a malignant parasite" (211). As the metaphor of disease suggests, the imaginary war would be cast as the struggle of national subjects in crises of identity.

Furthermore, national identity is bound up with the crises of the abject body, in a form that corresponds to the male horror of the feminine

Julia Kristeva describes in *Powers of Horror.* The success of the communist threat to "penetrate" the soft bodies of the ideologically vulnerable in the West "will depend on degree of cohesion, firmness and vigor which [the] western world can muster," Kennan's telegram continues (210). The West must choose reason over emotion—the "same courage, detachment, objectivity, and same determination not to be emotionally provoked or unseated by it, with which doctor studies unruly and unreasonable individual"—and health over disease—"communism is like a malignant parasite which feeds only on diseased tissue." Kennan is not advocating a specific foreign policy but rather an ideological approach to the struggle that cannot, above all, be admitted as ideology. Nonetheless, "this is [the] point at which domestic and foreign policies meet" (211).

The national subject as Cold Warrior will be hyper-male: reasonable, penetrating, vigorous, and healthy. Though the bomb seems not at issue for Kennan here, the Cold War is a kind of male creation, the birth of identity and power associated with the bomb. Klaus Theweleit writes:

> He, who has the power to destroy everything, HE, who is DEATH and LIFE in person, really can claim to have created HIMSELF. The makers of the bomb are the first men to have been really successful in bringing this oldest of male fantasies into material reality. ("The Bomb's Womb" 295)

George Kennan's language reveals that being realistic about Soviet ideology, not about Soviet economy or military preparedness, opens up a struggle of gendered bodies for dominance:

> Only in certain countries where communists are numerically strong do they now regularly appear and act as a body. As a rule they are used to penetrate, and to influence or dominate . . . other organizations less likely to be suspected, . . . a wide variety of national associations or bodies which can be dominated or influenced by such penetration. These include: labor unions, youth leagues, women's organizations, racial societies, religious societies, social organizations, cultural groups, liberal magazines, publishing houses, etc. (qtd. in Bernstein and Matusow 207)

Two weeks after Joseph Stalin's February 9, 1946, election speech seemed to signal increased emphasis not on (wartime) nationalism, but on communist ideology, Kennan warns that Soviet character was informed not by a logic of reality but by a "logic of force."

Kennan's telegram had a formidable impact because it spoke of threat in a tone of alarm that must have resonated both with a free-floating anxiety set loose by the apocalyptic nuclear end of the war—and with the sense of power. At last, Kennan seemed to provide a *realistic* assessment of the confusing Soviet policy, embodied in the idea of containing its malignant fluidity.[2] But was it the accuracy of his observation or the resonance of his language with gendered bodies that seemed persuasive? Since the American perspective was defined as objective, its dependence on interpretations of ideology became invisible. The critical activity of interpretive analysis itself came to seem un-American, unless it addressed the circumscribed space of a literary object. Policy would be objective truth, not interpretation.

The Cold War made the historical drama of the national subject its center.[3] Cold War rhetoric was characterized by a phobic, obsessive objectivity supported on a consensus subject. The rhetoric might be impersonal and abstract, but it was also a performance of *defense,* in the several senses of that word. The alienation from sensibility was marked by the threat—and supported by the power—of sudden, explosive violence. The hypermasculinity was a sustained posturing with a phallic shield (nuclear deterrent) that allocated the distribution of power in the interests of military-industrial stasis, not of catharsis or jouissance or progress, unless it was economic. The prompt of overwhelming anxiety was translated and personified as the act of the enemy, and the prompt of anxiety was the very locus of hallucination and paranoia, the threat of death and of desire—an unnameable Real that the bomb and the Holocaust shadowed forth.

The crisis of identity associated with such anxiety continuously threatens the very possibility of using language as defense. Cynthia Enloe thinks the Cold War reshaped relationships between men and women because it depended on citizens internalizing "an acute sense of danger" that would lead them to accept spending on the military, secrecy, the draft, and wiretapping, and "the construction of the world view that placed danger at its core relied on gendered danger as well" (16). Danger threatens to break down the boundaries of self and other and the differentiation that structures language. Anxiety might bring on a presymbolic access of uncertainty and conflation. At the very moment Kennan urges objectivity, the threat emerges in images of disease and fluidity. It is the waste of bodies—the growing hair and nails, excrement, menses, saliva, spilled semen, excess of nursing milk, blood—and their final reduction to waste, as corpse, that marks the act of definition, and difference, in the Cold War—the body as abject.

These figures of abjection point to an association between the body and the real that may also be suggested by Kennan's rhetoric. However, this is not a "real body" that might resolve uncertainty, but the threat itself. The body that appears in the post-Freudian theories of Jacques Lacan, Julia Kristeva, Luce Irigaray, Rosa Braidotti, Judith Butler, Elizabeth Grosz, and others connects us to reality not as concrete image or thesis or transcendental solidity, but as a material negativity. The effects of these discourses of the body are to deconstruct essential subjectivity while maintaining an access to/for experience and a site for referentiality. Thus this discourse is related to the Lacanian *Real* and to Jacques Derrida's *différance*. The Real is precisely that which cannot be known; matter and the body define the limits of cultural construction, what cannot be represented, and the excess, what disrupts the symbolic. As in Derrida, the difference of identity and the deferral of meaning form a chiasmus. The Real that Kristeva examines does not result in continuous narrative: history turns on the reiteration of loss, the return to dust, a certain mortality of meaning that is enforced by the Real. History depends upon the finite and repeated materiality of its subjects. After World War I, World War II, and the Vietnam war it has become more and more difficult to ignore that the modern subject has been shocked by trauma, that the bodied self has come as well to seem more and more "the body," as if we were all already at the limit of abjection: solid, dead, reified, corpse. Kennan's long telegram seems to speak this trauma and defend against it.

It is striking to notice how constricted the sense of bodies became as they were introduced into the aesthetics of spectacle and consumption during the Cold War. We may be used to thinking about the Victorian as the chief period that censored sex, although, as Michel Foucault argued in *The History of Sexuality,* sex entered then into discourse in a way that made sexuality ubiquitous. During the last half-century in the United States, however, there has been a distribution of physicality such that only certain people appear to have bodies worth mentioning. In magazines, the *Playboy* centerfold and the ever-erotic covers of *Sports Illustrated* (does the swimsuit issue provide a cover for the sensuality of the male athletes usually displayed?) have provided sustained examples of a voyeuristic tendency in modern audiences. Advertising has not only promoted ideal images of the body; its use of realistic media—photography, film—has effectively censored or abjected the majority of the population's bodies as ugly, old, fat, colored, disfigured, or abnormal, perhaps both producing alienation and demonstrating its benefits. The Cold War saw an immense heightening of idealized spectacle as advertising generated a consumer society and television supplemented the popularity of film in mass culture.

But this spectacle of pleasurable viewing has been shadowed by others, twentieth-century visions through photography of the dance of death and its cadavers: the concentration camp victims about to be liberated from Buchenwald, Dachau, Bergen-Belsen, Theresienstadt, and Mauthausen; the citizens of Hiroshima walking away from the blast with their burned hands stretched out before them; the Vietnamese child consumed with napalm, the starving Ethiopian, the Somalian mother with her baby. The desiring, dying body snaps into the field of vision in the codes of photographs that mark historical time. Simultaneously, even the most traumatic incision of experience into a lifetime casts off a meaningless, silent excess: body can only be represented within the mechanisms of definition available to us. The body makes its claims for compassion, for desire, for pity, for degradation, "the body" is rhetorical with a hysterical style. "The body" claims to be evidence of the real.

Some kind of persuasive anchor was necessary. All follows from the hypermasculinity of a national subject, defined in a relationship of mastery with an object that variously appears as communism, women, or nature. The object has a body, and the reality of that body (its nuclear capacity, its fertility, its complexity, its strangeness, its threat, its lack of boundaries) is what makes the distancing of hypermasculine mastery necessary, and what makes it realistic. The embodied, gendered language of national policy may seem amazing, given the stance of disembodied objectivity taken by public figures. But that purification of the body establishes a kind of paranoid mastery that seems to avoid the extremes of emotion and ideology, to be reasonable. The reasonable person keeps the threat of the Real contained.

In retrospect, the most bizarre characteristics of Cold War culture are those in closest contact with its war psychosis: the fallout shelters, the air-raid drills against nuclear strikes, the persecution of communists, the construction of a security state, the pursuit of spies, the vast filing systems of the FBI and J. Edgar Hoover's practices of extortion. The facts of the history reveal in exaggerated form how modernity's claim to the true/real might, as Kristeva theorized, rest on the hallucinatory instance of a foreclosure. The realistic policies of containment secured a frozen history, within which a generation grew up (from 1945 to 1965) watching McCarthy's charges, the executions of the Rosenbergs, and the nuclear testing on television news while entertainment presented the banalities of everyday life—Doris Day or *The Honeymooners*. The news might seem in retrospect less convincing than the sitcoms.

The imaginary quality of national realism required powerful means of persuasion. The Cold War was a disciplinary technology that served to articulate and distribute power and that used the mechanisms of surveillance in all the ways made possible by sophisticated bureaucracies and technologies invented for war. Perhaps J. Edgar Hoover's FBI was the most important link between military operations against an enemy and civilian governance. Anticommunism was orchestrated by the FBI together with a decades-old coalition of interested parties who emerged into cultural dominance during the Cold War. The coalition had begun to come together during World War I and had taken initial form with the "Red Scare" and the Palmer raids, directed against immigrants accused of being subversive—including, notoriously, Emma Goldman and Alexander Berkman. Hoover got his start in those years and began establishing his files on subversives with the seizures of radical archives he made then.

So important was the FBI's part in organizing the most extreme and far-reaching mechanisms of the Cold War struggle against the un-American that Ellen Schrecker has proposed McCarthyism should have properly been called "Hooverism" (*Many Are the Crimes* 11). But Hoover never let himself appear in the hysterical and extremist guise that McCarthy adopted. The chief characteristics of Hoover's FBI were its posture of nonpartisan objectivity, its claim to probity, and the tone of moral superiority as well as factual superiority that accompanied its every pronouncement. The FBI established itself as the archetypal Cold War subject. It was the very model of hypermasculine national realism—correct, powerful, self-contained, and reliant upon archival maneuver to project its criminal activities (break-ins, burglaries, illegal surveillance, manipulation of the justice system) onto the un-American others. The collaboration of the FBI, the military, and anticommunists in the government and private sectors worked to create a secret but powerful network that articulated the Cold War ideology of paranoia even liberals adopted. New security state measures extended the secrecy of wartime into a system of classification that even prevented adequate news coverage of national foreign policy.

Thus Cold War rhetoric defined an arena that would affect domestic life profoundly. As for relations with the Soviet Union: perhaps the Cold War maintained its stability and longevity because the participants depended upon it, as Mary Kaldor (building upon arguments advanced by E. P. Thompson and George Konrad) among others has said: the "two systems remained bound together in their conflictual embrace," resistant to change (6). Even the critics of Cold War policy agreed on the terms of what they call the "new reality" to a remarkable extent: "most of the critics and advocates shared a fundamental view with the architects of the Cold War. They saw themselves as standing in the middle between two extremes," as Hinds and Wendt point out in *The Rhetoric of the Cold War* (208). Walter Lippman devoted his influential journalistic practice to establishing a more workable plan for peace than the idealistic failures after World War I. He critiqued Churchill's "Iron Curtain" address, Truman's universal anticommunism, and Kennan's formulations, specifically the policy of containment. As part of the "realists' critique," however, even Lippman accepted the most basic premises of the new order and its language, and ironically contributed the most important metaphor of the period: he described the situation as the "Cold War" (219).

The national realism of the Cold War was a rhetorical stance that disclaimed its affiliations with rhetorical and literary conventions, particularly those of realism. National realism made an ahistorical appeal to the historical subject of reason, resting on a claim to be transparent, literal, and true that was enforced by police state measures. In other words, the conjuncture of an imaginary war that established national identity with claims to represent the transcendental subject of the symbolic order erected an Iron Curtain of its own, a discursive formation that was by its impossible conflation always under threat. National realism recalled and repressed in its assertions of reality (without admitting the textual history) the gendered literary conventions of the body, articulating desire and death, reinvoking narratives of sentimental domesticity and narratives of frontier adventure and discovery as artistic proofs of its authenticity. However, the struggle within domestic culture over the narratives of history took place in a neglected public sphere, the realm of mass culture: film, music, and non-elite literature. Male resistance to the banality of Cold War culture and its representations of patriarchal masculinity was, of course, widely thematized, its heroes ranging from James Dean and Elvis Presley to Holden Caulfield and Jack Kerouac.

Resistance also took shape at the level of form, in alternate styles of realism that did not practice the modernist break with a wide public. Significantly, "serious" middlebrow literature fell under particular suspicion during the Cold War, but at once from intellectuals and from conservatives. It belonged, perhaps, to the domain—of women's clubs and liberal groups—that George F. Kennan had listed as vulnerable to communist penetration. Literary works that were explicitly sentimental, and the genres of the Western, detective fiction, and science fiction were disavowed as "serious"—not, I am arguing, because they were too controlled by formula, although that was the charge, but precisely because they were too closely and obviously allied with the times. A number of critics have written in the last decade to show how such formula fiction—and films—reflected cultural history. For example, Frank Krutnik has argued that the film noir, derived from the tough thriller novel, was functioning to address "the non-correspondence between the desires of the individual male subject and the cultural regime of masculine identification," masculinity and the war's dislocation of men (85). But the New York intellectuals, writing for the public, and the New Critics, largely in the academy, disdained the mixed forms of cultural negotiation represented by genre fiction and Hollywood films. In particular, as Janice Radway discusses, they disdained the "serious" publications of the Book-of-the-Month Club, though they might endorse particular titles. Dwight Macdonald said in 1953 "There is slowly emerging a tepid, flaccid middlebrow culture that threatens to engulf everything in its spreading ooze," and Jackson Lears, citing this, points out that "the apocalypse in question was not the threat of nuclear war but the triumph of middlebrow culture . . . promoted by the Book-of-the-Month Club" (47).

The language of ooze associated with communism was used to characterize domestic culture. This signals the spreading influence of once-elite modernism, with its rejection of the feminine and the sentimental.

But the reason for the attack on the Book-of-the-Month Club, I'd like to argue, has also to do with its resistance to giving up realism as a literary style. The Book-of-the-Month Club published some titles that entered the highbrow canon of "literature," but it chose books written in a familiar style and chose nonfiction for over half of its selections—more popular, indeed, than fiction with its subscribers. In 1946, John Hersey's *Hiroshima* was given away to the membership as a free gift. Alan Nadel views *Hiroshima* as an early example of a mixed genre—the nonfiction novel— that will emerge with postmodernism, but in fact BOMC published such mixed genres regularly, books that implied "the *formal* failure of containment" (53). For example, Mari Sandoz's 1934 *Old Jules* (a BOMC choice) and 1942 *Crazy Horse* were both written as novelistic nonfiction. They risked being judged formal failures, however. I will discuss their pressure on the genres of truth-telling later.

Modernist literature came to dominate the aesthetics of the Cold War: it functioned as the bodied symptom of authentic trauma while the alignment of nationalism with science installed a paranoid realism at the level of the bomb's displacement across signifiers. But the middlebrow culture, far from imposing a banal normalcy on suburbanites, continued to dispute cultural history through the ongoing publication of works that were revising traditions of realistic narrative in the United States. The BOMC published *The Old Man and the Sea* in 1952—and Whittaker Chambers's *Witness*, along with Arthur C. Clarke's *The Exploration of Space* (186). In 1951, J. D. Salinger's *Catcher in the Rye* marked the advent of a critique of adults as phony. This is to argue that a struggle for control over discourses of realism in literature continued throughout the Cold War even though the academic party line disavowed any historical or political ambitions for the literary.

In the thirties, novels of literary realism written in the United States had explicit political references, but I am more interested here in the (overlapping) lineage of realistic writing that meant to be empirical and thus to claim association with Enlightenment discourses of objective truth rather than with rhetoric. Much realistic writing in the United States has been pragmatic, and yet responsive to an aesthetic of place too: it has had affiliations with the detail not so much of domestic commercial and economic interests (not Balzac, not Dickens) but with the detail accompanying an economy of exploration, of nature and landscape and settlement. Lewis and Clark's journals, Mary Rowlandson's story of captivity, Crèvecoeur's letters, Thoreau's nature writing and journals, some of Emerson's essays, Frederick Douglass, the autobiographies of slaves, much of Melville's description of whaling practices within his fiction, Mark Twain's travel notes in *Roughing It*, Theodore Roosevelt's *Ranch Life and the Hunting Trail*, Chesnutt's records of pre–Civil War plantation life, the letters and diaries of women on the frontier (who practiced herbalism and animal husbandry themselves, as well as teaching and the arts of community), Mary Austin's essays on the Southwest desert, Ernest Hemingway's *Green Hills of Africa*—these represent the genres related to recording discoveries that lay claim neither to verisimilitude nor to formal completion, but to productive fact—the journal, the travel narrative, the autobiography and memoir, the natural history—colonialism and capitalism in the field, as it were, and not from the perspective of the governing (European, urban) elite.[4] Bret Harte, Mark Twain, Sarah Orne Jewett, William Howells, Theodore Dreiser, Willa Cather, Jack London, Mary Austin, and Stephen Crane demonstrate the proximity of American fictional traditions to a regional and pragmatic aesthetic of nonfiction, with its claims to the representation of real—and useful—facts.[5] While there are women who have been significant writers in this tradition, it could be argued that its motif of discovery makes it masculinist.

This long history of realistic writing would precisely *not* be what the modernist critics of the Cold War valued as "literary," as the power to define the real was reallocated and submitted to government surveillance. The distinctions between fiction and nonfiction, literary myth and historical fact, literature and rhetoric delineated a frontier of denial to the powerful claims of literary modernism not only to represent the body of the world, but also to speak the true/real. During the Cold War, the effects of the modernist aesthetic, which had been shocking and disorienting in the twenties, were made less startling by the enforcement of literary boundaries. At the same time, literary modernism came to define the critical terms by which literature would be disciplined. The New York intellectuals, who reiterated their commitment to the "relevance" of literature, nevertheless ceased to think of literary realism as political (as it was in the thirties) and thought instead of literary realism in terms of the literary idea. Instead of imitating life, the work was its own, internalized context; its "ideas," then, associated with form and aesthetic feeling. Thomas Schaub, who analyzes literary realism and politics in *American Fiction in the Cold War,* points out that "in valorizing the literary idea the New York critics effectively endorsed the stylistic priorities of the New Critics" (33). The poetic context was contained within the body of the poem; irrationality was contained by the poetic body, its "ontology."

In other words, the literary body was womanly (since reason and emotion were gendered), and that emotional flow was contained by the formal properties of the aesthetic whole. At the same time that this genders authorship as male (a female author would loosen the boundaries of the object), it also submerges that gendering as part of the ideology of the aesthetic. Authorship would be the male fantasy of a bodied life. What C. P. Snow named "the two cultures" of science and the humanities seemed then and now, to everyone but the public and the postmodernists, self-evidently divided by their obligations to the real and the unreal. However, the formation of modernist literary aesthetics in the first decades of the century was deeply implicated with the history of the "real," not in opposition even to science: both assumed an impersonal subject and a real object.

Modernists had responded to the pressure of scientific realism by claiming to work on language itself, to rework the stereotyped formulations of everyday life so that the word might better approximate the real. T. E. Hulme, in "Romanticism and Classicism," argued that poetry's "great aim is accurate, precise and definite description," and that the "visual concrete" language of poetry is "a compromise for a language of intuition which would hand over sensations bodily" (732–33). Russian formalists had advocated *defamiliarization* as the poetic strategy that would be able to renew perception by changing the automatization of ordinary language. Modernist poems meant to escape the personal, but not the reality of the body; they worked to encapsulate the body's sensuous, emotional experience (alienated by the stratifications of modern life) in form. T. S. Eliot's "objective correlative" expressed the aspiration: "a set of objects, a situation, a chain of events which shall be the formula of the *particular* emotion; such that when the external facts, which must terminate in sensory experience, are given, the emotion is immediately evoked" (766).

Ezra Pound, T. S. Eliot, William Carlos Williams, and post-Coleridgeans such as I. A. Richards had from the first decade of the century begun to propose a modernism that theorized literature as the site of bodied experience, even though precisely *not* personal; rather, musicated through form into what Mallarmé had called the "new word." Literature then becomes, as William Carlos Williams argued in *The Embodiment of Knowledge*, an embodiment rather than a representation. Embodiment becomes a problem when subjects are alienated by an increasingly abstract, industrialized, bureaucratized public sphere. To the extent that white male subjects have been associated with the public sphere and the realm of production, and female, colored subjects associated with the private, with reproduction, or with the abjected, this version of alienation has had a race and a gender. Modernist literature from this perspective serves not only a nostalgic but, more importantly, a compensatory impulse. The body of the poem replaces the lost body of the rational self with a dissociated, fetishized linguistic practice—beauty and truth in touch with the real, or the true/real as an aesthetic hallucination. Modernist literature served such a purpose in the Cold War, but its radical critique of the public sphere was contained.

It is more than a little tempting to argue that both Cold War realism and the Cold War fixation on distinguishing American from un-American reflects a nativist concern with the racial stability of the family that

also explains its adoption of modernist poetics and its interest in the
ontology of the sign. Walter Benn Michaels has argued, in *Our Country*,
for the "structural intimacy between nativism and modernism" (2). In
his book Michaels sees both nativism and modernism as "efforts to work
out the meaning of the commitment to identity—linguistic, national,
cultural, racial— . . . common to both" (3). And indeed Michaels reads
the insistence on "reality" expressed by William Carlos Williams as part
of a nativist discourse signaled by the insistence on authenticity:

> For if rigidly linking a word to its referent is one way of in-
> sisting on the impossibility of substituting one word for an-
> other, then privileging the word over its referent is another;
> insofar as our interest is in the word itself rather than in what
> it signifies, we cannot replace it with another word that will
> seem to us to signify the same thing. (75)

The temptation to connect modernist nativism to the un-American-
ism of the Cold War is strong, but the cost could be great: Does it entail
accepting the ahistoricism of the modernist position? Does it entail as well
ignoring that liberals as well as conservatives adhered to the Cold War
logic? Instead, I want to emphasize the powerful discontinuities submerged by the Cold War consensus, in an especially exaggerated version
of the way a national project may—at least for a time—reread and re-
figure the available resources of language. The Cold War's national realism subsumed progressive, reform, and liberal assumptions about
referentiality together with conservative, reactionary, and nativist thought
under a governing certainty of threat. The consensus marked the elements
of discourses that confirmed the national situation. Even gendered manliness could contribute to this apparently ungendered consensus.

The New Critics insisted on the reality of the poem, but also on its
disconnection from history. W. K. Wimsatt in *The Verbal Icon* (1954)
argued against looking for theory's "special connections with the poems
of any specific period" to exempt poetry and its theory—that "deals with
universals"—from the historicity of rhetoric (170, 172). "The idea of the
circulation of the blood was expounded by Harvey in 1616, but we do
not conceive that it was about that time that blood began to circulate in
the human body" (170). Ezra Pound laid down the basic tenets of a modernist aesthetic not only in his theories of the image, but also in his bor-
rowing from the biologist Louis Agassiz's pedagogy of natural history,
in his use of Ernest Fenellossa's work on the Chinese character to advocate a more concrete representation, but (perhaps most of all) in his ubiquitous editing of other poets, from a Yeats cleansed of romanticism, to
Frost, H.D., Eliot, and Mina Loy, always removing abstraction. Pound's
every effort was to escape the muddle of subjectivity in order to ground

representation in the *real*, defined economically and anti-Semitically as that which was not usury.

In his influential essay on "The Concrete Universal," Wimsatt reasserted the ontology underlying Pound's natural science method: "A poem should not mean but be," and like a real thing "the real poem is a complex poem, and only in virtue of its complexity does it have artistic unity" (81). Cleanth Brooks wrote in *The Well-Wrought Urn* (1947) that "a true poem is a simulacrum of reality . . . by *being* an experience rather than any mere statement about experience or any mere abstraction from experience" (194). In his inquiry into new critical aesthetics, *The New Apologists for Poetry* (1956), Murray Krieger cited this passage from Brooks in order to talk about the notion of the self-fashioning poem making its own context—and to critique Max Eastman. It is perhaps too predictable that Eastman, advocate of revolution in the pages of the *Masses* in the years before the World War I "Red Scare," and writer of sentimental expression, might be found wanting. The nature of the critique was not that he had the wrong politics, but that he thought poetry referred to reality and located reality in the context outside the poem: "Although Eastman invokes a concept of experience similar to that of our critics, he has too primitive a view of poetry to ground this concept in a doctrine of context" (191).

The powers of context must be my theme. Michaels admits that neither Pound nor Eliot may be viewed as nationalists and that the ancestors to which they turn are international, yet he argues that "Pound's 'heritage' and Eliot's 'tradition' both participate in the genealogical discourse that nativism made central to the work of art and to the idea of culture" (102). The racial purity guaranteed by tracing genealogy is at issue. But Frank Lentricchia looks at Pound in relationship to a tradition that is, precisely, not native, pointing out that the "so-called virgin land was a nightmare to Pound" and styling him as a "reverse immigrant," who "fled the literary death whose name was natural immediacy" (202). The American absence, Lentricchia argues, makes Pound know "that there is no self anterior to representation to be aware of and that all the self that can ever be exists in the magical medium of representation" (203). The idea of nativism elides the question of the subject. However, if the subject is seen as the effect of systems of representation, then the representation of natural immediacy produces a psychotic break for the speaker of cultural traditions, an absence that is only fertile elsewhere.

The Cold War could make use of a nativist strain, legitimate ahistorical modernism, and indeed appear as an ahistorical stasis, spatializing all of history into the geographical conflict of capitalism and communism and simultaneously assimilate the discourses of evolution and progress. The Cold War consensus depends upon the reclaiming of the past itself as virgin land, to be colonized anew not as the wide open spaces, perhaps, but nonetheless as "freedom" for the New World reality of American postwar domination. The discursive formation of the Cold War installed a revised modernism at the very site of Pound's radical work, often leaving Pound out, and omitting the modernist claim that poetry could intervene in cultural politics by its explosive shock of the real.

The particular effort of the scholars in American studies that Donald Pease has called the "Cold War consensus" critics was the recolonizing of American cultural history in the name of freedom. Charles Feidelson Jr. argued, in *Symbolism and American Literature* (1953), for a historical refiguring that could show American literature as the native place for the history of a modernist aesthetics. His modernism (like Wimsatt's and Krieger's) cites Hulme and Eliot rather than Pound, even though all have clearly been influenced by Pound's formulations—evidence perhaps of the strategic disavowals of any overt connection to fascism that accompanied this particular construction of modernism. Pease first called attention to the "Cold War consensus" in *Visionary Compacts,* where he argued that the version of American cultural history assumed and conveyed by Feidelson and others emphasized a modernist struggle for freedom and a resistance to closure—a "Revolutionary mythos"—that had more to do with the Cold War than with the efforts to formulate the basis of a cultural renewal that characterized the American Renaissance writers (12). By the conclusion, with a rereading of Melville, Pease focuses on Ahab, the figure of excess rhetoric whose monomania would be read by the Cold War as totalitarian.

Associating powerful rhetoric with ideological threat suggests a major tenet of Cold War poetics. But to begin with, Pease looks at the figure of masculine protest that Leslie Fiedler associated with Rip Van Winkle, asserting that "Fiedler silently equates revolution with Rip's freedom from a variety of confining contexts" and so turns him into an archetype of the Cold War liberals who celebrate freedom as if they were returning soldiers on leave, "in terms of a continual furlough," "who need not distinguish the war of freedom they waged against Nazi totalitarianism from the domestic struggle they will wage when they return home—against inevitably dominant wives and confining home lives" (14).

This figure of masculinity—the Cold Warrior—joins military themes and domestic rebellion, the former soldier and the organization man, in a way that suggests how "beset manhood" operated. American studies scholars did not really disagree, but rather thematized the story of the free individual, R. W. B. Lewis's "American Adam," in a way that repeated the self-fashioning of the modernist real poem at the level of the real individual. The free, real individual acts in the arena of a challenge to authority that Ursula Le Guin—and Julia Kristeva—will see as adolescent.

This focus on the free male individual obscures the debt of national realism to a rhetorical history linked with more virulent identity politics. Before World War II began, the discourses associated with the war had begun to appear. The virulence of anti-Semitism overlapped with a new American politics of the Right. The media politics of attack and character assassination appeared in California in the opposition to Upton Sinclair's 1934 campaign for governor.[6] Father Coughlin preached fear and anti-Semitism on the airwaves.

The discourse of the Right inserted its accusations within a paranoid elaboration of truth-telling, proof, documentation, and apparent legalism. Ernest Elmhurst published a book called *The World Hoax* that purported to explain the Jewishness of Marxist plots:

> "You say Communism is Jewish?" challenges the Liberal-Minded Gullible.
>
> "I certainly do!" the wiser man affirms.
>
> "Well, *how can you prove it,* aside from the fact that great numbers of persecuted Jews flock into it to get them their rights the same as the workingman?"
>
> In nine cases out of ten, the more educated Gentile is immediately nettled and at a slight loss . . . where and how to . . . fetch forth documentary proof to support his contentions. . . . (11–12)

The interlocutor needs "facts" to defeat the gullibility of liberals. A certain politics of realism thus appeared in an oppositional guise that linked it to European propaganda campaigns. All during the war, for example, occupied France heard similar claims that linked anticommunism and anti-Semitism.

What World War II propaganda had instilled did not cease with the Cold War. In fact, the militarized state authorized by war and maintained by the Cold War had characteristics shared with fascism. Since it continues to serve as an epithet of great force, I want to distinguish two ways of thinking about *fascism:* the moral and the psychoanalytic. Cold War intellectuals connected the new enemy of communism to the old enemy of fascism by characterizing both as totalitarian. Hannah Arendt's analysis of totalitarianism and of fascism was especially influential. She helped shift the discussion from the terms of political theory to moral absolutes: fascism was simply evil. Ronald Reagan would later call communism the "evil empire," but his Star Wars stance was not so very different from that of many Cold War intellectuals in the fifties. Fear and self-defense would be a realistic response to the threat of an aggressive society run by absolute force. However, in earlier prewar days, *Partisan Review* writers had thought of fascism as not different in kind from other capitalist and imperialist states. Some feared that entry into the war would promote fascist practices in the United States.

On the other hand, perhaps the most threatening aspect of fascism is not its aggressive militarism, but its construction, through an aesthetics of propaganda and spectacle, of a ruthless national psyche based on anti-Semitism. Kristeva's psychoanalytic analysis of the "powers of horror" argues that fascist anti-Semitism arose not as a simple assertion of superior force, by a dominant group or ideology against a weaker victim, but as the defensive reinforcement of identity boundaries by an unstable subject, one threatened by the strangeness—the horror—of another who is not sufficiently differentiated from the self (like the abject mother for a child). Fascist identity would be both imaginary and extreme precisely because of the threat to its borders, and the threat of disintegration. Klaus Theweleit, in his research into the fantasies of men in the German Freikorps, found the torturer inflicted pain on another that he regarded as part of his own body, a bloody miasma or waste to be destroyed. The gendering was important: it was a male horror of feminine fluidity. This reinforces Kristeva's theories about the significance of the abject for a fascist orientation. Specifically, the imagery of their psychic life featured a horror of women, with their fluid excretions, their milk and blood. The struggle to stabilize identity would suppress precisely this fluidity, in favor of an identity contained by the stance of the Cold Warrior.

The figure of the Cold Warrior became the site of conflict about the nation and the individual. The warrior, he who exercises power through force rather than through persuasion, is gendered male (although women throughout history have taken up the role: from Fah Mu-Lan to Joan of Arc, they have cross-dressed to do so). Using rhetoric instead of force, on the other hand, is gendered as feminine. But the Cold Warrior often claimed to represent every man without gender. The hero appeared in the guise of antihero, but not without putting the manliness of the hero on trial.

It is not obvious that the thirties right-wing attack on the Left and on liberals, which might with justice have been thought of as fascist, should have any widespread effect on the scene of literature. What accounts for the extraordinary narrowing of canonical "culture" at the very moment when the United States emerged from World War II as an international power? Why did the poetry, prose, and theater of women, African Americans, working-class people, American Indians, and others disappear from view to those "interested" in culture? The suddenly uninteresting writers were an amorphous collection: Edna St. Vincent Millay and Willa Cather, writers of the Harlem Renaissance, Zora Neale Hurston, John Dos Passos, Meridel LeSueur, Mourning Dove, Sui Sin Far. They dropped out of the canon because they were not studied. The dominant genres of popular literature took on the aspect of the nonliterary: the Western, the detective story, the war story—genres characterized by their interest in dead bodies—romance, sentimental fiction, the Gothic—genres associated with women and a certain sensuality—and science fiction, another (cyborg?) kind of story.

This is to say that the cultural productions of communities "with bodies" were omitted from intellectual life during the first part of the Cold War. The bodies of these communities both disrupted the codes of public exchange and were disturbing for the stereotypical representations they inherited. The new denial of difference denied as well the history of identity politics that had portrayed bodies as gendered, colored, sexed, and normed. In *Sentimental Modernism,* I wrote about the effect on women writers of the modernist repression of the sentimental. During the Cold War, modernist repression joined with the hypermasculinity of nationalism to govern what readers, particularly in academic settings, might read.

The Cold War discourse became, in Gramsci's sense, hegemonic even though it was the invention of an anticommunist coalition, enforced and articulated by the FBI, and even though revisionary interpretation of our foreign relations appeared early. Criticism was contained. Cold War history was scarcely underway when revisionist historians began their analysis. William Appleman Williams suggested early on that the Cold War had its origin in the internal culture of the United States rather than in Soviet ideology. Williams argued in his 1952 *American-Russian Relations* that George F. Kennan's formulation of American policy toward the Soviet Union was not simply a realistic "containment," but called for "the application of a steadily rising military pressure to challenge existing Soviet leadership" (282). Power enforced the situation that was labeled *realistic.* Williams's challenges to Cold War discourse were themselves contained, although not censored, because they were Marxist and so un-American. The isolation of American history came to an end after World War II, and, Williams suggested, the "manifest destiny" of the frontier informed the new foreign policy. Ironically, American studies scholars who delineated the frontier, the wilderness, the pastoral garden, and the West as key elements of an American cultural mythology legitimated the condensation of soldier and cowboy rather than joining Williams's critique.

The old frontier logic was much altered in the new Cold War myth. It was dispersed across an ahistorical, polarized, and international block of states led and sheltered by the United States, an immovable coalition with little in the way of wide open spaces even though it was thought of as "the West." The displacement of the "Western" onto a more Eastern geography, the Cold War frontier of the West that came to an abrupt stop at the Iron Curtain in Eastern Europe, defined the sense of impasse that informed Cold War culture. The confrontation of the two major powers, East and West, in Berlin, could so resemble *High Noon* because there was no European space of another civilization and complexity to cross right after the war.

I am arguing that the Cold War took on the aspect of a melodramatic horse opera of good guys and bad guys because American culture was writing the script. The erasure of Native cultural history associated with the Indian wars extended all the way to Berlin. To bring this together with the question of realism and real bodies, I further argue that the frontier tradition, with its always-innocent hero undergoing trauma and triumph in his unacknowledgedly imperialist project, has shaped the history of bodies in America. Meaningful flesh in the Western drama is most often male, and subject to weather, accident, wounds, or death much more frequently than subject to sexuality—or childbirth. In this sense, the frontier narrative overlaps with the genres of real reporting that I described earlier. The frontier narrative, as William Appleman Williams had in mind, overlaps with the nation's violent history and its participation in imperialism. The innocent hero of the frontier is "haunted," as Toni Morrison has argued in *Playing in the Dark,* with a dark presence that has served to define his whiteness and his freedom, the histories of slavery and of Indian wars.[7]

Frontier stories posit a counter-space empty of human beings, a space of repression and denial, where the other appears as if without human consciousness, pure negation in the pursuit of identity. In Albert Bierstadt's sublime paintings of the Western vastness, human beings are either absent or dwarfed, and the Native American population is insignificant. The towering mountains are not home to anyone. This figment of the not-I mobilizes a subject in relationship to its limits, which may be multiplied indefinitely, and in the relationship of awe to a sight that inspires thoughts of death. It is, in this sense, utopian. Contrast the logic of I, not-I to the demonic struggle between two "superpowers" who elaborate their identities by an economy of personification, generating paranoia with its attendant borders and abjections: "communist," "capitalist." The Cold War took up both narratives of identity and invested bodies with significance accordingly. On the one hand, there is the story of a shoot-out at the O.K. Corral, or *High Noon,* with antagonists who might reinscribe the "manliness" endorsed by Teddy Roosevelt in American culture. On the other hand, there is a new *realism,* written in foreign policy by George Kennan and taken up by intellectuals as a willing resistance to the heroic.

There is good reason that the myth of the frontier seemed to Cold War Americanists to provide a continuous narrative for American history. Writers from Kennan to Richard Nixon and from Henry Nash Smith, R. W. B. Lewis, and Roderick Nash to Richard Slotkin joined with John Ford and John Wayne and the other significant players in film to reinvent a newly enlarged sense of the frontier as a myth fit to narrate the national history. This rebirth/revision of the frontier story made coherent the alliance of technology (the "endless frontier"), political life ("the New Frontier"), and capitalist consumerism (the new ranch house in suburbia). It is a regeneration through the violence of discursive reiteration. The paranoid construction of the frontier as a limit or border—or Berlin Wall—constructed not only the communists as "un-American." It was a defensive reinforcement of identity, and it made impossible not only the stories of difference that identity politics has dramatically restored.

A myth of the frontier also silenced other voices: the "endless frontier" of science replaced the scientists working for peace, such as Linus Pauling, but also pressed scientists away from pure science, toward the purposefulness of technology. The "New Frontier" represented by John F. Kennedy deployed the rhetoric of combat, reinvesting the increasing militarization of government with the idealism of war sacrifice: "Ask what you can do for your country." (I had not paid attention myself to the warlike stance of Kennedy's inaugural until a student told me that she "couldn't relate to it because we aren't at war now.")

Finally, the Theodore Roosevelt version of Rough Rider manliness was appropriated on behalf of a conservative politics. His son, Archibald Roosevelt, made the appropriation explicit in a pamphlet published by the Louisiana Sons of Liberty in 1968. Titled *On Race—Riots—Reds—Crime,* the pamphlet contained a number of Roosevelt quotes located by Archibald to support his own political sympathies, which were against the civil rights movement, the welfare state, and liberal politics: "It is true of the colored man, as it is true of the white man, that in the long run his fate must depend far more upon his own effort than upon of any outside friend" (8).

Archibald wants to use the egalitarian individualism of Roosevelt to argue against government assistance to the civil rights cause.

> The Indians should be treated in just the same way that we treat the white settlers. Give each his little claim; if, as would generally happen, he declined this, why, then let him share the fate of the thousands of white hunters and trappers who have lived on the game that the settlement of the country has exterminated, and let him, like these whites, who will not work, perish from the face of the earth which he cumbers. (written in 1886, 30)

Furthermore, he wants to enlist Roosevelt in a sixties policy of cutting aid to the Indians and eliminating their land and their tribal rights.

> I have scant sympathy for that maudlin sentimentality which encourages . . . the general continental European revolution-

ary attitude, which in governmental matters is a revolt against
order as well as against tyranny, and in domestic matters is a
revolt against the ordinary decencies and moralities even more
than against conventional hypocrisies and cruelties. (1906, 38)

Archibald doubtless wanted to view the sixties as "a revolt against order" and to think of everyone on the Left as "sentimental." Seizing upon
his father's individualism, however, he did indeed seize upon precisely the
ideological limit that would frame the sixties revolt and enable a return
to Cold War categories in the eighties and nineties.

The critical "Cold War consensus" of the New Critics and the New
York intellectuals might also be thought of as a consensus for a realism
that overlapped with the foreign policy realists. However, the criticism
and literature endorsed by Cold War critics functions in relationship to
that other material from which they resolutely turned away. They laid
down the rules of an aestheticism so tightly connected to the national
interest that the proclaimed end of the Cold War has brought about what
William Bennett hailed as the "culture wars." Thus the effort to reinstate
and prolong Cold War culture and renew the censorship of the bodied
word continues in the struggles over textuality, in the domain of the ideological where George F. Kennan had originally located the Cold War in
his "long telegram."

2

Cold War Modernism and the Crisis of Story

> [T]he characteristic element of modern literature, or at least
> of the most highly developed modern literature, is the bitter
> line of hostility to civilization which runs through it. . . . And
> perhaps I ought to admit at once that, as much as about mod-
> ern literature itself, I am talking about the teaching of mod-
> ern literature. . . . Indeed, if we are on the hunt for *the* mod-
> ern element of modern literature, we might want to find it in
> the susceptibility of modern literature to being made into an
> academic subject.
>
> —Lionel Trilling, "On the Modern Element
> in Modern Literature"

Modern literature, as Lionel Trilling thought of it, developed in the first
part of the twentieth century, but it entered the institutions of higher
education in the United States after World War II, together with returning vets, survivors of the Holocaust, and talented refugees. The men were
suffering from shell shock and the texts that Trilling taught (Conrad, Eliot,
Kafka, Gide) expressed despair, but both vets and literature found useful work. Literary criticism mediated the alienation by its own discipline
of distance. Lionel Trilling wrote about why he was reluctant to endorse
a class on modern literature—like his own at Columbia. He was worried
not only about modernist hostility to civilization, and its appeal to students,
but also—paradoxically—about the way that the modern by its very alienation was intertwined with the academic. The hostility to civilization that
Trilling marked would ally literature, one would think, with the forces
of the irrational and the unconscious, and with radical politics. Modernist
style was certainly conceived of as some kind of rupture of the conventional by its theorists, from the French symbolists through surrealism to
Theodor Adorno, and up to Julia Kristeva. The powerful alienation from
everyday life (symbolized by both theme and form in *The Waste Land*),
however, lends itself—at least in some forms—to an alliance with critical
distance and with the Cold War critic's political disengagement. Furthermore it both expresses and resembles the alienation of capitalism.

During the Cold War, university professors embraced alienation with chilling enthusiasm. This taking up of a certain modernism into the very structure of the discipline has had unexamined consequences both for literature and for literary theory. Above all, it has functioned to contain and defend against the rhetorical powers of literature: the powers of style and the powers of story. Even though literary criticism during the Cold War theorized an aesthetic that kept literature apart from the mean politics and the fearful history outside the ivy-covered walls, as if to protect its right to free speech, Cold War criticism had the same effect that McCarthy's anticommunism had: it silenced the speech of subversives in the interests of defense. In defense against banality and the public seduced by McCarthy, intellectuals were also alienated from the power of stories.

The loss of stories had been foretold by Walter Benjamin in "The Storyteller," where he described the communal sharing of experience provided by a storyteller such as Leskov, and its loss in the alienation produced by modern literate economies. Modernity, and not just the literary theory of modernism, shaped Cold War literature. However, the American Cold War culture generated specific forms of policing. Critics imagined a Freudian subject struggling to solidify the isolated ego against the forces of irrationality. They accepted a form of modern alienation for literature that established and maintained prohibitions against communal stories, stories that reproduced experience forming not individuals but communities. Bernard Malamud, for example, told stories that worked the edge between assimilation into American individualism and the invocation of Jewish experience. Ursula Le Guin, as another example, told—and tells—stories that aspire to speak to a communal experience: she addresses the homelessness of modernity in general and the Cold War politics of identity in particular. She articulates the intersection of imaginary and cultural symbolic without a claim to realism and thus inverts the continuing alienation of intellectuals from home, body, and experience as well as from stories—and each other. Both Malamud and Le Guin use mixed forms that include oral traditions—a form of address that emphasizes the dependence of the utterance on its connection to audience and destabilizes the isolation of capitalist authorship.

Writing as a disembodied middle-class subject, without claiming even his Jewish attachments, a critic such as Trilling might seem without gender as well and certainly without the ethnic stories that a Jewish heritage provided Malamud. Although the gendering of subversives is important in my reading of Cold War realism, this is not in order to claim that women were the most oppressed. One could hardly compare the aftermath of a general misogyny to the specific horror left by anti-Semitism. Rather, I am arguing, the too-familiar litany of race, gender, class, and sexuality has become the list of the oppressed now because they were conflated then—

conflated, made to provide the frontiers of a bounded identity, and eliminated from literary history, except as the effect of exclusion, a minority. In *Containment Culture*, Alan Nadel shows how a politics of narrative siting could impose identity by enforcing illegibility. Thus, in his chapter on "Race, Rights, Gender," Nadel discusses the variety of perspectives about masculinity available in African American writing, and the way a failure to read that complexity operates to contain and repress it.

> The problem, as we have been examining it, is not that blacks and/or women do not have narratives that comprise their personal history or sense of identity, but that those stories are not widely legible. If power is the negotiating of illegibility, then the personal becomes political not when it speaks of itself to itself, but only when it affects the dominant cultural narrative. (251)

Anticommunism instilled itself into the rhetoric of literature as a boundary-making logic, reflecting in cultural productions the logic of "containment" traced by Nadel.[1] Anticommunism shaped the literary discipline as an anti-rhetoric, a formalism, containing both the subversive and the conservative force of literary effects within the limited context of the aesthetic object and silencing the storytelling function, the artistic proof of ethical rhetoric, the communal conscience hailed and formed by stories.

The rhetorical logic is significant precisely because Cold War discursive strategies have perpetuated the rhetorical Cold War with its anticommunist orientation beyond the so-called fall of communism. Not only utopia, but also the modest hopefulness of a progressive liberalism continues to seem intolerable to a large number of readers: hence the cultural legibility of a postmodernism that might work for justice, rights, and fairness is still exceedingly limited, together with the complex stories and experiences of "minorities" whose representations continue to be contained by accusations of political correctness. This can be seen not only in the politicizing of multicultural stories, but also by the ease with which writers such as those I analyze later in this book—Hemingway, Sandoz, Malamud, or Le Guin— come to seem politically opaque, recuperated for containment narratives of an American culture.

Trilling worried about *both* the influence of the academy on modern literature *and* the influence of modern literature on his students. The academy, he wrote, can "restore to the old work its freshness and force— can, indeed, disclose unguessed-at power. But with the works of art of our own present age, university study tends to accelerate the process by which the radical and subversive work becomes the classic work" ("On the Modern Element" 268). This takes place because the university situates literature within the relationship between teachers and students. The most painful aspect of that relationship for Trilling occurs not when the student disagrees with a closely held belief, but when the students are all too glibly responsive to the alienation of modern literature and its despair. The interpersonal transaction Trilling envisions says much about how he imagines the student as a subject:

> Instead of prizing responsiveness and aptitude, we set store by some sign of personal character in our students, some token of individual will. We think of this as taking the form of resistance and imperviousness . . . a power which will lead a young man to say, "But is this really true—is it true for me?" And to say this not in the modern way, not following the progressive educational prescription to "think for yourself," which means to think in the progressive pieties rather than in the conservative pieties . . . but to say it from his sense of himself as a person rather than as a bundle of attitudes and responses which are all alert to please the teacher and the progressive community. ("On the Modern Element" 265)

That is, Trilling passes on the recoil against ideology that characterized *Partisan Review* ex-leftists after 1939 by the assertion that both progressive and conservative pieties might be avoided. The most powerful habits of thought about originality and the person come into play and in an exchange between an older man and a younger. Possibly such freedom from pieties would not seem so necessary for a young woman, if she were allowed into Trilling's class. Especially significant is the idea that a young man can demonstrate a "sense of himself" only through the power of "resistance and imperviousness." Being critical has to do with identity and gender and is only genuine if disconnected from pleasing the teacher or the progressive community. Modern literature, then, becomes a means of demonstrating that one is critical—but a *class* on modern literature threatens to turn alienation itself into a means of pleasing the teacher.

A conservative reaction to modernism, as well as to progressivism, then arises out of the teacher's very assumption that learning is dependent upon individual authenticity. Not commitment, but rather only resistance may be authentic. This has some affiliation, let us admit, with the general academic tradition of an agonistic rhetoric. But Trilling's language about the "pieties of progressives" also reflects the apolitical forms of the Cold War reaction against progressivism. His approach in the essay on modernism, as in *The Liberal Imagination,* was to separate out of liberalism whatever was salvageable from a political program Trilling rejected. In fact, what Trilling did was to reject the liberal subject in favor of a more disengaged subject, defined as the position between extremes—defined as the rejection of extremity.

We can see from the description of his course that something like an instantaneous set of "classics" was established, mostly not American, together with a way of reading them that acknowledged, reproduced, and so resisted the alienation they represented. Trilling taught Conrad's *Heart of Darkness,* Yeats, Eliot's *The Waste Land,* Joyce, Proust, Kafka, Lawrence, Mann, Gide, Auden, together with Frazier's *The Golden Bough,* Nietzsche's *The Birth of Tragedy and the Genealogy of Morals,* Herbert Marcuse, Norman O. Brown, Jacques Diderot's *Rameau's Nephew,* Dostoyevsky's *Notes from Underground,* and Tolstoy's *Death of Ivan Ilych.* His list includes more material related to interpreting culture than a course on modern poetry organized around American formalist aesthetics would have done during the Cold War, including Nietzsche and Freudian critics. However, he demonstrates for us the more clearly the strange doubleness about modern literature: it is at once a threat to the culture taught by university classes, and yet its most amenable form. There are no women or people of color on the list, and this reflects Trilling's mechanism of choice more than it reflects modernism itself.

Trilling thought that modern literature was part of a cultural warfare. If we admired literary style, we needed nonetheless to resist the crisis it produced and to support civilization, once we had acknowledged our discontents. "These structures were not pyramids or triumphal arches, they were manifestly contrived not to be static and commemorative but mobile and aggressive, and one does not describe a quinquireme or a howitzer or a tank without estimating how much *damage* it can do" ("On the Modern Element" 269).

The history of modernist literary interventions supports Trilling's warlike metaphor, but the Cold War functioned maximally to contain the threat. From the Vortex proclamations in Wyndham Lewis's *Blast,* to the declarations of Marinetti's futurism, to dadaism, to the theses declaring "The Revolution of the Word" in Eugene Jolas's *Transition,* to André Breton's decrees about surrealism, to the situationist history leading to Guy Debord, the repeated attempts to make some kind of cultural revolution are evident in the warlike defiance of the many avant-garde manifestos. Whether the culture wars thus asserted are related to Marx's *Communist Manifesto* or Hitler's *Mein Kampf* continues to be a matter of significant debate.

During the Cold War, however, literary criticism made an effort to ensure that literature was not engaged in any cultural warfare at all, and despite Trilling's apparent concern about the power of literature, he managed very well to contribute to its containment. The aggressive force of modern literature, the very stylistic ruptures that were meant to offend the bourgeoisie, were studied carefully by middle-class students at Columbia University, and the very alienation of the artist that was meant to represent the unconscious alienation of the modern individual became the self-conscious theme of proliferating academic discussions. Existentialism came to be the topic of widespread student interest, but Jean-Paul Sartre's Marxist orientation dropped out and it became another version of American individualism. This containment occurred together with the canonization of a few writers: "Modern Literature" was installed overnight as the object of a discipline. Furthermore, the discipline itself, of literary study, arose at the same time in the shape needed for critical scholarship on modernism, as a response to the challenge of modern literature. What we now think of loosely as modernist aestheticism was not just a focus on the artistic qualities of poetry and the arts, but rather a defense against the power of modern literature to rupture a cultural absolutism that was being installed. Literary critics studied alienation, but they were on the side of Cold War banality. In particular this can be read in the versions of modernity circulated around Marx, Freud, and Nietzsche.

Although Trilling and other literary intellectuals might seem to have been disengaged from foreign policy and anticommunist persecutions, in fact their work was permeated with the task of defense. In the intellectual culture of the Cold War, those who were most dominant were also those who were most *realistic* in an additional sense—that is, pessimistic about the progress of civilization. This consensus endorsing a tragic vision built not only upon the philosophical despair inherited from Schopenhauer and Nietzsche or the more contemporary representations of Reinhold Niebuhr, but more specifically upon the widespread disillusion of the Left, disenchanted with Stalin since 1939. Because it included the former Left, it powerfully disguised its exclusionary effect. Nevertheless, the critical agreement called the "Cold War consensus" both disallowed utopian desire and censored the writing of the hopeful. Furthermore, in the name of maturity and realism, what Schaub calls the "liberal narrative" erased the literary history of a wider, more inclusive liberalism. The Cold War consensus, with its opposition to liberal sentimentality, foreclosed not only political, but also gendered subjectivities, producing a civil society in relationship to voids. This returns us to the subject of Cold War individualism I discussed earlier: the hypermasculine subject manifests an identity circumscribed by the arena of aggression.

In Lionel Trilling's reading of modernism, for example, he emphasized the Freud of *Civilization and Its Discontents*, connecting antiprogressivism to hypermasculinity. In that 1929 essay, Freud blames women for distracting men from their work (for the good of civilization), and at the same time for thinking that civilization should be able to progress toward greater happiness. Human aggressiveness, not the uncanny, is the focus of Freud's interest. Communism, he says, is based psychologically on "an untenable illusion" that aggressiveness is connected to property, whereas it is a more fundamental principle of human nature. "It is always possible to bind together a considerable number of people in love, so long as there are other people left over to receive the manifestations of their aggressiveness" (*Civilization* 751). This explains anti-Semitism and also communist attacks on the bourgeoisie, he says. The 1929 essay gained in its tragic explanatory power from the view after Hitler, as details of the Holocaust beggared explanation. But the logic of communal identity referred to by Freud worked for the American nation as well; the people were bound together by the existence of communism, left over to receive the manifestations of aggressiveness as well as the blame. This overdetermined national subject was both hyperreal and hypermasculine, and it saturated even academic discourses with its new stain of the real.

The skeptical narrative of liberalism prided itself on being able to hold aloof from mass irrationality. Realism and reason seemed the defense against nationalist totalitarianism. Cold War liberals who read Freud emphasized the importance of the ego and critical arguments tried to separate reason from emotional appeals. As this ego psychology version of Freud prevailed, instinct, the unconscious, the pre-Oedipal, emotion, sexual desire, and the body were all condensed into a single primitive urge that needed to be mastered by the intellect—an irrationality located not only in a more primitive stage of culture, represented importantly by African American communities, but also in women's bodies. The identity of individuals seemed *real,* prior to culture, uncovered perhaps by psychoanalysis but not changed, except to strip away the confusions of neuroses and complexes. At the level of the individual, the self seemed defined by opposition to and difference from another; at the level of the nation, the national subject was also defined not by acknowledging the process of abjection and scapegoating, but by the "real" difference between capitalist and communist national identity. Thus the most significant element in the production of Cold War discourse, the involvement of pre-Oedipal processes of identity, became invisible and unanalyzable—and feminized.

The reception of poststructuralist psychoanalytic theory in the United States has been and continues to be distorted by the American version of individualism reconstructed during the Cold War. Jacques Lacan, breaking with the dominance of this ego psychology in the psychoanalytic establishment, posited the development of the ego as the assumption of the other, a structural alienation first realized in the "mirror stage." But projecting the strangeness of the self onto another continues as a theme of American identities. Post-Lacanian analyses of subjectivity from Louis Althusser and Michel Foucault through Julia Kristeva to Franz Fanon and Homi Bhabha have found the tendency of American ideologies of the individual tightly reinforced by a reality-principle Freudianism that disguises its debt to the security state formations. Secrecy has hidden the political valence of the hero's cultural arena.

Instead, arguments against psychoanalysis in the contemporary United

States are apt to repeat the criticism that Sidney Hook voiced in a 1959 symposium on the status of psychoanalysis and published in *Psychoanalysis, Scientific Method, and Philosophy*. Hook's introduction makes his sense of the context very clear:

> The liberation of nuclear energy has made the existence of human life and society problematic. This is comprehensible not as a consequence of a theory of natural science but as a consequence, for the most part, of a social philosophy derived historically, even if not logically, from the social doctrines of Marx. For good or ill, it is in Marx's name and in the name of those who have declared themselves his disciples that the most formidable challenge to the society of the free world has been made. (xii)

In his chapter, "Science and Mythology in Psychoanalysis," Hook cites a couple of notable (empirical) psychologists who had claimed psychoanalysis was *not* scientific—John B. Watson and H. J. Eysenck—and reports his challenge to psychoanalysts: "Describe what kind of evidence they were prepared to accept which would lead them to declare in any specific case that a child did not have an Oedipus complex" (216). Arlow's reply listed a number of consequences of a little boy's having no desire for his mother, including lack of gender and lack of social identification: "Considerations of masculinity or femininity would be minimal . . . impulsive emotionality and very meager identification with the standards . . . of his human environment" (217). In response to claims that psychoanalysis can discern what philosophers "really say, as against what they delusively appear to say," Hook replies: "Usually I find that what is at issue is some cultural or social or political problem. And if for the term 'real' we substitute the term 'reliable' or 'valuable,' many expressions that are difficult to construe make sense" (222). Thus psychoanalytic categories are subject to Marxist analysis, as science would not be, and dismissible as religion—or art: "The monistic dogma of psychoanalysis is palpably inadequate to account not only for the varied achievements of creative artists and philosophers and scientists, but also for the work of poetic mythologists like Freud himself" (223). The problem with psychoanalysis, Hook demonstrates, is its proximity on the one hand to ideology—and on the other, its proximity to Marxist analysis itself. Something real must be left behind of the self after culture has been subtracted.

I am arguing that the New York intellectuals supported a Cold War version of American individualism that put the old markers of identity, especially gender, under threat, together with any accompanying emotionality—the markers of Oedipus could become the markers of mythology. To be against communists was to be nothing less than transcendently rational as well as to be a hero of American patriotism. The new concept of leadership, as Sidney Hook argued for it in his 1943 *The Hero in History*, would combine a sense of the collective force of an economic system with a reliance on democratic individuals, a mutuality of individual and social effort articulated by reason. Irrationality was imposed by dictators—Hitler, Mussolini, and Stalin. In 1948, Hook went on to argue that anyone who supported communism was de facto irrational. The enormous impact of his argument will be traced in chapter 4.

This willingness to think about history in terms of the rational/irrational character of individual leaders shows how anticommunism came to be inflected with both psychoanalysis and gender for New York intellectuals who had once been interested in communism, including those (like Hook) associated with the *Partisan Review*. Even Jewish intellectuals such as Hook and Trilling were in this way caught up in a mode of thought related to anti-Semitism.

Cold War discourse links anticommunism to the logic of anti-Semitism, functioning by a rough identification that installs boundaries the more extreme and rigid because they are threatened, as Julia Kristeva has suggested in her analysis of Céline's fascist essays. But I do not mean to argue that Cold War discourse in the United States was the same as that of the fascists; Freud's analysis in "Civilization and Its Discontents" explains the cultural logic of anti-Semitism without imagining that it could lead to the genocide implemented by the Nazis, and Cold War discourse rested on elements of the wartime logic in ways that led to extremities of censorship, even purges, but not to genocide. Nevertheless, the Cold War discourse that circumscribed painful history and limited the threat of literature resembled in many respects the "banality of evil" that Hannah Arendt saw in her observations of the Eichmann trial.

Anticommunism's abuses were not limited to those who suffered persecution from the loyalty oath programs, the firings, the inquiry before the House Un-American Activities Committee, the blacklistings, the convictions and jail sentences and, in the case of the Rosenbergs, the execution. More widespread was the imposition of an anxious banality that made even liberal perspectives seem dangerously left. Then, as now, the political Right could impose sanctions against free speech, so that opinions that were not illegal nevertheless could serve as adequate reasons to fire, persecute, or otherwise censor academics, intellectuals, artists, and writers; then as now the ineffectual Left were blamed for extremism and political correctness. In 1948, Henry Wallace's Progressive Party campaign for president even generated student protest, and labor unions organized strikes—afterwards put down as communist. The rising banality of the fifties denied the significance of all this, as if the only desire of the American people were to have fun—but the case of Ralph Spitzer demonstrates how banality at Oregon State College was imposed from above after his 1949 firing stirred debate. Bernard Malamud's *A New Life* traces the forms of censorship, from the most intimate to the most public levels, set off by the rigors of enforced happy days.

The Cold War revealed itself, after all, to be about representation, power, and identity rather than about battles. The typical rhetorical structure of Cold War discourse has given us a model inherited by the identity politics of today. It is, as Christer Jonsson puts it in his 1982 analysis of foreign policy ideology, a conflict waged by "inferring the intentions of the adversary not so much from what they *did* as from what they *were* (imperialist/communists)" (104).

The modernist canon as it finally emerged in the English departments of the forties, as the Cold War took hold, provided the foundation for (even as it censored) identity politics. It omitted the historical tradition of literature, which was strongly redolent of marginal culture or un-American history. There was a kind of harrowing of difference, a purging of ambiguity unless it was thoroughly contained. Women writers, writers in the Harlem Renaissance, proletarian writers, immigrant writers, but also men such as Ernest Hemingway who gendered masculinity and attached it to the body—during the Cold War period all found themselves in a tenuous position as a single version of high modernism began to prevail. This was neither the result of ignorance about the variety of American literature nor of a tradition in literary history that left out all but a few. The *Cambridge History of American Literature* appeared in 1917–1921 with a whole chapter on Native American literature, recognition of women writers including Emily Dickinson, Margaret Fuller, Harriet Beecher Stowe, and acknowledgment of African American writing, even if patronizing, together with a chapter on "Dialect Writers" that had whites in the majority, using black vernacular. David Shumway is of course right when he calls the anthology "overtly racist" and "covertly sexist" and points out that the principle of its exclusions is "gender, race, and class" (91). However, the Cold War interrupts any narrative of greater inclusiveness we might want to make. Fred Lewis Pattee published the founding texts for the study of American literature in *The Century Book of American Literature* during the years from 1917 to the thirties. Relying upon a critical method influenced at least in part by the doctrines of nineteenth-century French critic Hippolyte Taine, Pattee considered "the man, the race, and the milieu" in these histories. He included large numbers of women writers in all these texts, both praising them for their leadership and condemning them to be just precursors to a future American greatness (a condemnation shared by the writers of the American Renaissance, however). In 1940, he published a volume on what he considered to be the most important decade of nineteenth-century literature, the 1850s, and he called it, for the significant influence of women writers, *The Feminine Fifties.*

The very concept of a national literature and what one might do to study it underwent such profound change after World War II that Pattee's extensive work seemed quickly just historicist by comparison to modernist criticism. Americanists who specialize in the literature before modernism, particularly those in American Studies, have never altogether lost sight of this broader perspective, though R. W. B. Lewis left the American Eve out of his *American Adam* and Feidelson read American literature as a precursor to the aestheticized version of European Symbolism that Edmund Wilson had condemned in his 1931 *Axel's Castle.*

With the postmodern opening up of literary studies, the old conception of modernism began to seem mysteriously narrow.[2] There is no need to argue about how literary studies in the fifties, and on into the seventies, counted only a few writers as the great modernists and almost all of them white middle-class males. Still, facing not only students, but also colleagues who cannot remember the bad old days when there were no women and no "minorities" on the syllabus or the curriculum, I feel it necessary to underscore how very focused on white men the curriculum became during the Cold War, and how easy it was to deny that there was any question of their gender or race involved. Without the obvious violence imposed by regimes that oppressed their writers, and indeed oppressed any form of critical expression, the culture of the West, and particularly of the United States, enforced a kind of censorship upon the arts. The reasons why the field of literature became so limited have implications beyond the literary.

The cultural logic of projection, scapegoating, and sacrifice intersects during the Cold War with a specific political and economic history. Clearly the reasons why an elite and gendered version of modernism prevailed during the critical decades when literary studies became established ought to shed light on the class formation of the profession. In the thirties and before, there had been troublesome aliens threatening the cohesiveness of the middle classes: feminists and new women, the "New Negro," the working classes, but also the large numbers of immigrants with their multiple languages and their experience with socialist, anarchist, and communist political aspirations. The strangeness of the avant-garde in literature overlapped with this other strangeness, multiplying the force of the manifestos threatening artistic "revolution" but also making it eventually necessary to draw more absolute distinctions between literary revolution and political upheaval.

The modernist canon did not prevail in the exuberant year of 1913 (publication of H.D., "imagiste") or the peak year of 1922 (*The Waste Land*) or even in the year of 1939, with the publication of the modernist way of reading in Cleanth Brooks and Austin Warren's *Understanding Poetry* and John Crowe Ransom's *The New Criticism,* and the *Partisan Review*'s repudiation of communism. The canonical version of modernism and modernist criticism prevailed after World War II, as departments of literature took up the responsibility for critical evaluation and launched a new, formalist pedagogy that contested the old ways of historical and philological scholarship. At that moment writers such as those I examine more closely in later chapters became illegible in a consequential way, because the alienation from shared experience made the communalism of storytelling problematic.

The writers I consider in later chapters all enjoyed a wide readership during the Cold War, so what I mean by "unreadable" refers to the dislocation of experience rather than to copies sold. Ursula Le Guin traces the trajectory of the dislocated story through her fantasies and science fiction. Writing in ways that both repeated and complicated cultural narratives of manliness and sentimental domesticity; writing in the domains of the well understood, how might a writer avoid the coercive reassurances of banality?

Even though women writers, writers of color, and working-class writers were obviously victims of what, in retrospect, can appear only as a kind of literary purge, what can account for their disappearance from critical discussion some twenty years or more after they wrote? Complaints about women writers are not new in literary history—but, then, neither are women writers. Yet feminist scholarship about the very numerous women associated with literary modernism had to assert the very existence of another modernism, other writers, uncovered material that was unknown. It's not hard to show that modernist poetics discriminated against women, or that modernist critics wrote scathing reviews of their work. Critics, however, do not usually succeed in eliminating the objects of their attacks so entirely from the landscape, no matter how ill-intentioned they might be. Critics, in fact, habitually write to advocate one set of values over another, and in an era of so-called relativism, or democratic pluralism, should scarcely be expected to prevail so very absolutely.

The modernist/Cold War purge was overdetermined. What lent it force can nevertheless be specified: a certain antagonistic relationship to the masses, a poetic that was differentiated from rhetoric, the growing professionalization of intellectuals, the coalescence of a mature American literature taking its place in the international scene, and—importantly—the gendered distinctions that served to organize a growing exclusivity against popular sentimentality. It is important, however, that modernist aestheticism kept it from acknowledging the sudden advent of a historical turn in the forties. At that point, the overwhelming influence of national politics on every aspect of intellectual life installed the local values of modernist poets and critics within a larger and far more oppressive cultural matrix. This took place not only during the heat of World War II battles, but even more massively during the Cold War that arose as its aftermath. The purge of strangers took place according to a logic captured by nuclear terror. Critical debates that might have been rhetorical, part of a conversation, became foundational. That is, they became part of a national realism.

The domination of this formation—and its gendering—becomes clearer in the careers of writers who appear to be in the mainstream, such as Hemingway, or representative of the times, such as Malamud, or those, such as Sandoz, who attempted to tell the real history, or those, such as Le Guin, who use the familiar to tell about the unfamiliar. The ubiquity and invisibility of Cold War ideology can be felt by its resistance to the very topics that might be raised by the strangers left out of literature— gender differences, for example. The paradox of the Cold War's hypermasculinity is that its use of gender eliminated or abjected and feminized all differences, making critical portrayals of masculinity or femininity appear disruptive, irrational, excessive, or politically misguided.

For the forties, fifties, and much of the sixties Cold War discourse prevailed. No feminists argued about gender in spite of the obvious propagandizing on behalf of what Betty Friedan finally labeled the "feminine mystique." Even though alienation was the topic of both popular and intellectual analysis, the forces of normalization silenced both strangeness and strangers. The extreme reductiveness of gender's either/or configuration dominated literary studies in the Cold War because gendering underwrote national realism. This was not, as often assumed, merely a continuation of a long history of patriarchy, or just an example of an eternal war between the sexes. There have also been, through history, periods of opportunity that were less constrained, when (for example) sentimental novelists, poetesses, new women, feminists broke free of gendered constraints to more inventive and explorative modes of writing. The Cold War consensus shut down a women's literary tradition that was flourishing when the modernists attacked it, and did not just go away under modernist fire. Feminist scholars worked hard in the eighties to articulate more complex distinctions than gender, theorizing the problem of "essentialism" in identity politics. Still, the efforts to acknowledge differences of race, class, sexuality, ethnicity, and so forth quickly were reduced to "difference," a single category, signaled by the mantra: race, class, gender. Feminists did not invent this reductiveness, just as they did not make gender decisive in the first place, because feminists do not come from outside cultural history. Gender continues to operate as a hidden structure, unknown in part because interpretation does not consider its own history. The hidden work of gender organizes the way we read along a hierarchical rift of inclusion and exclusion. Hypermasculinity functioned during the Cold War to shore up a national realism that could not, precisely, resonate with more than a rhetorical nativism, not in a culture of so many languages, so many histories, so much transiency. Hypermasculinity functioned to produce the fantasy of nativism as a national realism.

Just as the hypermasculine governed public discourse, in the form of disciplinary domesticity it overwrote the space of the interior. Home, mother, child came under the supervising gaze of Dr. Spock. Occupants of the claustrophobic house were threatened and contained by the new consumer manners of the nuclear family, and only the male escaped. It is not surprising that stories of adolescent escape could become definitive. The consuming male/warrior launches himself through cynicism, like Holden Caulfield. The young male must find a mode of rebellion that allows him to leave his mother, become a Medusa figure, "Mom." When Ursula Le Guin began to write her Earthsea stories in the late sixties, she imagined a return to other possibilities for the young initiate, the path beyond the arena of the Cold Warrior, but of course the hero still had to leave home to find his way. She reveals just how completely the site of "home" had been colonized and made risky by the Cold War. The domestic sentimental captured and stored away the vigorous political energies of compassion, segregated from the forbidden, which was the suspect public compassion for collectivities that even liberals tried to avoid. Where might the scientist or the intellectual live? What is the place for the body of reasonable thought?

Critical theory since the Cold War may be seen as working to recover from categories that arose out of very specific material circumstances but were transcendentalized. How to keep the discipline of interpretation and yet open up the idea of language? How can we keep a practice of interpretation that seems to depend, for example, on the "phallogocentrism" feminists have critiqued? Phallogocentrism seems to inform Freud and Nietzsche in spite of their modernity and to have informed the idea of reason for the whole history of philosophy. However, in opposing such male absolutism, a hypermasculinity that seems obviously incredible from the feminist point of view, critical theory has taken up a correspondingly ahistorical absolutism, finding logocentrism, most often with a phallus, in every kind of reasonable argument.

Part of my aim in this book is to show how rapidly the Cold War installed such problems of definition as policy absolutes, how recent and local is this critical history of empiricist foundations made *real* through political economy. I don't mean to argue that there has not been a long history of foundationalism in Western thought. I mean to argue that it has been contested, that often literary interpretation has been more influenced by rhetoric, pragmatism, progressivism, democratic revolution, or feminism than by epistemological absolutism.

The twentieth century has been marked by Diaspora, migration, and refugees, by issues of freedom and terror. In the United States, modern literature has been enlisted in the construction of a pluralistic nationalism. However, the ambivalence of what Lionel Trilling called the "liberal imagination" becomes evident by examining its complicity with the logic most fully dominant in the Cold War, a logic not only of anticommunism, but also of hypermasculinity. It was a habit of thinking about threatening differences that cast the stranger out of the plural identity in the name of being realistic. The pernicious result for American literary history was the exclusion of narrative complexity. The Cold War's hypermasculine mode of reading affected the reception even of exemplary writers such as Ernest Hemingway and Bernard Malamud, and insinuated itself into every aspect of literary inventiveness, elevating classic modernist poetics as formal criterion, but (in the name of a *modernism* enunciated by the Cold War) bringing the era of modernist achievement in poetry to a decisive close.

Cold War discourse forced its terms upon the structures of knowledge in this country at the most fundamental levels. Cold War discourse affected the common sense of the people more deeply than the real war, mobilizing a cultural revolution that produced—for an astounding forty-odd years—the unified national subject of its peculiar identity. Furthermore, by its psychologizing of the political, it reinforced the American ideology of the individual and set the terms not only for conformity, but also for resistance. It was a totalitarianism of the imaginary. It was inscribed in our habits of thought at every level by fear—not of punishment, but of the other. Children crawled under their desks in schools across the country to hide from a nuclear attack before Russia had the nuclear weapons to threaten. People built bomb shelters in their backyards and debated whether or not they would shoot their improvident neighbors to keep them out when the time came. Was it a collective nightmare about the Hiroshima we had ourselves produced? The danger that seemed so alien seemed also of the utmost concreteness, a matter of missiles that could be counted, warheads, nuclear devices that could be disarmed, all facts, requiring only intelligence and spy networks to discover the real truth. Cold War discourse was phobic, governed by an either/or logic, highly organized in a paranoid orientation. Perhaps it helped that Americans did not know what a communist was—it was dangerous to discuss either Marxism or Russian history and impossible not to conflate the two. Our history became the repeated drama of projection, removing the evil from within (commie sympathizers) and maintaining a posture of defense against the now externalized threat. The narratives of warrior and of domestic bliss became common sense. The appeal to common experience through story gave way to a hallucination of the void and the arena of a new nationalism that would be responsible for defining the real.

3

Theodore Roosevelt and the Postheroic Arena: Reading Hemingway Again

It is not the critic who counts, not the man who points out how the strong man stumbles, or where the doer of deeds could have done them better. The credit belongs to the man who is actually in the arena, whose face is marred by dust and sweat and blood; who strives valiantly; who errs, and comes short again and again; because there is not effort without error and shortcoming; but who does actually strive to do the deeds; who knows the great enthusiasms, the great devotions; who spends himself in a worthy cause, who at the best knows in the end the triumphs of high achievement and who at the worst, if he fails, at least fails while daring greatly, so that his place shall never be with those cold and timid souls who know neither victory nor defeat.

—Theodore Roosevelt, as cited for the frontispiece of
Richard M. Nixon's *In the Arena*

Richard Nixon invoked the heroic figures of American manhood that were associated with the strenuous life Teddy Roosevelt described, a manhood doubly informed by Harvard and by the North Dakota frontier. However, during the Cold War the political subject hailed by Theodore Roosevelt's still powerful call to the "man in the arena" underwent a decisive change. Ernest Hemingway's *For Whom the Bell Tolls* represented the last time a major American novelist could locate the arena of moral action on the Left, in the company of communists. Ernest Hemingway had a complex and critical—but intimate— relationship to that Teddy Roosevelt American. What happened to literature, and to political culture, as such figures of manhood increasingly came to be associated with the interpellation of anticommunist heroes, right-wing conservatives? Didn't manhood become as politically dangerous as the feminine?

After *For Whom the Bell Tolls*, even during World War II, Hemingway began to have problems with his writing. When *Across the River and into the Trees* appeared in 1950, with its portrayal of the aging Colonel Cantwell and the haunting specter of military failures, critics were quick to declare the book itself a failure. It certainly failed to replicate the "man in the arena," or to represent the increasingly stylized icon of the American male. Compared to the hyperbole, for example, of a John Wayne or the tough-guy extremity popularized by Mickey Spillane, Hemingway's aging Colonel Cantwell was all too realistic. But tough-guy readers were not the ones complaining. And Cantwell's personal failure was not what bothered literary critics, who were not looking for the replication of heroes. They would have preferred an antihero. The Cold War's "new liberalism," Thomas Schaub has argued, was constrained to "take greater account of conservative ideas, in which tragedy and moral ambiguity have long been uncontested assumptions" (21).

What made critics so uneasy that they called it a bad book was that it seemed perhaps insufficiently disillusioned and yet too critical of the military: too proud, too narcissistic. Maxwell Geismar, writing in the *Saturday Review of Literature,* said it was too "heavily weighted with the foolishness of grandeur," and not "the work of the man who was there" (Stephens 294–95). Hemingway criticized military decisions made in World War II, and the critics such as Charles Poore in the *New York Times* thought that seemed somehow aesthetically wrong: "His remarks on Eisenhower . . . show a certain lack of imagination" (Stephens 290). The *Newsweek* review said, "His indictments may be fair and true but they seem dissonant and awkward," "His memory of some incident of battle breaks into his quietness like a present reminder of the fighting in Korea. . . . This new style . . . may not be as effective as his old one has been" (Stephens 304–5). The spectacle of Hemingway jarred in the Cold War panorama, and the embarrassment was attributed to the decline of the writer. More than one critic thought that the "retread officer" in the fiction was like the rather unflattering portrait of Hemingway himself written by Lillian Ross for the *New Yorker* in the spring of 1950 before publication; more than one called it a "parody" of Hemingway, including Philip Rahv in *Commentary,* who added that the "legend suffers irremediable damage" (Stephens 319). Northrop Frye said in the *Hudson Review* that the narrator's lack of detachment meant "the most articulate character sounds like a mouthpiece for the author" (Stephens 333). Morton Zabel in the *Nation* made one aspect of the problem explicit: the reader has had "a complex conditioning," not only from Hemingway's other books, but also from the "dismal exhibitionism of the *Esquire* articles in the thirties or the self-exploiting public character of the interviews and photographs." "What one is left with," Zabel wrote, "is the impasse of routine mechanism and contrivance a talent arrives at when an inflexibly formulated conception of experience or humanity is pushed to the limits of its utility, excluding any genuine exploration of human complexity or any but the most brutally patented responses to character and conduct" (Stephens 297).

Hemingway at that point, about the same time that Philip Young was formulating the notion of the "code hero," had become unreadable for Zabel, who went on to suggest that his reputation would not stand up to that of his rivals, Fitzgerald and Faulkner. Novelists supported Hemingway: John O'Hara celebrated the book and looked elsewhere for the source of attacks: "Hemingway . . . has done nothing to protect himself against personal attack, or, more accurately, counter-attack. He has named some names, and made easily identifiable some others" (Stephens 303). Evelyn Waugh pointed out that the colonel was "the nemesis of the philistines" and Faulkner seconded Waugh—"the ones who throw the spitballs didn't write the pieces" (Stephens 323).

The hyperbole of the critics suggests that Hemingway had struck a nerve. It was not only that he portrayed the military in an unfashionably negative way. Norman Cousins, writing in *Saturday Review of Literature* with a tone of excessive disgust usually reserved by modernists for writing about women authors, demonstrated that by 1950 the Hemingway spectacle of manhood had become all too gendered for intellectuals:

> In sum, the Hemingway hero or real man is the spectacle of the ego run riot. It is a diseased and elephantine assertion of self. It is a world trying to drown itself in its hormones, a world in which people exist only in biological pairs—for the benefit of the male. (Stephens 317)

Far from being a protofeminist censure, Cousins's vituperative language about disease and hormones uncannily reiterates the terms of attack on communists, women, and Jews.

Across the River and into the Trees marked some kind of turning point for critics. Even though Hemingway enjoyed both success and notoriety during the Cold War, and even though the publication of *Old Man and the Sea,* the Nobel Prize, the increasing book sales, and the popular hunger for news of "Papa Hemingway" might seem to make my argument absurd, I am arguing that Cold War politics disciplined readers in ways that left no place for a certain Hemingway. At the same time that the reviewers and publishers hailed *The Old Man and the Sea* as a "classic," Philip Rahv said in *Commentary* it was "by no means the masterpiece," but simply a story whose participants' "existence is real" (Stephens 360); Delmore Schwartz limited his praise to the "vividness" of the experience in *Partisan Review* (Stephens 363); R. W. B. Lewis thought the book, and Hemingway, was slighter than imagined, a matter of a style that could catch the perception of experience (Stephens 364); and John Aldridge called it "minor Hemingway fiction" (Stephens 365). Finally, in 1953, when the *Hemingway Reader* appeared, Stanley Edgar Hyman wrote in the *New York Times Book Review* that Hemingway's pieces in chronological arrangement "graph a neat parabola of sinking into self-parody. And that makes a gloomy portent for the literary fate of Ernest Hemingway" (Stephens 374).

In the fifties, then, at the height of the Cold War, Hemingway had come to appear at once as the very emblem of traumatized manhood and the author of self-parody—in spite of the claim by his most insistent critics that his great contribution was a realism. When he wrote his influential study of American fiction, Richard Chase did not give Hemingway much space in his book, listing him in a tradition since Cooper as "the celebrant of the masculine life" (64) but making a harsh judgment: "You may be the perfect master of your language without being a great master of the art of the novel; Hemingway is an example" (204). He preferred Hemingway's old rival, F. Scott Fitzgerald.

Even though Hemingway criticism flourishes right now, the old denigrations also go on. Recently Marjorie Perloff has argued that his mentor, Gertrude Stein, made real contributions to narrative innovation through her "negative parataxis," blocking the connections imposed by habitual narratives at the same time that narration went on.[1] But she doesn't want to say the same for Hemingway. Was he just an imitator of cultural plots? Walter Benn Michaels assumes that Hemingway's notion of *aficion* and his efforts to distinguish real emotion from fake in *The Sun Also Rises* work to shore up notions of authentic male identity, not to put it into question:

> It is the easy substitutability of what I will characterize as the racial discourse of *aficion* (Cohn doesn't have it) for the discourse of homosexuality that I mean to stress here, as well as the interchangeability of both the aficionado and the homosexual with the castrato. All these figures can be equally (if differently) mobilized as blood supplements, as strategies for insisting upon a race-based model of identity when more literal strategies for preserving it have failed. (13)

It is not the hero, but the logic of discourse that has agency in this argument. The critique of a race-based model of identity or a virility-based model of manhood also reiterates them at the same time, and so Hemingway's Jake does not separate body from politics by being a traumatized hero. But the question is, what mobilizes such figures as "blood supplements" and "strategies"? Michaels attributes a kind of permanent rhetorical agency to modernism that at once personifies the strategy and closes off the possibility that the text might also exceed and undermine ideological nodes.

Some critics on the Left thought during the thirties that Hemingway substituted individual rebellion for social revolution. For example, Granville Hicks, writing in the *Nation* in 1932 (when he was still advocating Marxism), summarizes the message of *Death in the Afternoon* as: "If. . . you are troubled by the world, resort to personal violence; and if personal violence proves, as it usually does, to be dangerous, ineffective, and undignified, console yourself with drink—or skiing, or sexual intercourse, or watching bullfights" (Meyers 164).

When Ernest Hemingway went to cover the duel of two matadors, Luis Miguel Dominguín and Antonio Ordóñez, for *Life* magazine in the summer of 1959, he was returning to a scene that had become the emblem of his fiction: "the oldest and the most dangerous and the most beautiful." But does this scene put Hemingway on the side of a dominant warrior culture? On the side of a naïve individualism? The bullfight also provides an arena where the culture of another economy could be juxtaposed to advancing industrial capitalism. The craft of the bullfighter, like the craft of the storyteller, makes a disjunction in historical time that could disrupt the industrial determinism of modernity.

Hemingway's style displaces the alienation that undergirds military accounts of progress—and of heroism. Hemingway's style pays detailed attention to death in a culture that phobically put it off into the increasingly apocalyptic future. But during the Cold War, the strangeness of such writing became opaque, both collapsed into the familiar and consumed as an object of individualism. What versions of mankind became illegible during the Cold War? Ernest Hemingway may provide an exemplary, which is to say extreme, case.

I am arguing against the kind of discursive absolutism that the Cold War proposed, and even Walter Benn Michaels seems to assume. The contradictions raised by modernist primitivism, for example, opened up opportunities for various interpretations. The modernist primitive, from Picasso's Africanism to T. S. Eliot's use of dialect, arose from the break in nineteenth-century bourgeois time afforded by the contact zone of borders and frontiers—places such as Ireland and the American South, where an advancing capitalist literacy might be shocked into newness by its juxtaposition with a precapitalist culture of storytelling and craftsmanship, the resources of another political economy.[2] Hemingway uses a modernist primitivism on behalf not only of a reactionary nostalgia, but on behalf of more communal forms of living and a progressive politics as well. Robert Jordan, in *For Whom the Bell Tolls,* makes the analogy between the tribal knowledge of Pilar's European strangers—gypsies—and woman's knowledge about love ("the earth moved"): "I've known a lot of gypsies and they are strange enough. But so are we. . . . Nobody knows what tribes we came from nor what our tribal inheritance is nor what the mysteries were in the woods where the people lived that we came from" (175).[3] There is always a political doubleness about such frontiers and contact, the reactionary exploitation lying next to a progressive influence coming from the tribal, colonialism and nativism lining the civil while strangeness breaks alienation. In Hemingway, the strangeness comes from American Indians, Spanish bullfighters, the gypsies, the Cuban peasant fisherman of *Old Man and the Sea*—and sometimes from women. There is no doubt that his scenes of warrior intensity became Cold War stereotypes, not strange but all too familiar. So how did this doubleness and this strangeness become unreadable during the Cold War?

It was not that the Cold War critics were more liberal than Hemingway. What happened during the Cold War was that the ideology of extreme individualism ("resort to personal violence") for which Granville Hicks criticized Hemingway in 1932 gradually became the only model for a working-class man, a model that culminated with the hard-bodied hero of the eighties, Rambo. The contradictions disappeared. Hicks himself repudiated his former allegiances to the Left. Individualism had become hegemonic. It no longer seemed a matter for political debate or aesthetic representation, but rather a matter of personal—gendered, colored, ethnic, bodied—style. The style was tough-guy, film noir. During the Cold War, as modernism became dominant in academic departments, intellectuals redefined their class as a *distance* from personal style, as if no ideology or politics were involved. The *politics* of modernist style disappeared, at the very moment when modernism became an aesthetic standard. The politics of Hemingway's style were simply denied.

When Hemingway died, he left the results of twenty years of writing in quantities of manuscript unpublished before his death, and much that is significant is still unpublished to this very day. The list of posthumously published works is suggestively long: *A Moveable Feast, The Nick Adams Stories, The Fifth Column and Four Stories of the Spanish Civil War, Islands in the Stream, The Dangerous Summer, The Garden of Eden,* and *True at First Light.* Carlos Baker's 1969 biography gave evidence of Hemingway's difficulties writing, but he and everyone else—reaffirming Hemingway's worst fear—attributed the problems to aging and decadence, locating the political in the personal. I don't mean to suggest that none of Hemingway's writing problems were associated with his body. But the consensus of critics against him was not a matter of biology.

By 1970, Joseph Epstein could write in a consensus voice that "the experience of reading him is akin to watching a favorite actor—Humphrey Bogart, say, or Gary Cooper—on the late show," and decry confidently how his style had become "self-parody." The problem, Epstein wrote, was that "nothing about a writer's personal life ought to affect the way one reads his work" but that "Hemingway himself . . . sedulously encouraged the close identification between his own life and that of his fictional characters. . . . Hemingway's emphasis on his own excessive virility today seems merely embarrassing" (Meyers 559).

As a feminist critic, I have long been attentive to modes of silencing women writers—and women were greatly afflicted by the Cold War. But here I am finding evidence that the Cold War also had a silencing effect on Ernest Hemingway. I say "silencing" rather than something like "his reputation suffered its ups and downs" because the effect was not only to severely limit the political and social impact of what he wrote, but to keep a great deal of his work from being published. *Life* magazine consulted James Michener (!) before they published *The Old Man and the Sea,* worried that all the unfavorable reviews of *Across the River* would affect sales. "They not only blasted the novel . . . but they called into question his legitimacy, his right to publish any further," the *Life* man told Michener (4). Of course, no one can assess the extent to which these conditions kept Hemingway from writing at all, though the evidence of his problems writing is extensive, and his letters (the unsent even more than the sent) to Philip Young attest to the intensity of his concern.

The politics of a hypermasculinity made Hemingway embarrassing to critics such as Epstein, who were moving the liberal position to the Right. In particular, the Cold War separated Hemingway's critique of the nationalistic imperial discourse of manliness I am associating with Teddy Roosevelt from the ongoing influence of that discourse, at the very moment when the Rough Rider, the strenuous life, and the manliness of patriotism were being used together with reform progressivism and the objective, empiricist pedagogy of natural history (which I will discuss shortly) to reorganize and rejustify political life—not only the spectacles of the right wing, but also the liberal New Frontier. Hemingway's version of manliness was in competition with a patriotic exaggeration of Roosevelt that included no element of critique, as Richard Nixon's "man in the arena" exemplifies.

From the perspective of a post-sixties feminist, Hemingway seems all too individualistic, as well as masculinist, but from the perspective of Cold War anticommunism, Hemingway's political sympathies were dangerously sympathetic to communism. What is the significance of Hemingway's extensive FBI file? It contains repeated references to an incident in a bar, when Hemingway called a man widely known to be associated with the FBI "the gestapo." "It is likely that Hemingway is not friendly to us." Hemingway's intense conviction that he was being watched by the FBI and, later, the IRS seemed evidence of paranoia to those around him. The FBI opened the file in 1941, when Hemingway was reporting to the U.S. ambassador to Cuba about possible German submarine activity in the area. But we now know that his affiliation with the Abraham Lincoln Brigade members would have automatically brought him to the attention of J. Edgar Hoover.[4] His activities during World War II, using former members of the Spanish Republican Army on an antifascist mission looking for German submarines aboard the Pilar, marked both the beginning of the FBI surveillance and the onset of his problems writing. The long, unfinished postwar manuscript from which were carved out *Old Man and the Sea, Islands in the Stream,* and *Garden of Eden* returns in several ways to that critical moment when the adventurous individual, the writer, and the comrades who earned his loyalty came up against a national politics that could regard his activities and his critique as subversive.[5]

Hemingway writes from a position that complicates the willful simplicity of Cold War critical judgments. He became unreadable in the sense that I mean at the same moment that he entered into a sort of canonicity. His books came to seem the "melodramas of beset manhood" that also structured the critical narrative. At the same time that the American academy was preparing to take Hemingway into the university—Philip Young wrote the first postwar Ph.D. dissertation on Hemingway (and *Huckleberry Finn*) in 1949—the intellectual class was insisting on its own version of "containment," making a strategic withdrawal from overt political positions. He could not be interesting for his politics. If Hemingway wrote about the great difficulty civilized peoples have in relationships with others, the Cold War theme of alienation mistrusted social bonds altogether. Although Hemingway had written again and again about the shock and isolation experienced by the veterans of wars, the trauma after World War II dissociated individuals from history.

Granville Hicks wrote in 1944 that "for us, the sense of belonging is something to be achieved, not a heritage, and, as is clear in 'For Whom the Bell Tolls,' it is always precarious" (Meyers 373). By 1950, the problem of belonging no longer seemed a problem of the community, but rather a problem for the individual, to be thought about through isolated figures. Even more significantly for Hemingway, literary critics were also gladly dissociating themselves from referential discourses, such as political economy, science, or history, claiming instead the field of the imagination (for the myth and symbol critics) and the study of form (for the New Critics and the neo-Aristotelians). The new academic criticism tried to maintain rigorous distinctions between the organic whole within the poem and the chaos without, while Hemingway's style was in the arena.

The "arena" of conflict that Nixon would enter had been relocated by history; he hoped it was where the Roosevelt "strong man" could emerge, and perhaps as well the establishment man of privilege that TR, but not Nixon, represented. However, that killing field for Nixon was also inscribed with the events of World War II, the Holocaust, and Hiroshima. The confrontation with death required more grandiose denials about the sacrifice of innocence than Roosevelt had faced or than Hemingway had exposed. Furthermore, the very obviousness of Nixon's ongoing denials about the nature of that "arena" where he would define himself obscures the way that other aspects of Theodore Roosevelt's inheritance defined other—"liberal"—discourses of the Cold War. The industrial Security State enlisted mass spectatorship not in the service of ritual attention to the detail, the fragment of act, but in the service of making secrets. At the same time that the Cold War seemed to produce an extraordinary national consensus, it produced extraordinary denial and a repression of critical analysis so extensive that it continues to be difficult for us to examine. The hermeticism of the New Critical poetic object resonates with this secrecy. It, too, is "classified."

For Richard Nixon, the Roosevelt arena was both an opportunity and a trap. The Cold War was the conflict that could not be fought because it meant annihilation, and the substitute conflicts in Korea and Vietnam made all who participated, most especially Nixon, the inevitable butchers of the populations standing in for the absent enemy. The Cold War evoked and contained the warrior as a founding prevarication, to stand for the impossibility of taking action, the impossibility of the very manhood thus evoked. Nixon occupied the site of the lie.

But the authority to speak about what is real was perhaps the most significant part of Theodore Roosevelt's legacy, the secret force that lent conviction to an ethos through the "objectivity" connected with not only journalism, but more importantly, with natural history writing. What happened to Hemingway had to do with the way a certain ethical speech was suddenly no longer possible, with what it might mean to write not only truly, but also about the real. Richard Nixon could become the "man in the arena" because disillusioned liberals no longer believed in heroism. Hemingway could no longer engage the intellectual arena because his critical readers no longer believed that literature could refer to a reality that mattered or could contend with ideology, except by resisting the spectacle of mass culture—increasingly filled with tough guys. Hemingway's popularity with the Spillane-loving public only endangered his critical status further.

The United States has inherited a confluence of powerful discourses about progress that Theodore Roosevelt helped to commingle by his multiple interests and involvements. Roosevelt's influential journalism (and he was an extraordinarily prolific writer) asserted the value of manliness, nationalism, conservation, and the western experience of strenuous activity in the out of doors together with the more global, imperialist, and capitalist aims made spectacular by the filmed charge up San Juan Hill and inscribed by the construction of the Panama Canal. The language of natural history helped make claims of objectivity for his version of the progressive that continue to obfuscate the way the United States has read its politics. He established through his writing, his political life, and his advocacy of natural history—embodied in his memorial at the Natural History Museum of New York City—what Donna Haraway has called the "Teddy Bear Patriarchy," dedicated through the museum to "preserving a threatened manhood" through "exhibition, eugenics, and conservation" (283)—that is, by mounting a resistance to decadence, and not in the name of politics, but in the name of a manliness that embraces science. But it is in the arena of the threatening confrontation that Roosevelt most defines American individualism, as Haraway points out: "In the upside down world of Teddy Bear Patriarchy, it is in the craft of killing that life is constructed, not in the accident of personal, material birth" (241).

Nixon was able to borrow Roosevelt's man of action as an icon in part because the male body had been so decisively turned into a hallucinatory image of the real man by postwar culture. It would always have been hard to imagine Nixon hunting buffalo in North Dakota—or reforming Tammany politics in New York, for that matter. I do not mean to trace the continuities of policy from TR to Nixon, but, on the contrary, to call attention to the markedly new use for the old narratives. Roosevelt's American had been forward-looking and confident; he had conserved the possibility of manliness together with its site in the natural landscape by his conservation ethic and his program of establishing national parks. Furthermore, together with his friends Owen Wister and Frederic Remington, and other members of the Boone and Crockett Club, Teddy Roosevelt had used the powers of the Eastern Establishment to reinvent the American West and make it available as a myth of progress and reform.[6] Teddy Roosevelt was probably more like John Kennedy than like Richard Nixon.

But Ernest Hemingway's texts had always had a critical relationship to the Roosevelt narrative of manliness and progress. At the same time that Hemingway took the Roosevelt hero as his theme and the discourse of natural history as an important paradigm, he wrote to unsettle that ideology of manhood from within, and he reversed the positivism of nature writing. After World War I, *In Our Time, The Sun Also Rises, A Farewell to Arms,* and *For Whom the Bell Tolls* constituted, in fact, a modernist, expatriate revolt against much of the optimism about progress, American frontiers, and the effects of the "strenuous life" that Teddy Roosevelt had advocated, particularly against the cheerful entry into heroic militarism. Hemingway debunked the glory of war and even associated it not with an access to the paternal, but with a loss of fertility. In these works, Hemingway also elaborated a complex but thoroughgoing critique of the Rough-Rider manliness advocated by Teddy Roosevelt. I rehearse these generalizations not because they are new insights, but precisely because they are widely accepted and yet contradict the reading of Hemingway that would emerge after 1945, with the Cold War.

Thinking about Ernest Hemingway together with Theodore Roosevelt, as Michael Reynolds in particular does in his book on the early years,

The Young Hemingway, elucidates both Hemingway's situation in cultural history and his more radical situation in literary tradition. Hemingway resists Teddy Roosevelt's advocacy of a nationalistic manliness that would value the right politics, but he is indeed like Roosevelt too, and particularly in continuing a tradition of natural history writing that is connected to the literature of the West, a pursuit of accurate description that would record an act of discovery, the frontier of writing. The location of the "real" in Roosevelt's natural history and Hemingway's fiction changes, however.

Let me take a moment here to look more closely at the discourse of realism as it developed in Theodore Roosevelt's life. It is the discourse of a truth that belongs to a certain body, and to experience defined by as well as defining the bodied subject. Roosevelt went to North Dakota in the 1880s to heal, not only from childhood asthma, but more particularly from the loss of his mother and his beloved wife, and found there the metaphoric resources of a Rough Rider approach to the national future. In this he followed a prescription for neurasthenia followed by Owen Wister too, among others, and advocated widely by S. Weir Mitchell. Notoriously, Mitchell's treatment was gender-specific. Men became more manly by going west. Women, however, such as Charlotte Perkins Gilman, were confined.

To turn away from the powerlessness of soft and decorous (Eastern) female bodies and their discourse of sentiment, Theodore Roosevelt sought to discipline the male body that might be discovered and proved in the course of the strenuous life. From then on, he displaced the challenges of ranch life and the Western frontier onto the narrative of modernity. This Roosevelt realism was a peculiarly American discourse. The "frontier" operated like the other spaces of imperialism and colonialism, but the proof of its virtue was in the production of a manly life. Progress was not equated with more and more civilized behavior, but rather with strenuous effort. Or civilization itself became, as Gail Bederman argues, implicated with discourses of manhood and racial prowess. The narrative of modernity equates evolutionary progress with *fitness.* The Roosevelt/American version of progress thought not in terms of reproduction of the species, but in terms of the manly striving that reproduced an American individual. Owen Wister portrays his "Virginian," for example, as a naturally superior man. For both Wister and Roosevelt the West breeds a hierarchy of the fittest based on abolishing (unnatural) privilege:

> It was through the Declaration of Independence that we Americans acknowledged the *eternal inequality* of man. For by it we abolished a cut-and-dried aristocracy . . . we decreed that every man should thenceforth have equal liberty to find his

own level. By this very decree we acknowledged and gave freedom to true aristocracy, saying, "Let the best man win, who-
ever he is." (147)

For Roosevelt, the "arena" corresponded to both physical and epistemological action. The narrative of the hunter overlapped with the narrative of the scientist: the great scientists of the nineteenth century gathered their specimens for collections by killing them. As Donna Haraway
reminds us, in her analysis of the institution of natural history, the struggle
for life depended upon death.[7] They murdered to dissect. Audubon, of
course, drew his birds not from life, but from death. And Theodore
Roosevelt began in childhood to shoot enormous quantities of animal
specimens for his collecting; he began shooting big game not as a hunter,
but as a natural scientist.[8] The famous story of his refusal to shoot a bear
that had been selected for him to hunt, that resulted in the gift of the first
"Teddy bear," makes it seem as if his hunting were most of all for sport,
but the story distorts the more significant and extensive practice. This
hunter of scientific discovery who proves himself in the act is the subject
of the heroic American nation in its moment of ascendancy to world domination, taken up in its imperial aspect as the very subject of the endless
frontier announced as the Cold War got under way. And this hero of invention and discovery continues to support American nationalism in both
subtle and obvious ways. It is too easy to read Hemingway as appropriated by this manly imperialism, even though Hemingway's reading of
Roosevelt is characterized by resistance.

At a time when linguistic philosophy began to think in terms of structures that carefully distinguished logical truths from claims about reality, Roosevelt collapsed the distinction between representation and reality by emphasizing the reality/truth of the act. Half a century later, this
performative dimension of an American realism had enormous consequences for the public discourse defining the Cold War. It meant that the
manly individual had a superior claim to knowledge, superior even to
scientists. It meant that the George Kennan school of realism in foreign
relations invoked the realities of power rather than the realities of nuclear
discoveries or the truths about international knowledge of such weapons taught by nuclear scientists. The performative dimension of such a
realism wedded denial to struggle; truth would emerge with the dare.

The significance of credibility in the long history of Nixon's involvement with anticommunism and the Cold War perhaps needs no argument.
But how are these words connected to what I am calling a Roosevelt realism? Nixon's career is marked by the assumption that crisis (of Voorhis
or Hiss or Cambodia) is a good. He substitutes the act for the cause. In
Six Crises he wrote, "A man who has never lost himself in a cause big-

ger than himself has missed one of life's mountaintop experiences. Only in losing himself does he find himself" (xiv). Both the banality of his sentiments and their clear attachment to Christian principle may lead us to ignore their connection to modernist desires for escape from the personal. Crisis may make us impersonal: "The very fact that the crisis is bigger than the man himself takes his mind off his own problems" (xiv). This is the hypermasculinity of the Cold War, and the way—as Donald Pease has pointed out—that it functions not simply as a politics, but as the arena of cultural meaning. The man puts himself in the arena to become more than himself. Superseding the personal, he becomes modern. Hemingway resists this extremity because he writes literature, makes language the arena, because he takes the Roosevelt attachment to the texts of natural history and puts pressure there, on the textual claim of the true/real.

Theodore Roosevelt was the hero of the generation before World War I, and of the Oak Park of Ernest Hemingway's childhood, where he seemed the advocate both of a manly national life and of the strong middle-class family. Teddy had been a child—as Hemingway would be—more than slightly taken up by the adventures of natural history. As a child, Roosevelt specialized in writing a natural history journal, collecting specimens to describe as Audubon had done, by shooting them. The Roosevelt family was closely connected to the establishment of the New York Museum of Natural History. Young Hemingway had his own connections to natural history in the Field Museum in Chicago, where Dr. Hemingway took his children sometimes on weekends. Michael Reynolds tells us that Hemingway was assistant curator of the Agassiz Club at the age of ten (*Young Hemingway* 30). And is it entirely irrelevant that Hemingway wanted to disguise the *Pilar*, in 1942, as a vessel belonging to the American Museum of Natural History in order to search out the German submarines? Hemingway owned a large number of natural history and travel books, including Teddy Roosevelt's 1902 *The Deer Family* and his 1910 *African Game Trails*.[9]

Hemingway's relationship to Roosevelt was intense but not simple. *Green Hills of Africa* clearly recaptures for the thirties the 1909 safari taken by Roosevelt, with this time the writer, not the politician, emerging as the key cultural icon (Lynn 503). Hemingway never wrote about his home town of Oak Park, but he clearly wrote about the dreams of the little boy who dressed in safari khaki in 1909 and took a strong interest in Roosevelt's adventures. He even hired Philip Percival, Roosevelt's own guide, when he went to Africa. But Hemingway's participation in World War I as an ambulance driver for the Red Cross ruptured the idealistic views of war that Roosevelt held.

Roosevelt would have doubted Hemingway's manhood, as Hemingway came to doubt the warrior ethics Roosevelt attached to war. Roosevelt specifically thought serving in the Red Cross was a role best left to the unfit and to women. Neither Roosevelt nor the generation of Hemingway's parents who idolized him understood the difference between the strenuous life of courage and the miserable life of the soldier in World War I, and on that pivot the century turned.

However, if Hemingway was disaffected with Roosevelt the legend and the cultural history, he was not—far from it—to lose faith in the writing method endorsed by Roosevelt and grounded in the methods of natural history. The true reporting of experience, of the active life carefully observed—that was a moral basis for writing itself that Hemingway translated into the literary tradition. In this respect he might be connected not only to the literary modernists, but also to Roosevelt's old friend, Owen Wister, who wrote Roosevelt's biography and *The Virginian* to describe the American hero of the active life—and, moreover, to locate it not in Roosevelt's native New York, but on the frontier, in the narratives of the West.

Hemingway only saw Roosevelt as a boy, but he knew Wister, in the twenties. Darwin Payne describes the relationship. Hemingway visited Wister in Shell, Wyoming, in 1928 on a western trip with Pauline after he heard that Wister had praised *The Sun Also Rises* and the story "Fifty Grand." They met the next year in Paris and began a correspondence. Wister read the galleys for *A Farewell to Arms,* made suggestions for revision (including that the profanity be omitted), and provided praise that was used to promote the book—an intervention that at first bypassed Hemingway altogether and made him furious (320–21). Nevertheless, in 1956 Hemingway stated again that Wister had been "the most unselfish and most dis-interested and the most loving" of friends. The personal closeness was accompanied early by a certain public merging in the film image: Gary Cooper appeared in *The Virginian* in 1929 and two years later in *A Farewell.* Wister himself was just publishing his *Roosevelt: The Story of a Friendship.* It was thirty years after the days when Wister was writing *The Virginian* and seeing much of Roosevelt, then president. Wister's novel had brought together the cowboy tale and the love story, the Eastern Establishment and the West: he represented the progressive appropriation of the frontier that his close friend Roosevelt was carrying out in the political realm. Hemingway's relationship to Wister, like his relationship to Roosevelt, was more than an Oedipal rewriting—Hemingway doubted the frontier mythology itself. Michael Reynolds compares the old progressive frontier ideal to Hemingway's critique: Wister thought the country's "salvation rode on the marriage of eastern culture and western grit. For Hemingway, the marriage was unconsummated" (*Young Hemingway* 74).

On the other hand, Hemingway's early interest in natural history locates him within the epistemology of discovery connected to Louis Agassiz. The method described by Ezra Pound advocated that readers practice the kind of careful observation of a text that Agassiz exacted from a student who was required to return again and again to look at his specimen. In *ABC of Reading*, Ezra Pound introduces for pedagogical use, "impersonal enough to serve as a text-book," a scientific approach to studying poetry: "The proper METHOD for studying poetry and good letters is the method of contemporary biologists, that is careful first-hand examination of the matter, and continual COMPARISON of one 'slide' or specimen with another" (11, 17). Pound takes as his model the storied pedagogical method of Louis Agassiz, the legendary scientist of natural history:

> A post-graduate student equipped with honours and diplomas went to Agassiz to receive the final and finishing touches. The great man offered him a small fish and told him to describe it.
> Post-Graduate Student: "That's only a sunfish."
> Agassiz: "I know that. Write a description of it."
> After a few minutes the student returned with the description of the Ichthus Heliodiplodokus, or whatever term is used to conceal the common sunfish from vulgar knowledge, family of Heliichtherinkus, etc., as found in textbooks of the subject.
> Agassiz again told the student to describe the fish.
> The student produced a four-page essay. Agassiz then told him to look at the fish. At the end of three weeks the fish was in an advanced state of decomposition, but the student knew something about it. (17–18)

This story featuring the intensity of prolonged close attention was also the oft-repeated initiation into apprenticeship under Agassiz at Harvard. Men who studied with Agassiz recorded their accounts of the experience, and the same tale was told by many prominent scientists who had apprenticed under Agassiz: Nathaniel Southgate Shaler, Samuel H. Scudder, Henry Blake, David Starr Jordan, Addison Emory Verrill, Burt G. Wilder.[10] As the scene of an initiation, the call to close observation became the guarantor of a certain reliance on individual experience that might be coupled with claims of scientific objectivity. The initiation into close observation also relied not just on a specific text, but on the whole metaphor of the world as text.

For Agassiz, such a mode of inquiry kept science and religion together. The scientist in examining the world around him saw the design and the hand of the designer.[11] Agassiz's relation to "natural theology" was well known but further publicized by John Greenleaf Whittier's poem "Agassiz's Prayer," in which Whittier reported the words pronounced in Agassiz's opening lecture of the Penikase Summer School for Teachers. This lecture and this summer school idea, once started, would be responsible for propagating the Agassiz method throughout public education in the years to come.

Modernist literature was interested in the objectivity of science, but it also functioned as a kind of replacement for the religious discourses that were so seriously interrogated by science. So there is more than just the assertion of the value of experience in the Agassiz story told by Pound. The initiation into the Agassiz method of close observation at once laid claim to a scientific and empirical realism and yet repeated an obstinate theological resistance to Darwinian evolution, with its displacement of man and God from their positions in a stable and objective hierarchy. Agassiz himself resisted Darwin to the last, notoriously, insisting that the taxonomy of species, read off the text of nature, never changed and that thus man could not be kin to apes. Natural history writing was becoming more a public and literary rather than a scientific discourse at the same transitional moment. Perhaps the influence of Agassiz persisted as nature studies boomed toward the end of the century not in spite of his anchor in theology, but because of it. Agassiz's method was, furthermore, a marvelous pedagogical tool and inaugurated widespread educational reform in science instruction. Students would study the plants, rocks, and animals in the field, not in the classroom. Or they would study through the collections made available in natural history museums—the one Agassiz founded at Harvard had that pedagogical, public aim as well as its scientific purpose. All over the country museums of natural history proliferated: Theodore Roosevelt at the age of seven already dreamed of establishing such a museum.

The genealogy of the Agassiz story shows how natural history might be affiliated with the Eastern Establishment as well as with modernist texts. At Harvard, the inheritors of the Agassiz experience passed it on. William James was Agassiz's student; as a young scientist he went to Brazil on an adventurous expedition up the Amazon to collect species. Agassiz's wife, Elizabeth Cary Agassiz, (who had been a student at Elizabeth Peabody's school and would later assist in the founding of Radcliffe) wrote up the story of the expedition and told how miserable and seasick James was on the voyage. The young James wrote to his father that Agassiz "has a great personal tact too, and I see that in all his talks with me he is pitching into my loose and superficial way of thinking" (Teller 79). Both Nathaniel Shaler and William James were Roosevelt's professors at Harvard. And, of course, James was also the most significant influence in the academic career of one Gertrude Stein, engaging her in experiments on writing and attention. Theodore Roosevelt entered Harvard an ardent naturalist; he not only studied with Agassiz's student Shaler, but also visited him in his home. In his senior year, Roosevelt gave up on science in order to pursue his interests, writing "at the time Harvard . . . utterly ignored the possibilities of the faunal naturalist, the outdoor naturalist and observer of nature. They treated biology as purely a science of the laboratory and the microscope." But Paul Cutright points out that his natural history teachers were surprised at such an allegation (127). In any event, Roosevelt continued in science not as a career, but as a life-long practice.

A significant aspect of natural history writing for Roosevelt was its truth. While he was president of the United States, Theodore Roosevelt found time not only to go to Yellowstone with John Burroughs and to Yosemite with John Muir, but also to enter with Burroughs into the "nature fakers" debate over the veracity of stories about animals. By that time, in the first decade of the twentieth century, nature studies had achieved the status of a social movement, there was a tremendous market for nature books, and reviewers began to complain about "goody-goody books of the natural history kind" and "mawkish sentimentalism" (Lutts 37). Is it too much to suppose that Roosevelt feared not only for the veracity of nature stories, but also for their manliness? Burroughs defined the danger as "putting in too much sentiment, too much literature" in an article in the *Atlantic*. Roosevelt encouraged the opposition to the "nature fakers" behind the scenes. There ensued a vigorous debate, in the course of which Roosevelt went public in an interview. The *New York Times* and the *Washington Post* carried stories that promptly lambasted TR as a "gamekiller" (Lutts 108). After more violent debate, Roosevelt assembled a panel of naturalists whose testimony could appear in print. The naturalists wrote that "all who know the truth and who care for the honest nature study or for literary honesty should raise their voices against such writings." And TR's own article appeared together with that panel, asserting the danger to the schools of propagating misinformation in nature stories: "We abhor deliberate or reckless untruth in this study" (Lutts 129).

Perhaps the young Hemingway, involved himself in nature study, took such a lesson to heart. The fakers were not scientists, and their manhood was in doubt besides. Hemingway's obsessive concern with a truth that many thought he regularly distorted may be thought about in the context of this debate. In the painful father-son story, "I Guess Everything Reminds You of Something," the father's admonition to the son to "Write about something that you know" means, specifically, that he should know about the type of gull in the story he wrote, and it is the fact that the boy could not have known such a gull that first arouses the father's suspicion about plagiarism (597).[12]

In natural history we are talking about a textual tradition, but the specific syntax of method is thus traceable in stories of personal apprenticeships as well, including perhaps not only Hemingway's youthful encounter with Agassiz's method and Roosevelt's model, but also his early exchanges with Gertrude Stein and the friendship with Owen Wister, which developed in the twenties. Agassiz's method had wide influence, and his method was that of the explorer. When he wanted to study glaciers, he took students out to a glacier and set up camp on it.

We are also talking about a history of exploration that had intimate connections to power. Before Agassiz ever arrived on the scene, Lewis and Clark recorded careful observations in their daily journals. They wrote under the imperative of another American president, Thomas Jefferson, who like Roosevelt saw the political interests of exploration coincide with the scientific techniques of natural history. In particular, those Lewis and Clark descriptions elaborated their very objectivity and botanical precision from a vivid sense of interest. What plants might have value as food? Which might be poisonous? Which might have medicinal qualities? After Jefferson and Roosevelt, Hemingway: his interest in the world he explores has that same desire for precision, objectivity, and purposefulness. If Hemingway takes up the discourse of the American frontier, however, he does so with a difference, without the confident faith of the legendary Teddy in the righteousness of war or the power of the strenuous life to protect the hero from harm, with no confidence that the eastern establishment carries out the morality of a Western principle. What are the politics of this style?

Natural history is a method to be distinguished from literary writing that advocated the powers of the imagination and the resources of fantasy, dream, and the unconscious—not artificial paradises, as Pound said. Natural history writing aimed to bring together practical knowledge, scientific nomenclature, the careful, sustained attention that made the senses organs of true knowledge, and a style that drew upon precise and concrete naming. Writing a modernist prose that resonated with the discourse of natural history, Hemingway represented a difference from the European symbolist and surrealist modernisms, with their derangement of the senses. Nietzsche called such empiricism metaphorical, but Pound first called his poetics "imagism" in order to emphasize the close, *realistic* articulation with the senses of an Agassiz-influenced concrete style. Hemingway's style has always crossed the boundaries between high art modernism and the public adventure, a crossing that would embarrass modernist critics.

Viewed from the perspective of a writing tradition intimately bound up with the history of nationalism and associated with the frontier, Hemingway's work represents both a continuation of certain principles and a significant questioning of the national project. Masculinity is thus split as well. As Reynolds argues, the moral values of "courage, love, honor, self-reliance, work, and duty" continue to ground Hemingway's version of the strenuous life and they also frame the authenticity of a writing that would avoid faking it. Hemingway's rhetoric of honest observation does not take place in an ethical vacuum. The rhetoric should be associated with literary modernism's ethics of authenticity. The provenance of that ethos appears more clearly when it is a matter of the authenticity that natural history writing claimed, a real/true that could be violated. Roosevelt's participation in policing the "nature fakers" episode while he was president demonstrates how important was the claim to write the real.

On the other hand, Hemingway diverges in important ways from Roosevelt's association of manliness with the victorious nation. Roosevelt never considered the human cost of manliness as he defined it; his own asthma and his bad eyesight might have seemed like frailties he was able to overcome, but in fact Roosevelt as a small child was not only, at intervals, asthmatic, but also already strenuously energetic, as David McCullough tells us. Roosevelt was not only an excessive optimist, but also a tireless advocate for his particular American myth.

In *Ranch Life and the Hunting Trail*, Roosevelt reported his experiences with life among the cowboys in the Badlands of North Dakota. It isn't one of the books we *know* Hemingway read, but it is related to *The Deer Family*, which he did, and an earlier work than the *African Game Trails* that followed Roosevelt's safari in 1910.[13] Illustrated by Frederic Remington, Roosevelt's descriptions of the West probably were important to the young Hemingway. The books constituted a major entry in the canon of American mythmaking.

Roosevelt's descriptions of domesticity in the North Dakota Badlands assume the scientist, the hunter, and the hungry consumer are one:

> Sometimes strings of sandbill cranes fly along the river, their guttural clangor being heard very far off. They usually light on a plateau, where sometimes they form rings and go through a series of queer antics, dancing and posturing to each other. They are exceedingly wide-awake birds, and more shy and wary than antelope, so that they are rarely shot; yet once I succeeded in stalking up to a group in the early morning, and firing into them rather at random, my bullet killed a full-grown female. Its breast, when roasted, proved to be very good eating. Sometimes we vary our diet with fish—wall-eyed pike, ugly, slimy catfish, and other uncouth finny things, looking very fit denizens of the mud-choked water; but they are good eating withal, in spite of their uncanny appearance. We usually catch them with set lines, left out overnight in the deeper pools. (*Ranch Life* 42–43)

Of course, the most representative moment of the North Dakota strenuous life for Roosevelt was the cowboy's "rough riding" on unbroken stock—not something he did himself, in truth:

> Up rises the bronco's back into an arch; his head, the ears laid straight back, goes down between his forefeet, and, squealing savagely, he makes a succession of rapid, stiff-legged, jarring bounds. Sometimes he is a "plunging" bucker, who runs forward all the time while bucking; or he may buck steadily in one place, or "sun-fish,"—that is, bring first one shoulder down almost to the ground and then the other, —or else he may change ends while in the air. (*Ranch Life* 53)

One of Remington's illustrations has TR riding the bronco in full buck, an unlikely pose. Roosevelt's *Ranch Life and the Hunting Trail* is also noteworthy for describing a world without women, and apparently without any kind of sexual desire. Juxtaposed to Roosevelt's writing, Hemingway's fiction seems greatly concerned with love, sexuality, and women, as filled with Eros as with Thanatos.

In 1921, Hemingway wrote "Up in Michigan," a story about a hunting trip that ends, carelessly, in a lovemaking so much more like hurting the young woman than like love that today it would probably be called a rape.[14] The indifference of the hunter to the woman's perspective suggests the emergence of Hemingway's critique of manly single-mindedness. On the one hand, there is Liz's romantic thinking about Jim:

> All the time Jim was gone on the deer hunting trip Liz thought about him. It was awful while he was gone. She couldn't sleep well from thinking about him but she discovered it was fun to think about him too. If she let herself go it was better. The night before they were to come back she didn't sleep at all, that is she didn't think she slept because it was all mixed up in a dream about not sleeping and really not sleeping. When she saw the wagon coming down the road she felt weak and sick sort of inside. She couldn't wait till she saw Jim and it seemed as though everything would be all right when he came. (60)

On the other hand, there is the disappointment of the hunter's arrival:

> Jim said "Hello, Liz," and grinned. Liz hadn't known just what would happen when Jim got back but she was sure it would be something. Nothing had happened. The men were just home, that was all. Jim pulled the burlap sacks off the deer and Liz looked at them. One was a big buck. It was stiff and hard to lift out of the wagon. (60)

Later, after some drinking, Jim takes her for a walk down to the dock by the lake and they have sex, over her protests. Then he falls asleep, won't wake up, and she walks back alone. "A cold mist was coming up through the woods from the bay," the story ends (62). Juxtaposing the failure of love with the hunter's success, the woman's narrative of romance with the man's narrative of adventure, the story brings both of the gendered plots into question (62).

Hemingway introduces a doubleness into the fine carelessness that permeated Roosevelt's enthusiasm for the West, and a doubleness about the Roosevelt advocacy of manliness with which Hemingway has so often been associated, but which he also critiques. In "The End of Something," Nick has taught Marjorie her considerable knowledge about fishing. On this trip along the lake to the site of a closed-down lumber mill, however, he declares that "It isn't fun any more," not even the love, and she goes away without a scene (81). Bill then appears: it is apparently the end of love and the beginning of a male bonding. Not fishing trips, however, but the scenes of war in the brief "Chapter III" and "Chapter IV" that precede and follow the story frame its significance, with its turn to a purely masculine relationship. The scenes of war enable the slightly nostalgic aura of fishing trips with Marjorie to function as critique.

Hemingway describes the natural world with great care, as does Roosevelt, and like Roosevelt when he went to ranch in Medora, North Dakota, Hemingway turns to the good place for healing. But only Hemingway is able to bring together in writing the accurate intensity of the good place together with the intensity of the pain that needs a refuge. "Big Two-Hearted River" shows the method. The wonderful, careful detail gains another resonance through repetition:

> the trout keeping themselves steady in the current with wavering fins . . . many trout in deep, fast moving water, slightly distorted as he watched far down through the glassy convex surface of the pool, its surface pushing and swelling smooth against the resistance of the log-driven piles of the bridge, . . . big trout looking to hold themselves on the gravel bottom. (163)

The grasshoppers in the fire zone "all turned black from living in the burned-over land" (165). Like Thoreau, Hemingway uses the description of nature as a means of thinking about larger issues, with Thoreau's critical view of the human community. One can read the descriptive passages, as one can read Thoreau, two ways. First, the report needs no other purpose than to approach as near as possible to the accuracy of natural history. The intrinsic value of the natural world requires nothing of the observing Nick and his attentiveness thus displaces the question of value away from the self. But like Thoreau, Hemingway selects the details of nature for their resonance with other levels of significance. This is true as well in his nonfiction, even though Hemingway distances himself from the too-literary versions of nature writing, including Thoreau.[15]

Thus Hemingway returns to the *locus amoenus* of American pastoral. But it is a place where the town has burned down, the forest has been reduced to stumps, and the grasshoppers match the charred landscape. It is not just a mirror of Nick's postwar depression, however. Even though this is fiction, the description works as true nature writing to prompt an environmental sensibility. The unspoken trauma has not just damaged Nick. The war, indeed, comes to seem part of the industrial juggernaut that has cut down the pines. The restorative power of the North Dakota ranch for Teddy Roosevelt only thirty-five years earlier rested on the assumption that the wildlife and the river he described so attentively were more permanent than the person in pain who escaped through his engagement in those narratives of discovery. Hemingway's nature is more vulnerable, though he is not sentimental about the vulnerability. He uses a hopper for bait, after catching them early while they were still too cold and wet with the dew to jump: "Nick took him by the head and held him while he threaded the slim hook under his chin, down through his thorax and into the last segments of his abdomen" (175). The truthful representation of nature holds significance for the man by the very placing and repetition of the words, just as the landscape holds him.

Other stories give further information about Hemingway's nature writing. In "Now I Lay Me," Hemingway tells the trick of remembering the trout-streams and fishing them to make it through the night during the war in Italy. All the stories that seem, then, at first like the vivid description of experience might also, from this perspective, take on the aura of vividly remembered experience, imagined so realistically not just in pursuit of accuracy, but also as respite for the imagination from the real sounds of war. In "A Natural History of the Dead," descriptive writing serves with almost surreal irony to undermine the reassuring tone of some writers in the naturalist tradition. Hemingway will resist the tendency to denial. He sets out to write "a few rational and interesting facts about the dead" as if he will write a bitter reply to his parodically sentimental question: "can any branch of Natural History be studied without increasing that faith, love and hope which we also, every one of us, need in our journey through the wilderness of life?" (335). The story also challenges the "Humanist" elevation of human culture: "Hit badly enough, they died like animals, . . . from little wounds as rabbits die. . . . Others . . . lie alive two days like cats that crawl into the coal bin with a bullet in the brain" (338). The tone in the story goes from satire to horror to eloquence. Hemingway does indeed use the methods of natural history to describe the dead, we see. This story, which appeared also as part of *Death in the Af-*

ternoon, includes a number of terrible scenes portrayed with terrible accuracy—a genre that appears widely elsewhere in Hemingway's fiction: the mules drowning in the water at Smyrna, the explosion of a munitions factory, a recaptured battlefield in Italy, a death from influenza, a still-living man consigned by the doctor to a cave with the dead—and a catalogue of burials. The mixed genres of this story overlap natural history as fiction and nonfiction, while Hemingway's critique of earlier naturalists suggests his revision of earlier sentiment about reading the text of nature.[16]

In the first decades of the century, modernist style, whether on behalf of a reactionary politics or a revolutionary politics, had aimed to upset the hegemony of normalized writing. The shock of style was not to make it unreal (standard language was already unreal, because automatized), but to make a renewed contact with experience possible. Hemingway attacked in particular the hegemony of frontier and natural history realism. He took the observational style that had once been scientific and positive and made its reference not fishes or glaciers themselves, but something left out and unspoken. Nora Robertson argues that his simple language put him in contact with the mother's body—that is to say, with negativity, or death.

In Hemingway's text, the "true sentence" of natural history writing is revealed not as completion or truth-telling, but as a delay and reserve that, precisely, does *not* name its object. So it is an unmaking of positivism; the detail of contact swerves away from the narrative of closure with nature and mastery over it. The "symbiosis with the natural world" associated romantically with Native Americans is at once true and not describable. Glen Love has charged that Hemingway represents a Darwinian individualism implicated in survival of the fittest, and that he imposes tragedy on nature (205). But Hemingway records "truly" what even some of us as environmentalists would like to disavow, that the contact zone between twentieth-century individualism's narcissistic economy and a wider ecology resonates with violence and death.

Does Hemingway write so closed a narrative as tragic Western individualism? In "Indian Camp," the young boy's initiation into his father's practice of modern medicine takes the form of incompatible lessons. The doctor opens up the Indian mother giving birth—inflicting terrible pain but enabling the survival of a live baby and mother. There is the careful description of the procedure: "Nick watched his father's hands scrubbing each other with the soap" (68). Is his cleanliness like that of the scrupulous storyteller? The doctor has no anesthetic; he says, "But her screams are not important" (68). Is the lesson stoicism? Racism? Life's necessary trauma? The event is so extreme that the boy loses his curiosity—a failure indeed if this is an initiation into the discourse of modern science. But the Indian husband has slit his throat. Has the husband failed the test (perhaps of manhood)? Does he represent a race that is too primitive to understand modern medicine? Or does his death testify to a violation too extreme to survive, and to an empathy the doctor, and his step-by-step instruction, ought to have included? Finally, what about the Indian woman? Is she the true hero of the story (as she is the center) because she can survive the pain? She isn't passive—she bites Uncle George in the arm "and the young Indian who had rowed Uncle George over laughed at him" (68). The laugh reverses the ethnic hierarchy too for a moment and reveals that pain has been on only one side heretofore. The spare detail fills the scene and makes it more and more difficult to assimilate to a single-minded reading.

Other Hemingway scholars have noted his connection to Roosevelt. I would like to emphasize that the connection is *double:* one of emulation but also of disillusionment. Jeffrey Myers lists "striking similarities" between Hemingway and Roosevelt, but without qualification, as if Hemingway simply continued the legend of the strenuous life. And this is precisely the legendary trap that would reduce Hemingway's work to a much less complex and less historically significant intervention than it was. Kenneth Lynn says that Hemingway "tapped into the twentieth century's enormous nostalgia for the manly virtues of earlier times, as defined in America by the pathfinders of Fenimore Cooper, the foretopmen of Herman Melville and the cowboys extolled by Theodore Roosevelt, Owen Wister, and Frederic Remington" (9). This is to say that Hemingway is a Western writer, but I want to be careful about the sense in which this is meant: the association of the Western with nostalgia may be misleading. The nostalgia of modernism for a lost innocence is neither specific to Hemingway nor central to his path-breaking style. Instead, I might argue that Hemingway renovates virtue where he can find it rather than adopting the antiheroism of modernist narrative; if innocence is lost, nostalgia does not replace the sense of writing as a powerful act and a remedy to nostalgia. Roger Whitlow argues that Hemingway exemplified the "man in the arena" that Roosevelt admired, and shared with Roosevelt the sentiment that "it is not the critic who counts." However, even Hemingway's resistance to academic criticism was more modernist than Roosevelt's. Taking Hemingway as representative of his times may be valid; to some extent he helped produce the modern cultural history he is taken to represent. However, to take him as representative of a particular link to Roosevelt, a certain kind of male subject, risks confounding cultural, natural, and personal histories.

There is, in other words, a sense in which we ought to think of Hemingway as a Western writer, and yet it's not the sense that would identify him as yet another cowboy or worse, yet another famous myth whose legend would do better without the realities of his existence. The comparison with Roosevelt ought to alert us as well to the ways Hemingway diverged from the Roosevelt legend. Hemingway's West is invested neither with innocence nor with the escape from death. Hemingway's West is not the Cold War West and he does not practice anticommunist or nativist politics. The danger was, and is, that a version of manliness promoted by Teddy Roosevelt entered American mass culture, partly because Roosevelt promoted it so widely, and that mass-culture macho is dangerous for any communication of complexity. Worse yet, this manly overcoming of crisis warrants the claim to speak really truly. It underwrites the paranoid extremity of anticommunism, disguising the psychotic rupture.

The cultural success of Roosevelt's manly ideal had as much to do with new technologies of mass communication as with heroic acts. Roosevelt's strenuous life in North Dakota was, as a ranching enterprise, an economic bust, but his stories for *Century* magazine, illustrated by Remington, captured the public imagination. Roosevelt was interested in the portrayals of the Wild West, and in Buffalo Bill Cody's Wild West show as well as his "Rough Riders." "Roosevelt negotiated with William Cody to enlist all of his Rough Riders in the First Cavalry. Before leaving for Cuba, the First Cavalry picked up two other important recruits—a pair of photographers from Vitagraph, one of the world's first motion-picture companies" (Gibson 19). He took the filmmakers from Vitagraph along with him to San Juan and they filmed the famous charge up San Juan Hill. When it turned out to look like a confusing mess rather than a victorious rout, Roosevelt had it staged again, with the original enemies now deprived of their bullets. It was the *staged* film of the charge up San Juan Hill that helped make Theodore Roosevelt and his Rough Riders famous. Celebrity was written into the Roosevelt codes of masculinity from the start. And Hemingway was skeptical early on about the validity of the legend. His 1921 poem, "Roosevelt," which appeared in *Poetry* magazine, established a certain skeptical distance from the heroic figure: it ended with the lines "and all the legends that he started in his life / Live on and prosper, / Unhampered now by his existence" (193–94). Ironically, the problem of the celebrity legend was to become Hemingway's problem as well.

Hemingway, after three decades of establishing a style that dominates modern prose, after his columns in *Esquire* and pictures of his safaris, bullfights, boxing, and fishing expeditions, and after almost three decades of films made from his stories that starred the heroes of Hollywood from Gary Cooper to George C. Scott, emerged after World War II as the figure of "Papa Hemingway," the very model of a certain tragic masculinity. In the case of Hemingway, he himself contributed to this celebrity image as the masculine ideal, perhaps less in his fiction than in his nonfiction essays on fishing and hunting big game. Hemingway's participation in the construction of gender is undeniable.

Arguing to absolve Hemingway would be as beside the point as reducing him to reactionary versions of masculinity. Louise Westling has recently taken Hemingway to task for the "imperial nostalgia" of his Indian stories. Jamie Barlowe objected when she heard me argue that Hemingway had been a victim of Cold War hypermasculinity, that I seemed to overlook the misogyny, the anti-Semitism, the homophobia, and the unfairness in so many of Hemingway's texts. So I need to clarify: I don't mean to argue that Hemingway's writing was not blameworthy in any respect, or that his texts didn't include discourses of misogyny, anti-Semitism, nativism, or homophobia. I argue that Hemingway's writing—and that includes his later, Cold War writing, such as the much-vilified *Across the River and into the Trees* and the nonfiction *Dangerous Summer*—exceeds the ideological predictability of a masculinized individualism in many significant, interesting ways and that it does so at the level of style as well as thematically, in contact with a cultural unconscious. And I mean to argue that when his writing came under the governance of Cold War cultural narratives, the complexities of Hemingway's critique became inaccessible, forcefully repressed. Masculinity—like the American identity—became ontological, rather than set of contested narratives.

Hemingway's writing constructs life on the site of killing, as Roosevelt did, though not with the same abandon. Hemingway would substitute the arena of the bullfight, a defamiliarizing relocation to Pamplona of the conflict between hunter and hunted. He touches death with a postcombat disillusionment about the arena of modern war (though at least part of his life he is indulgent about the hunt). It is war as craft, preindustrial war, and a form of encounter with death that can be met by an extreme attention. The attention is aesthetic, as the attention to the violence of a non-anesthetized cesarean in "Indian Camp" is aesthetic, because it lends intensity through language to the concrete situation without imposing a thesis. Its danger is that aesthetic intensity will become unfeeling distance. Or that it will be overtaken by an ideology it fails to resist explicitly. In *The Dangerous Summer,* Antonio repeats the encounter daily:

> Any man can face death but to be committed to bring it as close as possible while performing certain classic movements and do this again and again and then deal it out yourself with a sword to an animal weighing half a ton which you love is more complicated than just facing death. It is facing your performance as a creative artist each day and your necessity to function as a skillful killer. Antonio had to kill quickly and mercifully and still give the bull one full chance at him when he crossed over the horn at least twice a day. (141)

It's an allegory of the artist, perhaps *the* allegory for Hemingway. In the arena is reenacted the fate that is ambiguously chosen/not chosen. The arena rewards the exemplary and gives the measure, which is closeness to death. The preindustrial craft of storytelling/bullfighting requires an arena that will define its risks and its victories within a communal bond. Equally important, bullfighting requires attentiveness from the matador as from the writer. That apotheosis of attention was precisely the theology of the true/real that Pound took from Agassiz and that brought natural history and modernism together in the absence of any other godly manifestation, as a realism different from the artificial paradises of symbolism. Hugh Kenner, quoting two instances of "Le Paradis n'est pas artificiel" located in the *Cantos,* wrote:

> God himself, evidently, did nothing but shape interdependent details, fleas and corollas and the unfolding wonders a microscope offered to Agassiz' attention but not, it would seem, to others with similar microscopes. God is concentrated attention; a work of art is someone's act of attention, evoking ours; there have been great feats of attention. (53)

I want to underscore my sense that gender is far from the whole story here, that indeed part of the problem for Hemingway is that social critique has been read as nothing more than masculine posturing. My interest in Hemingway was reinforced at the MLA a few years ago when I heard Cary Nelson play the tape of Hemingway's 1947 address to the Abraham Lincoln Brigade. The period from the end of World War II to the sixties, phase I of the Cold War, was characterized by a far-reaching purge of works from literary history. When we turn to Hemingway, we can recognize the staggering scale of our Cold War losses. Americans learned their own intellectual history only as myth, and hence as the most real or the most deterministic of imaginaries, as if it had no openings. The association between manliness and nation produced by Theodore Roosevelt has a rhetorical history, but its reproduction in the discourses of nationalism takes on the inevitability of the unconscious without a reproduction of the historical struggle around traditions of manliness, warfare, the frontier, and narrative that Hemingway, for example, engaged in. The legacy of Cold War repression has produced a feminist response that would, in turn, exclude Hemingway from the canon.

The Cold War reveals itself, after all, to be about representation, power, and identity even more than about battles. The rhetorical structure of Cold War discourse has given us a model inherited by the identity politics of today. What is at issue is not just a misreading of Hemingway, but the way the discourse of the Cold War enforced this hypermasculinity so that men were subjects of it and women silenced by it and men and women alike unable to speak outside of its parameters. By its extremity, Cold War polemics set up a big-stick discourse that exacted hypermasculinity of its speakers. Misreading the Hemingway code into a new system of compensatory rhetoric, the Cold War reader gradually turned the more nuanced Hemingway text into an exaggerated allegory of hyper-masculinity and national defense. This phallic distortion has made Hemingway an endangered writer himself, in spite of resistance from the numbers of critics who have insisted not only on nostalgia, but also on complexity and labored to correct the hyperbolic myth. Literature appears as the "melodrama of beset manhood" to the retrospective feminist perspective because we see the gendering of the allegedly transcendental subject.

One can even understand why the popular nostalgia for a lost American heroism coalesced around Hemingway in the postwar Cold War culture of diminishing affect. Hemingway's work did not succumb to the lure of boredom as a cover for terror. He was writing, insistently, in the face of a claustrophobic literary scene, about a more open vista—not about the insides of houses, or of minds, but about land, sea, and sky; and he was writing about struggles that externalize the drama of embattled self and other. He was writing about war. He located the American novel on the streets of Paris, in Spain, in Africa, in the Caribbean, in Cuba, and doing so portrayed the new international scope of American responsibility—and power—in terms more critical and less extreme than the nuclear showdown imagined as government policy in the buried tombs of government offices. If his terms sometimes seem a throwback to Teddy Roosevelt's embrace of manliness as a cure for fragility—if, indeed, carrying a big stick seems something of a prevailing motif—still, Hemingway like Roosevelt had taken from Louis Agassiz's method of natural history a discourse that assigns "realism" not to the melodramas of nuclear plots, but to the intensity of sustained and repeated—one could even say impassioned—observation. The trauma of nuclear threat would make observation itself hallucinatory, a surveillance of secrets and the hidden—a dark apocalypse scarring over the metaphors of well-illuminated perception.

No one was more conscious than Hemingway of how he might become a stereotype, a legendary figure inscribed in public culture and perhaps, finally, gradually, a figure he himself took on. This allegory or melodrama fixed manhood in a deadly apotheosis of manly power without consequence, an empty transcendence. In this reduction of identity to propaganda, as well as in the more obviously political difficulties, Hemingway was a victim of the Cold War. He recognized the reductiveness of imposed identity. It threatened his ability to bring his writing to the public, even to a publishable state. His worries, in letters, about how the portrayal of himself in Philip Young's 1952 biography might affect his writing—his strenuous resistance to the idea that his heroes might, in some way, be himself—suggest how porous he felt, how vulnerable to the mirroring of his readers. It is perhaps in this transcendent guise that Hemingway as writer appeared in *Life* magazine for September 1952, where the text of *The Old Man and the Sea* was published for what seemed like "half the country," he said. When the book won a Pulitzer for him, it confirmed his own feelings that it was a true success. He wrote in a 1954 letter that "It always reads to me, then, when it's very good as though I must have stolen it from somebody else and then I think and remember that nobody else knew about it and that it never really happened and so I must have invented it and I feel very happy" (*Selected Letters* 896). The success was not a victory of manhood, but of the writer's death into his own immortality: "I still can't read it without emotion and I know that you will believe that this is not the emotion of someone admiring what he has done, because he did it, but because I was reading it as completely detached as though it were written by someone who was dead for a long time" (837). The earlier work, with its losses and woundings, gives way to something else, to an aesthetic objectification of human acts that caught even Hemingway. Perhaps, as he feared, his very success was precisely what would let the readers take him away from himself and make him the emblem of the Papa that American culture at that moment so fervently desired.

Theodore Roosevelt used celebrity and mass culture very adeptly, but becoming a celebrity icon of a certain masculinity worked against Hemingway. What made Hemingway particularly vulnerable, perhaps, to being appropriated by Cold War discourse is the way his works seem to reenact the double valence of that consensus. Grossly, at the level of an imaginary masculinity, he seems to give us a melodramatic heroism—and the Cold War narrative structure is fundamentally melodramatic, relying upon a clear identification of roles, good guys and bad guys, of heroes and heroines. Hemingway's image as "Papa" responded to the consumption of private life that was increasingly appearing. But closer up, in fact, Hemingway's fiction reveals instead of polarization into two sexes or two sides precisely the opposite. The men and the women are alike. In the postwar *Garden of Eden*, that cross gendering becomes decadence. Catherine keeps cutting her hair shorter and shorter, in visits to the hair salon that are compulsive and erotic, like forays into the dressing room of a theater of forbidden pleasures. She takes the hero with her, to have his hair cut the same way, so they are the same, and they enact the role reversal in the night's lovemaking—he becomes her girl. But the earlier Hemingway, with, for example, the earlier Catherine of *A Farewell to Arms*, portrays this gender ambivalence in a way that is less explicit and yet that gives the woman access to the heroic code. Perhaps, as Sandra Spanier has argued, Catherine is the code hero of *Farewell to Arms*. In

The Sun Also Rises, the fact that Jake is castrated and Lady Brett the tough guy has greater significance for the location of the subject in modern narrative, in the narrativization called war, than for the thematic literature of war wounds. It is the male speaker whose power is wounded.

Hemingway's texts ought not to be a good anchor for the Cold War aesthetic because they contain a very large proportion of what will seem the feminine: not only that submersion in the materiality of experience, so that the sensation of the fight is more important than who wins, not only the gendered masculinity, but also compassion, a political compassion that could be suspect to traditional critics, and literary pleasure. Joyce Carol Oates thinks of Hemingway in order to define literary pleasure. She describes a young student's reaction to "A Very Short Story": "This is love, that look on your face, again, always, what pleasure" (65). She worries, however, about that myth of the persona:

> How one feels, for instance, about his highly stylized religion of machismo (the glorification of the bullfight as a ritual of beauty; the camaraderie of men who are bonded by their "superiority" not to women but to most other men as well); his rites of personal risk and exotic adventure . . . the equation of masculinity with greatness in literature. (303)

What is important to underscore is that masculinity in Hemingway calls up rather than represses the bodied, and sometimes the abjected, identifications of gendering. Michael Reynolds has argued that masculinity in Hemingway's work did not function to purify itself of the feminine:

> Ernest was most interested in female sensibilities. His first mature story, "Up in Michigan," took a young girl's point of view, and Molly Bloom's long, erotic soliloquy at the end of Ulysses was, for Ernest, the best part of Joyce's book, the part he came back to time and again in his later fiction. . . . To write, a man must cultivate that feminine side of himself, become both male and female. (*Hemingway, the Paris Years* 98)

Hemingway's preoccupation with authenticity, and his fear of biographers, has notoriously been juxtaposed with the lie—particularly with respect to an autobiographical book such as *The Moveable Feast.* Thinking of Hemingway together with Stein and Pound suggests the modernist way out: truth and lie may be contained by the boundaries of aestheticism. Therefore it is important to recall the enormity of the struggle Hemingway was waging, against and within a realism that disguised its ideological imperialism. Did he want to give up on the claims to the true/real associated with the ethos of natural history writing? His extraordinary overwriting of *The Dangerous Summer* in 1960 (100,000 words when his contract with *Life* called for 10,000) suggests, to the contrary, that attentiveness to detail had become his chief mode of defense. Within modernism, he established a style that haunts contemporary prose. The famous parataxis works for Hemingway and for Stein to rupture narrative control and locate continuity instead at the level of syntax, substituting the performative—the everyday act—for more mythological stabilities. He wrote both within and against the moral legacy inherited by him and by American culture from Teddy Roosevelt.

The discourse of liberal reason during the Cold War borrowed the notion of ideology from Marxist categories, but tried to put itself outside ideology, and furthermore to punish those who were ideological. In literary criticism this took the form of the argument that literature was not political and should not be. Mass culture was suspect, irrational at best and prey to groups such as unions and civil rights movements, marked as ideological. But intellectuals also supported a far more dangerous formulation, claiming that reason ought to be objective, free of self-interest or left-wing politics, and of course separable from the forces of cultural history—and therefore, nonobjective thinkers had no right to demand access to the institutions of reason, such as universities. As I will discuss further in the next chapter, Sidney Hook made the most influential and damaging form of the argument: communists were clearly ideological, submissive to the party line, unable to reason. It was legitimate, Hook wrote for the *New York Times* in 1949, to fire communist professors at the University of Washington and Oregon State University because they were the agents of a subversive ideology ("Academic Freedom"). Those who were not communist would not be harmed. The argument was repeated again and again and had a far greater influence than McCarthyism in legitimating the persecution of the Left.

Furthermore, the argument continues to be used to counter revisionary histories of the Cold War that expose the extent of the persecution. In 1991, for example, Stephen Whitfield—writing about the culture of the Cold War from what he called the liberal perspective—repeated the claim that good literature had been unaffected by anticommunist harassment:

> The historian can nevertheless draw the happy conclusion that the culture of the Cold War was by no means synonymous with the culture of the 1950s, and in that asymmetry one can distinguish a relatively free society from a political system with totalitarian tendencies. The drive to inhibit art and thought left much untouched, and what was exempt from the scorched-earth policy of the patriots remains among the adornments of American culture. (12)

He lists Hemingway among the "exempt," but the historian needs to attend more closely to the forms of censorship that operate in a liberal society and that the Cold War patriots were able to maximize.

Ernest Hemingway had written himself into the arena that Roosevelt defined, even though he was critical of the deadly obligations of manliness. After World War II, the proliferation of Westerns and war movies in the fifties would suggest that the manly virtues endorsed by Teddy Roosevelt at the beginning of the century were in popular ascendancy again, an instance of the "hard bodies" described by Susan Jeffords that defined the Reagan era. The literary sphere was so dominated by the male perspective that women's writing nearly disappeared. But the segregation of mass culture from intellectual life split versions of gendering as well. Furthermore, liberal and conservative political divisions replicated and amplified the complications through foreign policy: as advocates of realism and containment (during the Truman years) deployed a global imperialism that feminized national culture while Republican advocates of nuclear power plays, led in particular by John Foster Dulles, insisted upon a manly nationalism—a distinction that carried over into the later divisions of doves and hawks.

In other words, even though gender functioned to mobilize political discourses in struggles for domination, and the feminine everywhere came to serve as the losing term, Nixon's political "arena" defined the oppositions quite differently from liberals and intellectuals. In fact, the obvious masculinity cited from Roosevelt could serve as a screen for the claims of liberalism to be universal. I do not mean to blame Roosevelt for Nixon, nor do I mean to claim that we can simply do without the Roosevelt legacy I am pointing to. Masculinity, like femininity, has been constructed within a cultural history that is changed as it is also reiterated. In fact, I would argue that natural history in particular continues to support, by its premises, much of environmentalism, that Ralph Nader in many ways is carrying on the reformist and progressive legacy of Theodore Roosevelt and uncritically reproducing some of its identity politics as well.

The vocabulary of liberal reason and realism posited a nonideological transparent subject, without class, gender, or ethnicity. But the national subject was propped on the patriotic manliness relayed by Theodore Roosevelt, now become a hypermasculinity without history whose gendering was denied. This hypermasculinity emerged as national identity in the arena of nuclear showdown. Meanwhile, the popular images of the real man and the tough guy promoted in film and fiction were declassed: they appealed to the working class and became a marker of class distinction that would eventually enable Republicans to appeal to the "individualism" of those men. Richard Nixon thought himself the American everyman in this drama, the representative of a Theodore

Roosevelt progressivism, but more importantly, the very figure of the American individual, he who must battle against a feminized society and an untrustworthy press.

Cold War intellectuals did not claim the gendered manliness that Theodore Roosevelt made patriotic and Nixon tried to appropriate. Liberalism in particular, but also the realisms of diplomacy as well as of science were constructed through the abjection and elimination of gender, race, ethnicity, and class from a neutral universal subject—the symbolic phallus that borrowed its authority from manly history but was separated from gendered bodies. The gesture of universality operated as a gesture of repudiation at the same time.

What happened to manliness? Masculinity began to take on the aura of the abject, of a beset manhood. Toxic, seductive, impure, the image of heroic manhood in figures such as John Wayne solicited the addictive identification of a working class whose other identity had become un-American, who increasingly needed through the fifties to deny the bonds of labor and learn how to enter the privileged relations of the middle class, taking up the gendered subjects and the interiorities of family relations that were just then being repudiated by modernist intellectuals together with the artifacts of mass culture such as *Leave It to Beaver* or *I Love Lucy*. Richard Nixon appears on the public scene as an agent of the forced transformation to a populist nativism of the American labor-identified working class, although he looks moderate by comparison to extremist spokesmen, from Joseph McCarthy to George Wallace. Nixon's advocacy for the House Un-American Activities Committee and his identification with Roosevelt are linked to the declassing of masculinity. That other reader of Theodore Roosevelt, Ernest Hemingway, was caught in the strong currents of this realignment. The very fact that his writing entered into the discourses of gender, even though critically, gave him the popular appeal that would attract *Life* magazine (which published *The Old Man and the Sea* and *The Dangerous Summer* as a three-part series) and make him problematic for the emerging consensus of intellectuals.

Both critics and ordinary readers have tended to exaggerate an easy identification between Hemingway and stereotypical national ideals, as if he were precursor to John Wayne rather than to Tim O'Brien or Raymond Carver. Some feminist criticism has accused Hemingway of advocating sexist cultural codes of manliness. But Cold War codes of reason show us that the manliness you see may be less threatening than the gendering you don't see. A legendary manliness in the narrative tradition promulgated by Teddy Roosevelt, together with its politics of heroic nationalism, has threatened to overwrite the more complex Hemingway. What I want to suggest is that Cold War logic made Hemingway "unreadable" for a number of critics precisely because it limited interpretation and occluded the contested history of culture, identity, and gender—the Theodore Roosevelt tradition—that Hemingway so extensively brought into question.

The hypermasculinity of the Cold War consensus in literary criticism is not demonstrated by overt gendering, but rather by the assumption that all subjects are male, that human nature will naturally identify with beset manhood. Hemingway violated these conventions of hypermasculine transparency. Hemingway gendered men and wrote about women. His writing made gender visible, but that threatened the newly globalized ideology of the individual with its American claims to universality. The sense that Hemingway is a masculinist was not invented by feminists, but feminists have not been able to successfully dispute it either, suggesting how thoroughly both Hemingway and feminist criticism together have been caught in the discourses of gendered extremisms. It has seemed uncannily in discussions of the contemporary canon as if the last word on Hemingway (that he is too masculinist to be interesting) had been pronounced no matter how many feminist critics such as Linda Wagner-Martin, Sandra Spanier, Jamie Barlowe, Debra Moddelmog, Abby Werlock, Nancy Comley, and Susan Beegel have written about Hemingway. So I am trying to describe an invisible barrier of Cold War gendering, a gesture I hope is made possible by the weakening of its hold.

Hemingway both constructs and subverts gender. It is a double movement that is characteristic of modernist writers, particularly the women. The Hemingway style promotes what Peter Schwenger calls a "fundamental ambiguity":

> Hemingway's style is in one sense an extension of the masculine values he depicts: the restraint of emotion, the stiff upper lip, the *macho* hermeticism. At the same time, that style preserves in each story a truth that one is made to feel can never be fully known. That quality of truth is one that has already been denominated feminine, eluding as it does any masculine control. Masculine reserve thus modulates imperceptibly into feminine unknowableness. (*Phallic Critiques* 50)

The transformative effects of Hemingway's style continue to attract our attention and our analysis. On the level of plot, theme, and style his work ought to make us think about the complexities of gender.

However, to read Hemingway from a feminist point of view, as an avant-garde writer whose style unsettles identity and sexual relationship, one must first address the reduction of his text to a singular and exaggerated masculine coding. Does this reductiveness occur in the codes of his work or in the codes of reception? Despite his criticisms of war, his flight from Oak Park, and his questioning of gendered identity, Hemingway has been closely identified with American emblems of manhood. Thus the warning in *Across the River and into the Trees* seems singularly applicable. In that 1950 novel, the Colonel returning to the old scenes of his Italian campaign refuses to reinscribe the categories of the war. "Whenever you oversimplify you become unjust."

Although he had helped produce the reductiveness of celebrity, the very complexity of Hemingway's writing made him more susceptible to hyperbolic misreading. After World War II, Ernest Hemingway was vulnerable to being stereotyped, not because he wrote prescriptively like Roosevelt, but because he wrote about gendered crisis. Hemingway's political compassion, in particular his association with the Abraham Lincoln Brigade in Spain, made him ironically out of step with the Cold War critics who had rejected their former leftist affiliations. Hemingway claimed he was under surveillance. Though others scoffed, the opening of FBI files has revealed that Hemingway was not just being paranoid. Hemingway's loyalty was suspect and his great novel, *For Whom the Bell Tolls,* could not be read in the sympathetic political context that the Spanish struggle of the Left against fascism demanded. In 1941, the Advisory Board recommended *For Whom the Bell Tolls* for the Pulitzer Prize, but Columbia University president Nicholas Murray Butler said, "I hope that you will reconsider before you ask the University to be associated with an award for work of this nature," and there was no Pulitzer Prize for fiction awarded that year. The book was declared unmailable by the post office ("Censored Books").[17]

The problem of gender overlapped with this political suspicion. He was working on material, as *The Garden of Eden*'s publication suggested, that included gender changes and sexual experimentation very much at odds with the Hemingway identity assumed by the critics of his masculine codes. Nancy Comley and Robert Scholes take an extensive look at Hemingway's stories involving homosexuality, untangling a clichéd homophobia from what they argue is a more differentiated, and more engaged, representation: "He was especially interested in the alternatives to 'normal' sexual patterns. Contrary to his own statement about the sameness of abnormality, his stories show that there are so many varieties of normal and abnormal that the whole distinction is threatened by them" (*Hemingway's Genders* 137). Comley and Scholes make the post-consensus question about Hemingway's genders obvious: why would a literary critic want to assume that Hemingway was anything but various and often contradictory?

The scene of the warrior contains desire and its powers of displacement or condensation. Hemingway's return to the problem of a "real" defined in terms of death opened up a scene so fatally attractive to the men of American letters that it may be seen as the very unconscious of criticism. Daniel T. O'Hara argues that point in his analysis of "Reality in Theory," yoking Fredric Jameson together with Lionel Trilling and Harold Bloom as critics who,

> sounding vaguely like frontier preachers, define the Real as what Emerson first termed in his finest later essay, "Fate," the "Beautiful Necessity"—that awful figurative representation of reality as the power of death which is always so delightfully fitting for the ascetic spirit of criticism in America to behold. (198)

Nothing could have been more seductive for Cold War modernists than the deadly necessity foretold by the bomb.

The true/real that is the effect of Hemingway's sustained attention is not death itself, but the unspeakable that is not yet an object (or a corpse). Soliciting the approach of the unspeakable by the closest of turns risks death, and most of all that dying into the arena of language that appears as the known, the object, an abject, or the abject of critical language, the cliché. In a story such as "Hills like White Elephants," the method of a close pass seems at times like a riddle that can be solved by the addition of the unspoken word: abortion, they are talking about *abortion*—but the word makes the attentiveness of the story collapse. In a related story, "The Sea Change," a "brown young man" uses the word "vice," and then "perversion" to describe the girl/his lover's desire for another woman, and she objects: "You don't have to put any name to it." When he insists, "That's the name for it," she says, "We're made up of all sorts of things. You've known that. You've used it well enough." He also has refused the word for an unspeakable act that could be called *vice* or *perversion* in their relationship. This disavowal and this close avowal of the word is the turning point of the story, what makes him let her go and makes him "a different man" (304).

In "God Rest Ye Merry, Gentlemen," Hemingway tells the story of a young boy who has tried to castrate himself, and who may die from loss of blood. The intersection of religious and scientific discourses is marked by absolute dissonance: the boy's conviction that his "awful lust" is a "sin against purity" and the Jewish Dr. Fischer's reassurance: "It's a natural thing." The boy is a sacrifice to Christianity, but Dr. Fischer is also in trouble, for violating Federal statutes on the coast: the missing word is probably *abortion* here too. Since the boy "didn't know what castrate meant," he mutilated himself, and the incompetent Dr. Wilcox "was unable to find this emergency listed in his book"—Doc Fischer calls it "the amputation" (300). What was deadly—was it the Christian word of purification, the failure of the scientific word "natural" to convey morality, the absence of this emergency from normal codes, or the fatal reliance of Dr. Wilcox on the words of *The Young Doctor's Friend and*

Guide to make up for his lack of knowledge? The humorous cynicism with which the two doctors describe the case suggest that the unspeakable is what their merriness itself covers over: a death that threatens from the true/real of lust as signifier of sin. What is deeply problematic about manhood for Hemingway has to do with the consuming power of desire when it is imbricated with the death drive as Freud has tried to show us.

The world of natural objects split in the Cold War, becoming on the one hand the opaque objects of a technology that would turn them into resources—to mine or log or use in experiments; or, on the other hand, the transparent symbols of a mythology that belonged to American pastoralism and marked the contours of a landscape made to conquer. Hemingway kept the two entangled together, like the love and destructiveness of desire. In *Islands in the Stream,* he describes how the artist, Thomas Hudson, burns driftwood.

> It was whitened by the sun and sand-scoured by the wind and he would become fond of different pieces so that he would hate to burn them. But there was always more driftwood along the beach after the big storms and he found it was fun to burn even the pieces he was fond of. . . . On the floor his eyes were even with the line of the burning wood and he could see the line of the flame when it left the wood and it made him both sad and happy. All wood that burned affected him in this way. But burning driftwood did something to him that he could not define. He thought that it was probably wrong to burn it when he was so fond of it; but he felt no guilt about it. (5)

The Real burns like driftwood, the more affecting as we are fond of what burns. Hemingway's attentiveness requires a witness to record—a witness within the well-established traditions of manly witness, to be sure. Though his willing assent to destruction may seem allied to the imperialism of a Roosevelt, the attentiveness itself to that mixture of affect turns realism away from such directness of action and situates it, instead, in the arena of a repetition, a turning on itself, a writing.

Thus I am pointing to double levels of reading here: on one level, there is the text—in this case, Hemingway's—a site of complex and multiple intersections with culture, and of many possible readings. On another level, there is the Cold War consensus, a remarkably stable and oppressive set of agreements about interpretation that insisted upon a national identity established by binary extremism. I am not arguing that there was nothing written that escaped the Cold War consensus—to the contrary, I am arguing that the potentially oppositional work that was written even by a figure as powerful as Hemingway could be made unreadable. Since Cold War intellectuals both Left and Right—that is, from New York intellectuals to the New Critics—defined themselves in relationship to a mass society from which they were alienated, it was not obvious that they acted out a melodrama shared by other cultural players such as Richard Nixon. It was, in fact, extremely important for critical intellectuals to keep the boundaries well disciplined, to avoid overt identification with the state. Writers who violated this discipline to engage gender identity or the political economy seemed unliterary. The Cold War consensus agreed that literature was different from history or politics. Hemingway stirred up both.

4

Unsettling the West: The Persecution of Science and Bernard Malamud's *A New Life*

> In every case the storyteller is a man who has counsel for his readers. But if today "having counsel" is beginning to have an old-fashioned ring, this is because the communicability of experience is decreasing. In consequence we have no counsel either for ourselves or for others. After all, counsel is less an answer to a question than a proposal concerning the continuation of a story which is just unfolding.
> —Walter Benjamin, "The Storyteller"

> Americans from one part of the country we call the United States appear as strangers, almost foreigners in another part of the country. That tells you something about the nature of man; he is frequently afraid of faces he does not recognize.
> —Bernard Malamud, speaking at Oregon State University in 1967

In his 1961 novel, *A New Life,* Malamud wrote about what happens to a liberal Jewish teacher from the East, Sy Levin, when he tries to reform the English department of an "unknown town in the Far West." Labeled a troublemaker, Levin ends up being fired—but he also leaves town with the prospect of better times. He is an antihero, but he points ironically to a more heroic antecedent. The larger political implications of the novel have been obscured by critical tendencies to read it as a myth of individualism and by speculation about its autobiographical specificity. Malamud himself was not fired for being a troublemaker, but he could have had a model who was. A young professor of chemistry at Oregon State College, Ralph Spitzer, was fired for being a communist in 1949, in the year that Malamud arrived to begin his teaching career there.[1]

The loss of memory that accompanied the Cold War had to do not only with the way that the literary and religious discourses of romance, myth, and symbol were withdrawn from counsel, but also with the way that the discourses of science and information became the arena of warlike (and suppressed) rhetorical struggle. The traumatic aftermath to the events of World War II required testimony of some kind, but instead an atmosphere of terror found its secret place in the rigidities of bureaucrats. Scientists involved with the weapons program published their hope to avoid a weapons race by sharing scientific information in 1945. John Hersey published *Hiroshima,* with its accounts of survivors of the atomic blast, in 1946, and the Book-of-the-Month Club distributed free copies to its members. And yet news of the nuclear aftermath entered everyday life not as a thoughtful reflection on national responsibility or the effects of militarized science, but as a threat to American futures. Bomb-shelter emblems on public buildings and schoolchildren's rehearsal of air-raid drills helped make ordinary citizens feel like victims of the nuclear era and not responsible parties to it.[2] As the war ended—but the culture of war quickly renewed itself—there were stories of the concentration camps too, of their discovery, of some who escaped, of the many who died, and Anne Frank's diary (which was published in 1952). Still, many—perhaps most—survivors of the Holocaust have gone for decades without speaking of their experience, as Felman and Laub among others have discussed. A narrative of disillusionment captured Cold War fiction. It was a story that avoided its context of historical extremity.

There was information, but it had little to do with a truth that might give counsel. The solitary individual presumed by literary modernity moved in existential extremity. What accounts for the sudden renaissance of Jewish writers during the Cold War? Could their emergence in part have to do with the largely unspoken community they formed: a heritage of storytelling, and a story too terrible to tell? Heard or not heard, from refugees and survivors, the stories of World War II left memory itself traumatized.

And then the Cold War itself, however imaginary, began to produce casualties: the spectacular execution of the Rosenbergs imposed, like McCarthy, violent governance through spectacle. By 1961, when Bernard Malamud wrote *A New Life* about the firing of a professor, the anticommunist political terror that had been inflicted on American intellectuals was but one layer of the trauma. At work on the filaments of memory, he unraveled a narrative banality that substituted for cultural recollection.

By 1961, Cold War politics had all but silenced the various manifestations of the political Left, from communist through popular front, anti-Stalinist, Trotskyite, socialist, to fellow traveler. The most significant elimination of radical perspectives might have occurred in the domestication of everyday life. The working class was effectively cut off from political critiques and encouraged to identify with sexually defined consumerism: the (middle-class) discourses of family that both evoked sentimentality and denied the progressive historical resonances of sentimental power—and the individualist hypermasculinity that disconnected men from working communities. Nearly as radical a break took place among intellectuals. Anticommunist persecutions and surveillance helped force scientists to accept the governance of national interest, and the covert operations of economic influence may have impinged even more on scientific freedom of thought.

Malamud used historical fantasy in the service of a moral reflection on the Cold War life of intellectuals. His character's defense of the liberal arts in *A New Life* parallels Ralph Spitzer's vigorous defense of free speech for scientists. Malamud's redemptive storytelling recalls Walter Benjamin in that he refuses to follow the withdrawal of the critics into a separate cultural sphere.

Walter Benjamin quarreled with Theodor Adorno during the thirties over the status of art in class struggle, arguing that mechanically reproduced art such as film could advance the cause ("The Work of Art in the Age of Mechanical Reproduction") and that art could, perhaps, release the closure of historicism and make experience materially available to a present caught in the "storm" called progress ("Theses on the Philosophy of History"). Benjamin thought the opponents of fascism also promoted it by, "in the name of progress," treating it as a historical norm (257). Benjamin's concept of banality does not (as Alice Yeager Kaplan thinks Hannah Arendt's does) conceive of fascist art as simply unsuccessful—devoid of imagination and a sense of reality (Kaplan 49).

Hannah Arendt linked the problem of banality to fascism and the Holocaust in her discussion of the Eichmann trial. The book was published after Malamud wrote *A New Life*; however, some of her observations seem to overlap with Malamud's thinking. Eichmann's evil did not leave any mark on his air of ordinariness. The lesson is that evil does not necessarily appear in a Gothic spectacle of blood and deformed physique; evil does not even necessarily interrupt the rounds of bourgeois normalcy. It does not necessarily appear as the irrational or even the antisocial. There was nothing *unheimlich*, nothing uncanny about Eichmann, Arendt reported when she first saw him (329).[3] Malamud uses storytelling to introduce a foreign space into the banality of the Cold War in Cascadia. In opposition to golf, football, and grammar, Sy Levin introduces foreign films, sexuality, and literature in the composition class. Appearing as representative of the unwelcome and the *unheimlich*, Levin makes trouble, but evil belongs to what banality repressed: the larger history of un-American persecution and global trauma that ought to have haunted the classroom. Anticommunism invaded every aspect of community, but indirectly, as the largely invisible and abstract support to banality.

The Cold War reinforced the solitariness of the novel and its incapacity to convey the experience of community. Walter Benjamin thought the advent of middle-class literacy informed the novel as a genre that was isolated from community. However, as I have discussed earlier, modernism depended strongly on the bringing together of other cultural forms that would break up the closed narrative of historicism by their juxtaposition of the incommensurable. A strong political consensus such as Cold War nationalism impacted storytelling by its pervasive abstract construction of everyday life.

The most startling form of censorship took place as a collective amnesia on the Left. The "New York intellectuals"—Lionel Trilling, Philip Rahv, Mary McCarthy, Sidney Hook, and Irving Howe, among others— had repudiated former associations with communism. But they maintained themselves as the site of radical discussion in journals such as the *Partisan Review, Commentary,* and *Dissent,* and in novels demonstrating their disillusionment with communism, such as Trilling's *The Middle of the Journey* and McCarthy's *The Groves of Academe.* The former Left rewrote the analysis of Marxism and Marxist thought together with the history of American communism before the Cold War.[4] Bernard Malamud found a welcome from the journals of the New York intellectuals, but he was not a member of that former Left. Far from repudiating a previous extremism, he presses humanely for critique.

During the fifties, Elvis Presley seemed radical. Youth culture seemed radical. The Beats seemed radical. The "San Francisco Renaissance" of the Beats foregrounded protest through style and a break with tradition, but they were also part of vernacular culture, not in the academy except when students read them surreptitiously, as Michael Davidson reminds us. Norman Mailer called the "new hipster" a "psychopath" because he saw the Beat revolt as necessarily antisocial. *Playboy* magazine emerged as a voice of progressive critique, with its articulation of "the Playboy philosophy," its publication of Left perspectives, and its questioning of the domestic consensus.[5] The civil rights movement represented progressive politics but repudiated the history of support from communists together with W. E. B. Du Bois. Martin Luther King's rhetorical appeals were to Christian and enlightenment traditions. Linus Pauling and others continued activities on behalf of international peace right through the fifties, under considerable pressure, eventually forcing the United States into a certain embarrassment—they had to grant him a passport—when he won both the Nobel Prize for chemistry and the Nobel Peace Prize.

Nevertheless, when the "New Left" arose in the sixties, it had almost no continuity with the past, and the theorists of the new social movements looked to Europe for the kind of critical and philosophical discussion that worked through analysis of the historical moment. The political "realism" of those (such as Trilling) who repudiated utopian progressivism transferred onto a historical realism that censored political optimism from the intellectual record. The troublemakers of the sixties seemed simply manifestations of disorder to such Cold War realists.

Consider this fixity an element of what Murray Krieger, in 1960, called "the tragic vision." Reading the modern from Kierkegaard and Melville through Dostoyevsky and Kafka to Malraux, Krieger argued "Justice has passed from the universal to the rebellious individual" (*Tragic Vision* 7). This plunged literature into an extremity that "produces the uncompromising hero who in turn produces an action falsely conceived in purity so that he is compromised utterly" (264). Like Trilling, Krieger argued that the extremity of the modern would destroy civilization in the name of justice. In *Man's Fate*, André Malraux, for example, showed the dilemma of the revolutionary hero as a Nietzschean struggle between will and destiny, "not a political response but an existential one" (61). Even in Ignazio Silone's Christian/Marxist *Bread and Wine*, Krieger found a tragic enthusiasm: "The assertion of a private ethical from outside all ethical structures . . . is already a demoniacal assertion" (84). It is significant that a writer such as Bernard Malamud, who wrote for the *Partisan Review*, should write a retrospective novel in 1961 that made the troublemaker into something of a hero.

In his youth, Bernard Malamud was the storyteller of his neighborhood. He gathered the other young people to him in long evenings on the front steps of his Brooklyn apartment and made his first reputation there.[6] Perhaps the conviction of his storytelling role sustained him later, during the nearly two decades before his career as a writer solidified in the early fifties. Although Malamud is part of what some called the "Jewish Renaissance" that occurred after World War II in American letters—and thought, indeed, of the Jew as the postwar Everyman—he also said he was not a Jewish, but rather an American writer. He is closer to the stories of an immigrant childhood than Saul Bellow, not so publicly political as Norman Mailer, more responsive to a cultural history than the younger Philip Roth.

In his earlier novel, *The Assistant*, and a collection of short stories, *The Magic Barrel*, that won the 1959 National Book Award, Malamud had seemed to find his proper subject by writing about the lives of urban Jewish immigrants such as his parents. His stories had a fantastic quality that would later be thought of as akin to Latin American magic realism. In them, everyday life was plunged into a morally charged intensity. Malamud visited again and again the question of justice for the common person, which was the possibility of a better life. He took the extremity of modern ethical dilemmas into his narratives but addressed them in the voice of a Jewish storyteller, the voice of spiritual experience and surprise, with counsel for his audience.

But in *A New Life*, Malamud also wrote a reply to the Cold War academic novels of the forties and fifties. Though the project of a new life would become comic and even somewhat absurd in his hands, he did not turn it to the Cold War realism of disillusionment with utopia. He brought the perspective of the Jewish immigrant to the American myth—that is, the myth of the frontier—doubting innocence, but not the desirability of justice. He located the Western myth in its double dimension, in the genuinely moving natural landscape, and in the oppressive banality of Cold War institutions. Far from exempting higher education from complicity, he showed the true ubiquity of anticommunist censorship and its relationship to prewar anti-Semitism.

Malamud made his antiheroic protagonist from the very object of American anti-Semitism, the troublemaking radical. Before World War II, for example, Ernest Elmhurst argued in *The World Hoax* that Jews promoted Bolshevism to create unrest and discord, an argument that characterized European anti-Semitism:

> Exploiting material advantages in Gentile countries during times of unrest and strife has always been the Jews' best opportunity. Indeed such conditions have most usually been created by them for this express purpose. . . . "Wars are the Jews' harvests." . . . It has become his chief ambition to carry the seeds of unrest and discord into every country. . . . He is busily engaged—through the promotion of "democracy" and universal suffrage—in planting the germs of Bolshevism everywhere *for the sole purpose of advancing his own race.* (120–21)

Linking the troublemaker, the Bolshevik, and the Jew, as Malamud did in *A New Life,* carried a certain risk. But it also reinvoked the critical moral consciousness that Malamud thought was the specific contribution to modernity of Jewish thought. The book resists political allegory by the multiplication of resonances—political, spiritual, ethnic, unconscious. Malamud was influenced not only by the storytelling of immigrants in his childhood, but also but the way Sigmund Freud had exposed the significance of the irrational. Freud himself had attributed such a heritage to the Jewish religion, as he wrote in a May 1926 letter to B'nai B'rith. Like Malamud, perhaps, Freud did not think of himself as a believer, but rather thought his ties to Judaism gave him a critical perspective, particularly on the effects of nationalism:

> Whenever I have experienced feelings of national exaltation I have tried to suppress them as disastrous and unfair, frightened by the warning example of those nations among which we Jews live. But there remained enough to make the attraction of Judaism and the Jews irresistible, many dark emotional

powers all the stronger the less they could be expressed in words, as well as the clear consciousness of an inner identity, the familiarity of the same psychological structure. And before long there followed the realization that it was only to my Jewish nature that I owed the two qualities that have become indispensable to me throughout my difficult life. Because I was a Jew I found myself free of many prejudices which restrict others in the use of the intellect, as a Jew I was prepared to be in the opposition and to renounce agreement with the "compact majority." (qtd. in Diller 119)

What Bernard Malamud had found when he moved from New York to Corvallis, Oregon, in 1949 was that the Far West did not escape the un-American persecutions or the "compact majority's" acquiescence. Malamud taught at Oregon State University (then Oregon State College) for twelve years, made his reputation there, and—as I have argued elsewhere —was always grateful to the place and the people who enabled his own remarkable new start as a successful writer.[7] Malamud's own career probably did not suffer from conservative persecution or even anti-Semitism in Corvallis, but he saw evidence of both. He discovered, in fact, that Cold War America was un-American everywhere, there was no hiding place out West. For the first time, in that place of a certain exile from the intellectual life of the East, he succeeded in publishing the books and stories he had been working on for so long; his arrival coincided closely with the beginnings of notice from publishers and editors. His novels and stories were all filled with a Chaplinesque sense of the discrepancy between the American dream and everyday life, but in *A New Life* the very content of the everyday is threatened by Cold War versions of banality. What marked these works with Malamud's particular genius was not only his open-eyed gaze at the painful truth, but his resistance, through humor, to dogma in its representation. As he left Oregon in 1961, he published *A New Life*, which soon made best-seller lists in New York and Los Angeles.

The novel has obvious, if complex, relationships to the real life he had been living in Corvallis as a teacher at Oregon State. This last of the four books Malamud published while he was in Oregon gives us not the pain of immigrants suffering in the Eastern cities, but the pain of oppression and prejudice set against the hopeful aspiration of the journey west. The book is not only about the Spitzer case, or about the particularities of Cold War persecution of free speech, but the context of the Spitzer firing shows the connections Malamud makes between the dangers of the Cold War and a more personal history.

There are several correspondences between the details of the Spitzer case and the book's story of a past firing, as I will later show. Malamud obviously alluded to the Spitzer case. But first I need to address a pressing question: why hasn't anyone talked about the relationship of the case to Malamud's book before? Critics may not have made the connection because they haven't known about the firing, though the case was famous enough in 1949. Many who knew about Spitzer and about Malamud's book had good reasons to deny any relationship: by 1961, a culture of secrecy had become a culture of tactful forgetting—and perhaps Spitzer himself was just getting on to his own new life and would have been impacted by fresh revelations. Most importantly, perhaps the specific politics of the Cold War are simply not Malamud's subject. That, in fact, has been the critical consensus. What I want to explore in this essay is the possibility that Malamud's mythmaking has some kind of relationship to that other narrative that emerges from the documentary record, a historical context that joins the Spitzer case to the myth of renewal in defiance of the alleged separation of "two cultures." The consequences would be to make clear just how the Cold War consensus has made it difficult to read any utopian stories, or to form alliances between the communities of science and storytellers. The loss of political context for Malamud's novel shows how the loss of power for oppositional forces worked.

Granville Hicks, for example, had been one of the foremost Marxist critics before World War II. In 1935, he himself had been fired from Rensselaer Polytechnic Institute. He was, furthermore, Malamud's friend. Yet his review of *A New Life* almost totally ignores the book's treatment of being "suspected as a radical," with only the brief mention in these words. This fact makes my argument seem suspect. Surely, if the theme were significant, Hicks would discuss it, at least? But surely the significance of anticommunism is precisely why he did not discuss it. When the book appeared in 1961, Hicks had long since repudiated his former radicalism. Any discussion of it plunged the writer into the ongoing history of the crisis on the Left. Malamud's book did not participate in the suppression of the issue. But friends such as Hicks and the *Partisan Review* group were not forced into a corner by Malamud's book, either. Hicks, for example, could talk about something more comfortable, like Levin as "a hero of our times . . . escaped from despair, only to find himself surrounded by triviality" (20). What Hicks left unspoken and unargued is the assumption that Malamud agreed with him about the treatment of literary radicals. A certain discomfort is manifest in Theodore Solotaroff's review of *A New Life* for *Commentary*. He wrote at great length about Malamud's strengths as an author, citing Norman Podhoretz that *The Magic Barrel* represents "an act of spiritual autonomy perfect enough to persuade us that the possibility of freedom from the determinings of history and sociology still exists" (197). Then he called *A New Life* a failure. It exhibited a "kind of malice toward Levin and . . . everything else in Cascadia" but also failed to make the real point—"the collision . . . of the post-ghetto sensibility and the culture of the hinter-lands"—"'Jew' is never mentioned in the novel" (203). This prompted a letter from Malamud, pointing out "There is no malice of mine toward Levin, nor to Cascadia, nor even to Gilley; there is no malice in the book," and "The word *Jew* is several times mentioned. The Jewish theme is visible and important" (February 21, 1962). Indeed, the Jew had become the figure of radical social critique once occupied by the communist.

Critics of *A New Life* have often made the same mistake that a few of the readers in Corvallis made when the book first appeared: they have imagined not only that Malamud is Levin but that the book just reflects Malamud's indictment of an inferior academic culture and a small town.[8] The book does not quite fit into the Manichean narratives in which Cold War history has been told.[9] Sympathy for the troublemaker would suggest sympathy for the Left. But it might also suggest sympathy for the Eastern intellectual who brought enlightenment to an unintellectual West. Malamud has not condensed a number of elements into the single figure of Levin; rather, he has made Levin the (flawed and ordinary) representative of the critical internationalist Jewish intellectual. This is a figure more heroically represented in the book by the character of Duffy, whose story Levin imitates on a diminished scale—and in history by the events surrounding Ralph Spitzer, events I will describe in detail shortly.

When Bernard Malamud arrived at the then-called Oregon State College in the late summer of 1949, he was already thirty-five years old, with only a few stories published. Yet he had the conviction that his life's purpose was to write, as he soon told others (and indeed his stories were at that moment gaining editorial notice). It may be that he felt himself already late, delayed by the Depression and the war. His stories were long in coming, he had been poor, and he had worked hard teaching high school in Brooklyn and in Harlem before he took the job in Oregon, his first college teaching position.[10] The place was a retreat to the Far West. Had he also retreated from the larger issues of modern history—the war, the Holocaust, the nuclear terror?

Malamud's realism has a mythical dimension that suited Cold War criticism. His moral stories even appealed to academic critics who thought that fiction should avoid any preaching about ethical purpose, that alienation was pervasive and ambiguity the only art.[11] In such a context the New York intellectuals seemed to be fighting a rearguard action to keep some sense of historical and cultural context in view. But we ought to wonder about a line of interpretation for Malamud that assumes "freedom from history" as we chart the shape of his conviction from beginning to end, from a short story like the 1940 "Armistice," through *The Fixer* and *The Tenants*, to the postnuclear *God's Grace*, and, lastly, to *The People*, a book that would have identified the American fate of the Nez Perce with the fate of the Jews. Malamud's resistance to demonology takes the form of a veering away from the tragic vision described by Murray Krieger. His narrative practices preserve a comic space within the grotesque reality of the Cold War for utopian aspiration, however modest. Thus does he resist anti-Semitism, anticommunism, and racism.

In *A New Life,* anticommunism is virulent because it is the visible coding of a submerged danger, enacting a more generalized antipathy to strangers. Malamud's fragile hero finds it all too easy to become a scapegoat. Sy Levin arrives in the little western town, "in a strange land," filled with doubt and hope about what he might do but ready to fight for progress. "Formerly a drunkard," he is a stranger, a Jew, "from the East" (1). He worries that he might reveal something about his past that would endanger his career, but he is also unable to keep from upsetting his superiors, advocating liberal humanism in a department that emphasizes grammar. "How can we . . . teach what the human spirit is, or may achieve, if a college limits itself to vocational and professional education? 'The liberal arts feed our hearts,' this old professor of mine used to say" (28). He is warned: "What we don't want around are troublemakers. If someone is dissatisfied, if he doesn't like what we do, if he doesn't respect other people's intimate rights and peace of mind, the sooner he goes on his way the better" (37). Furthermore, Levin is single, and so his department chair feels compelled to talk to him about sex, recommending that he hustle to get married and above all not date students or prowl among faculty wives.

Again and again Levin hears about his predecessor, Leo Duffy, a troublemaker who was probably Jewish, who taught Marx in his classes, who was fired—a ghost of past radicalism and a cautionary tale. Sy identifies with the absent figure and as he learns what happened to Duffy, he sorts out his opinions about the rest of the faculty. Levin wants to pursue his chosen career as a college teacher, but he gets increasingly enmeshed in the struggle for the liberal arts on campus. Must he endanger his career if he works on behalf of a progressive future?

The book unsettles everyday life on a number of levels. Levin is threatening not only for his liberal politics, but also for his violations of the sexual constraints his department chair had warned him about. He has a brief and comic encounter in the office with a female colleague, and then a more dangerous and seductive excursion to meet a student at the beach. His adultery with Pauline Gilley, and his final theft of her and the children from her husband, the director of composition, contribute to the end of his career. The relationship begins when Levin encounters her unexpectedly out in the forest. Their thoughtless lovemaking out under the trees gives rise to the whole affair and overlaps with Levin's other challenges to community life. If such desire is, in the Freudian sense, an irruption of unconscious life, it is also a radical force that resembles the power of political desire. When Levin discovers that Pauline had loved

Duffy before him, however, the question of love ceases to look like a natural unconscious and becomes, like politics, a question of ethical choice. The political and the psychoanalytic narratives of history converge.

When he takes up political action, Levin's criticism of the English department incites a faculty member to say he is as bad as Leo Duffy, to call him a "'Lousy goddamn un-American radical'" (318). As he presses for change—for open discussion of ideas, for literature in composition classes, for foreign films and bookstores, for a more democratic department—he risks his career. What Levin must finally do to make things right is not to give up on either his crusade or his love, but to follow both through to the end, losing his job and the ecstasies of first encounters alike but setting off with Pauline and the children to take on his responsibilities. If it is a comic finale, it nevertheless suggests that a new life is not so easy to come by. Furthermore, Levin leaves the college behind with its vocationalism intact and Marion Labhart, its crusading president, still in charge.

Malamud was never fired himself, but he was thought of as a troublemaker by some, and he must have felt something like Levin's trepidation, asserting the need for progress (as he did) when he was, as he said of Levin, a stranger, a Jew, from the East. Malamud wrote the book with a kind of seriousness to which readers have responded. It is more than academic fiction. Critics have written about the themes of rebirth, the pastoral, the problem of the hero as schlemiel, the innocent who goes West. The book rewrites the deadly rhetoric of the Cold War, bringing a more cosmopolitan knowledge of human experience and political violence to the debate without adding any distance to the experience of identity.

Some of Malamud's strategies are characteristic of other fiction in the fifties, avoiding rhetoric, but also thereby sequestering art away from political significance. The sense of struggle—the contradictory emotions, the long unsettled debate with self over department politics—is internalized, mobilized by love and hate, by the body's sublime and abject gestures, and by place, here the rain and flowers and green mysteries of the West. But *A New Life* is not in other ways typical, and its differences are related to Malamud's uses of the real, both the "real" of public history and the "real" of the unknown, that is, a "real" that is composed and communal, visible in institution and convention—in language, and a "real" that is like the Lacanian Real, unconscious and pressing.

Malamud rejects the intellectual position that sided with nationalistic anticommunism and portrays it not as rational or universal, but as allied with anti-intellectualism. And he rejects the naturalized hypermasculinity that thought of free sexuality as a means of subverting bourgeois marriage; his Levin must recover from the impetuousness of his affair and accept responsibility.

Malamud locates Levin—the lightening—the source of shock and challenge to business as usual on two levels: the conscious, political order that may be debated and where power may be contested by ethical encounter, and the unconscious, personal order where desire evokes the abject and the sublime. But we here see how the public order may itself be repressed. The events covered on the front page of newspapers (in Corvallis, but also in New York and San Francisco) have been forgotten. The Spitzer case and the wider political context for this book as for a generation of fiction published in the fifties, has been made unconscious by being ignored. The wider political context for Spitzer and for Malamud is dark indeed, for it includes the unspoken memory of the Holocaust and the unspoken problem of nuclear destruction. Against that darkness the banality of the fifties appears as phobic defense.

A New Life looks back on the American public university of the fifties and sees not an elite culture threatened from without by totalitarianism and mass hysteria, but a suburbanized academic culture of pragmatism, vocationalism, and narrow self-interest, threatened most of all by the willful and frightened suppressions within. Academic liberals were in a difficult, conflicted position. What curtailed academic freedom was not only the militant hysteria of nonacademics. It was the safety of a bureaucracy that demanded only conformity. The oppressive force of banality joined with a liberalism that supported persecution, the liberalism of the New York intellectuals first and foremost. It was an academy that needed the critique liberalism of the more Left-leaning kind might have provided.

Malamud himself, as a *Partisan Review* writer, was publishing his stories exactly where the most painful arguments were being articulated by writers who still saw themselves not primarily as academics, but rather as public intellectuals. Yet these critics—the voices defending the articulation of literature together with history as anticommunism was gathering force in the late forties—failed to provide the ethical stance needed to resist the ensuing persecutions. In fact, some of them provided the rationale for the persecution. The majority of literary critics drew back from the public arena altogether—neither Cleanth Brooks nor R. S. Crane could be thought of as a public intellectual, however influential their work inside the academy. Others—including the scientists who suffered from their political action, such as Linus Pauling—did not falter. Faculty at some institutions resisted anticommunist pressures. At the University of California faculty successfully challenged the imposition of a loyalty oath, though not without damage to some of them.

Down the road from the Oregon State College, the University of Oregon—"Cascadia University at Gettysburg" in *A New Life*—prided itself on its resistance to anticommunism and its tradition of academic freedom, letting Oppenheimer speak, and also American Communist Party leader Gus Hall. At times, *A New Life* seems to support the argument that the liberal arts university provides a better basis for academic freedom than the land-grant college. If *A New Life,* on the one hand, argued that anticommunism and the struggles of the city are everywhere, extending even to the West, the book also, on the other hand, allowed some readers to get off the hook and imagine that only the western college could be subject to such provincial persecutions. Malamud, however, regarded America in general as provincial and unconscious. In *Long Work, Short Life,* he describes how his trip to Italy, while he was thinking about *A New Life,* made him vividly aware of the personal suffering of Italians during the war and brought him into contact with the Holocaust with an immediacy that made him realize what a naïve American he had been.

A decade after the firings of communist professors, Malamud's novel revises the disquieting questions about critical intellectuals prompted by the history of anticommunism, questions that would grow even more pressing as the sixties went on.[12] His work refuses to participate in the normalizing of discourse represented by anticommunist liberalism. At the same time, he does not, like Pauling or other hero/victims of resistance, articulate an adversarial position. He directs our attention instead to the fate of those without sufficient power to resist successfully. Perhaps he felt himself one of those (especially in those early years of the fifties, before the books, the National Book Award, the reputation). Against an American provincialism taking refuge in the Western, his attention is on the suffering and the hope of ordinary people, the struggling victims of Holocaust and war and terror. After such betrayals, is a new life possible?

The Un-American in an Unknown Town

> He knew what the news was and preferred to forget it: The Cold War blew on the world like an approaching glacier. . . . The country had become, in fear and self-accusation, a nation of spies and communists. Senator McCarthy held in his hairy fist every man's name. And there were rumors of further frightening intercourse between scientists and atomic things. America was in the best sense of a bad term, un-American. Levin was content to be hidden amid forests and mountains in an unknown town in the Far West.
> —Bernard Malamud, *A New Life*

What Bernard Malamud showed in *A New Life* was that un-American persecutions had become intermixed with the ordinary life of the most unpolitical of faculties, in the nicest of small towns. In spite of recent post-Cold War interest in the ravages of anticommunism, few academics know

how widespread and politically directed was the policing of intellectuals. But the confluence of paranoia, anti-Semitism, and suspicion of intellectuals—most especially scientists—made deep inroads into American free speech and civil rights. Long before McCarthy stumbled onto
the media bonanza his accusations created, the Tenney Committee was
gathering material on fellow-traveling intellectuals and entertainers in
California, Truman instituted a loyalty oath to protect the Democrats from
Republican right-wing accusations of disloyalty, and J. Edgar Hoover put
the resources of the FBI in contact with college administrators nation-
wide in a campaign to ferret out disloyal faculty. This overt persecution
prompted and supported the wide-ranging suppression of critical thought
that took the form of an unthinking, apparently unpolitical convention-
ality. Malamud's book makes clear the connection between the very political and that banality. Thus Malamud's book operates in a space between
the devastation of the Holocaust and banality, the dangerous American
willingness to enforce conformity to the right side of the Cold War. It is
a critical perspective that violates novelistic orthodoxy and violates the
orthodoxy of liberal opinion as well.

The fifties concealed a mean and dangerous political history under an
outpouring of consumerist banality, and the local events in the Corvallis,
Oregon, of the late forties and the fifties demonstrate how that worked.
We call this phenomenon McCarthyism, as if only he violated civil rights
in the name of patriotic excess; but as David Halberstam writes, McCarthy took the spotlight "to lend his name to a phenomenon that, in fact,
already existed" (49). When President A. L. Strand fired Ralph Spitzer
from his job as a chemistry professor at Oregon State College in 1949 (before, in fact, the advent of McCarthy), most of the faculty took the president's
side, and pictures of cheerleader candidates replaced the political headlines of the student newspaper, the *Barometer,* within a few weeks. Not
only did Spitzer lose all his appeals for some kind of justice, but the general climate of opinion changed rapidly.

In 1948, much of liberal opinion was probably still on the side of a
cosmopolitan openness to every kind of political argument, including
communist arguments. Supporters of Henry Wallace's Progressive campaign for president only came to seem obvious subversives in the next
few months, in the aftermath of increasing attacks. In 1948, the AAUP's
Committee A issued a statement on academic freedom that called "political discrimination" against communists the "wolf's paw" that "might
presently extend to other forms of heterodoxy." The committee worried,
all too prophetically: "Faculty members in general might take alarm and
sagaciously conclude that they cannot afford the luxury of ranging thoughts
and bold speech."[13]

In the next few months, the wolf's paw opened the door wide, as former

Progressives together with communists suffered the fate of the heterodox. Just as the AAUP committee had feared, the firings of individual communists or "sympathizers" soon extended the opprobrium to anyone who looked like a troublemaker. In fact, the general catastrophe extended even to silence mysteriously the investigations of the AAUP itself in the years that followed. The imposition of a seamless banality erased history. In Corvallis, the memory of the firings disappeared—or, because people who suffered from anticommunism everywhere continue a traumatized silence to this day—remained unspoken.[14] Malamud's book aims to recall, in 1961, how a troublemaker was not only made marginal but erased from history in an American academy that began to seem as if it loved football players better than scholars.

Some members of the English department at Oregon State remember Malamud, and I have spoken to many of them at length about his career there. Those who were in the department when he was teaching in Corvallis have provided me with vivid details about his disciplined work habits, the department's composition policies when he labored under their strictures, even showed me his homes and the places he walked. No one, however, talked about that long-ago upheaval in Corvallis, when Linus Pauling's brilliant young protégé, Ralph Spitzer, found himself not only out of work but subsequently hauled before the House Un-American Activities Committee. Was it so very insignificant an event, then? So beside the point? I think, on the contrary, that its reverberations have lingered, that it was one of those traumatic breaks about which testimony cannot easily be given.

The Spitzer case is not one of the most famous of the anticommunist firings, but it was both central and in many respects typical. The treatment of Spitzer shows how even committed liberal academics were driven to take stands against academic freedom. When, in early 1949, the University of Washington fired three professors for being communists, and then Oregon State College fired two professors for being fellow travelers, the academic world was split. In the intellectual circles of the East, limits that would distinguish the liberal from the communist had begun to seem more necessary than boundless ideals of freedom. Under pressure from the Republicans, Harry Truman had already imposed a loyalty oath on government employees and set into motion the investigations. Academic intellectuals were also under pressure. Sidney Hook provided a rationale for liberals to move toward the center that was widely seized upon as institutions deliberated policy in the wake of loyalty oaths and firings. His anticommunism was especially persuasive because he had been one of the foremost Marxist philosophers in the country since the thirties. In the *New York Times Magazine* of February 27, 1949, Hook responded to the University of Washington's firings by arguing that communists should not be extended the protection of academic freedom because the nature of the party line violated the most basic principles of academic freedom.

This question of the party line has not ceased to engender acrimonious debate, appearing decades later in accusations of "political correctness." Hook's article "Should Communists Be Permitted to Teach?" claimed to uphold the standards of academic freedom, reiterating the premise upon which his mentor, John Dewey, and Arthur T. Lovejoy had organized the AAUP: that university professors must be free to exercise professional competence in their research, subject only to review by peers, and not to limits or constraints imposed by others in or out of the institution. However, Hook argued, such freedom implies "duties correlative with rights" (24). Membership in the Communist Party, he said, is different from questions of belief because of "what is entailed by the *act* of membership" (24). The Communist Party controls thought, demanding that professors follow the "party line." Hook provided models of such party line thinking: that "politics is bound up, through the class struggle, with every field of knowledge," so that a scientist, for example, would be required to "relate his subject to the growth of technology, its impact upon social divisions," and so forth (26). He turned to the public letter of resignation from the party in which Granville Hicks (*New Republic,* October 4, 1939) protested that the party refused to allow him to oppose or even remain doubtful about the Nazi-Stalin pact.

Indeed, Stalin's sudden agreement with Hitler had been a watershed moment for the Left, enforcing a disillusionment with communism of the Stalinist kind that had been debated throughout the thirties and conflating it with the other communisms that Trotskyites and anti-Stalinists had supported. Many of the ex-communists not only severed the affiliation, but also repented. This generation of the disillusioned to which Hook belonged was defined as much by their postwar opposition to communism as by their promotion of liberal principles. They failed to acknowledge the dangers posed by anticommunist demonology. Was it because the anticommunism in the United States was so inconsequential a persecution by comparison to the anti-Semitism of the Nazi Holocaust or Stalinist oppressions? Or was it a form of denial—because in fact American anticommunism rather specifically repeated the propaganda used by fascists before and during World War II, and it probably contained an anti-Semitic component—Jews were more likely than others to be persecuted as communists. Malamud's book shows the overlapping dangers.

The oppositional logic is at work in Hook's argument. Why might the "*act* of membership" curtail free thought? Hook seems to assume that a single individual is the ground for academic inquiry—a vision of a heroic isolated thinker that he himself had already critiqued (in *The Hero in History*), and that certainly did not fit the exchanges necessary to science.

Thus, as the Cold War took hold, even such a careful thinker as Sidney Hook extended his opposition beyond membership in the Communist Party to certain forms of knowledge associated with communism. The spectacle of Soviet persecutions led to his revulsion, and the growing fear of their increased power made his position a phobic opposition. But such an intellectual stance against forms of inquiry had widespread tragic consequences. That is, Hook's argument contributed not only to the loss of jobs, but also to a severe narrowing of the kinds of research that might be possible. A scientist such as Ralph Spitzer, who took an interest in relating his subject to its social history and to its relation to technology—as indeed Spitzer did—was suspect. But of course he might not simply be following a party line; social history is an important aspect of knowledge, even of scientific knowledge. In other words, the notion of the "party line" (like the notion of "political correctness," a term from the thirties that has resurfaced) assumed a coherence of position that is not only political, but also divorced from thoughtful analysis and criticism, as if no form of political engagement could produce knowledge. Ironically, the critique of such a party line adopted the very form of oversimplification it ostensibly rejects.

Anticommunism damaged academic inquiry because ruined lives struck terror in others, and because that terror acted to enforce political quietism. Furthermore, the political Right were all too happy to take advantage of liberals such as Hook, adopting the rationale for paranoia to justify widespread surveillance of scientists and intellectuals who were far from being members of the Communist Party. Linus Pauling, twice a Nobel Prize winner and the teacher and mentor of Ralph Spitzer, provides a singular example of the damage. He spent most of the fifties in ongoing difficulties with the passport office. The "two cultures" that C. P. Snow described of science and the humanities were alike in their need for freedom of inquiry and shared the experience of being under attack by anticommunists.

Even before World War II had ended, many scientists had made known their concerns about the interaction of nuclear weapons and a global organization of nation-states. The cosmopolitan, internationalist discourse of science found itself increasingly at odds with the nationalist interests of the political sphere. It did not take many years of the Cold War for scientists' desire for a free exchange of knowledge to come to seem like subversive activity. On April 22, 1945, Ralph Spitzer wrote from Wood's Hole, Massachusetts, to Linus Pauling about discussions there of the statement released by scientists at Los Alamos:

> We . . . have come to essentially the unanimous conclusion that the only solution that will not lead to a catastrophic armament race is to internationalize knowledge on atomic en-

ergy (and preferably all weapons) and demand as a price for
our sharing our knowledge free access to laboratories and
factories all over the world, with reciprocal rights for other
nations. . . . It is going to take a lot of effort to get the idea to
people that . . . there is no use to talk about winning or losing a war in which the contestants can wipe each other out
in a day. (April 22, 1945)

Pauling replied on September 26, 1945—and in the interim, Hiroshima
and Nagasaki had ended the war—"The only solution to the problem,
the only way of avoiding an atomic war which would devastate the
world, is the formation of a democratic world government . . . not a union
of nations."

In the interest of peace, Pauling joined forces not only with other scientists such as Harlow Shapley, Albert Einstein, Henry Pratt Fairchild,
and John Peters of Yale, but also with artists and entertainers, members
of the "Hollywood Independent Citizens Committee of the Arts, Sciences
and Professions" such as Humphrey Bogart, George Burns, Eddie Can-
tor, Gregory Peck, Orson Welles, and Dalton Trumbo.[15] Trumbo would
be blacklisted after HUAC made him testify for its hearings. In 1949,
Pauling argued, in a letter to chemist Milton Burton at Notre Dame, that
the key to peace was not conflict, but cooperation: "If we are to hope
that the United States and Russia can ultimately learn how to get along
in the world without war, then individuals, such as myself, must learn
how to get along with communists."[16] Pauling's continuing idealism may
seem both courageous and naïve, in retrospect, so conditioned are we after
McCarthyism to remember the virulence of anticommunism and the
danger of association with communists. To admit that he belonged to
what were described as "Communist-front" organizations, to advocate
collaboration with communists, defied the very assumption that such a
collaboration was guilty and disloyal. But neither Pauling nor Spitzer
operated under such an assumption.

In 1948, Spitzer and his wife campaigned for Henry Wallace's Progressive Party and were activists in the Oregon State campus group of "Young
Progressives." Spitzer planned to embark on a research project in the
history of science, a form of study that would come to seem subversive,
but that Pauling, as he wrote to Milton Burton on February 28, 1949,
apparently encouraged. He continued to be an activist in the scientific
community as well, arguing for an international approach to science and
against the increasing stigmatization of Soviet science. He argued against
the denunciations of Lysenko that—in response to Soviet political coer-
cions—were defining a new political line among geneticists, including the
president of Oregon State, August L. Strand. In the January 31, 1949,

issue of *Chemical and Engineering News*, Spitzer published a letter in reply to H. J. Muller's editorial charging that science was being destroyed in the Soviet Union. The letter argued that "the heated, not to say hysterical, charges which are now being made are reminiscent of previous assertions that the Soviet Union was, for example, destroying art, music, and economics." According to Spitzer, the proper scientific response to the debate was to read Lysenko and make a decision from his reports, not from the political reports surrounding him.[17]

The debate among scientists had political ramifications not only because Lysenko was Russian, but also because he was arguing that human interventions could change genetic characteristics. It had economic implications for Soviet development in agriculture, which Spitzer addressed. The genetic debate also had political implications inside the United States that Spitzer did not mention. While most scientists might not use the gene as the emblem of a racial identity, the argument that immutable identity was carried in the genes could support racist and nativist models, and the politics that accompany them.

On February 8, 1949, the president of Oregon State College, August L. Strand, called Ralph Spitzer and his wife, Terry, an undergraduate, into his office and told Spitzer his contract would not be renewed. Was Terry a greater threat than Spitzer himself? She was an outspoken activist. Like Linus Pauling himself, whose wife, Ava, persuaded him to speak out about peace, Spitzer was influenced by his wife's progressive politics. Strand announced that he was canceling the appearance at the Young Progressive meeting on campus of Coos Bay ILWU officer Don Brown, under suspicion of being a communist. Then he added that Spitzer would not be rehired the next year. Let me point out here that the purge of labor unions intersected, here and elsewhere, with the purge of the academy.[18] The case also involved L. R. LaVallee, in Economics.

Since both Spitzer and LaVallee had been active in Progressive politics, working for Henry Wallace's campaign, there was an immediate movement to protest what seemed to be a political firing, and newspapers became interested, soon to include not only Oregon papers, but also those in major cities. Spitzer defended himself vigorously, if with a degree of innocence about the growing power of those who would finally be enlisted to anticommunism. He pointed out that cases such as his own served to damage academic freedom in hundreds of invisible ways as faculty members learned to be afraid. Spitzer immediately turned to the AAUP on campus, which declared itself without jurisdiction, and asked the Appeals Committee of the OSC Faculty Council to investigate. He made four points: the head of the chemistry department was not consulted; the acting head had no complaints about his work; he had been promised a leave for a fellowship; and he had been promoted to associate professor. Procedures had clearly been violated. Nevertheless, the Appeals Committee supported President Strand.[19]

At first the president's office denied the political aspect of the firings, issuing news releases that claimed, for example, on February 17, 1949, that year-to-year faculty were released frequently for various reasons without particulars (which might damage their chances at finding new jobs); that the local chapter of the AAUP found the procedure fair; that the two men involved had chosen to make an issue of the case but that Strand did not intend to be "drawn into a controversy" and that "men and women of greatly diverse political and religious beliefs are on the O.S.C. staff now as always."

Ralph Spitzer was apparently shocked that he would be fired for his political activities, and he protested his firing on behalf of academic freedom. He wrote to Linus Pauling that he would not "steal away quietly and not cause ourselves any trouble on the campus" as the local AAUP had suggested. "My conscience would give me little peace if I felt that I had succumbed to terrorism of this kind, and left the rest of the faculty here wondering when it was their turn" (February 9, 1949).

The ensuing debate took place around the issue of academic freedom, however, not only because Spitzer defended himself, but also because Oregon State president Strand eventually chose to argue the case on this basis, after first declining to give reasons for his action. Although Spitzer was an associate professor, he did not have tenure. It was within the legal rights of the president to refuse to renew his contract without any reasons given but not to give, as a reason, political activity. One must assume that Strand entered the debate because he thought he was in the right and not just because he knew he would have widespread support from Oregonians grateful to see those "pinkos cleaned out" of their state colleges, as he did. In fact, by giving his reasons for dismissing Spitzer, Strand exposed himself to possible AAUP censure.

Strand entered into the argument powerfully, calling together the entire faculty of the Oregon State College to tell them what he had done and to present the case—a dramatic act that got front-page coverage in the next day's papers. The *Corvallis Gazette-Times* ran the headline: "Strand Lashes at Commie Professors." In the extraordinary seventeen-page speech he delivered to the faculty on February 23, 1949, and at length, in his extensive replies to letters and news stories, Strand drew upon contemporary debates within science as well as upon the larger debates about academic freedom and the firing of communist faculty to make his case.

President Strand's argument against Spitzer to the faculty of the Oregon State College was a model of Cold War rhetoric. His portrayal of the enemy made no attempt to balance perspectives and so tended to enhance phobia rather than understanding. He set out not, primarily, to prove the question of Spitzer's competency, but rather to denounce Soviet science and anyone who would give it credence. Examining Soviet debates over genetics—"the losers have been liquidated"—and the rise of Lysenko, Strand argued that communist Russia had set out "to eradicate the unpopular, idealistic Weissmanist-Morganist tendency in biology."[20] Strand documented his case for the academic audience with references to scientific journals, giving dates, volumes, and pages, aiming to prove himself more objective than what he sarcastically labeled "the capitalistic press."[21] In general, he wanted to show that Soviet science, and particularly Lysenko's genetics, was founded upon the ideology of a party line, however, not that Soviet science was faulty science.

Then Strand tried to convince the faculty that Spitzer was associated with that communist ideology. Reading Spitzer's entire letter to his gathered faculty, dramatically, with the presumption that it was self-condemning, President Strand declared that it presented conclusive evidence of party line thinking: "Why should a chemist bother to stir up controversy in the field of genetics? I can tell you. It is because he goes right down the party line without any noticeable deviation and is an active protagonist for it" (12). Spitzer's defense of controversy missed a report from the Soviet press of August 27, 1948, Strand goes on to say, that condemned the Soviet Academy of Sciences because *"they forgot the most important principle in any science—adherence to the party point of view, fell into apolitical and objective positions"* (14). Spitzer had abandoned objectivity to follow the party line in a scientific debate, and that made the letter of "unusual significance," Strand claimed (16).

With respect to the question of academic freedom, Strand followed the logic enunciated by Sidney Hook. He asked: "How about freedom from party-line compulsion?" and quoted University of Washington's President Allen that academic freedom demands of the teacher "an absence of restraints placed upon him by his political affiliations, by dogmas . . . or by rigid adherence to a 'party line' that sacrifices dignity, honor, and integrity to the accomplishment of political ends." All of the seventeen-page speech is taken up with the recital of Soviet misdeeds and his reading of Spitzer's letter, associating him with the enemy.

President Strand's argument shows how Cold War rhetoric insisted on the possibility of a pure, scientific rationality separate from ideology without addressing scientific issues. Strand concluded with a peroration that revealed, if not the hysteria of which Spitzer wrote, at the least a recasting of the problem into the terms, not of science, but of heroic resistance to communism: "Many men in Soviet Russia besides Vavilov have died in concentration camps, or by other means, because they would not accept the untruths which Dr. Ralph Spitzer has chosen to espouse" (17). This astounding appearance before a meeting of the faculty was followed by vigorous defenses of the dismissal wherever Strand had the opportunity to express himself, and those who took the other side were themselves called fellow travelers.

After Strand's speech to the faculty accusing him of following the party line, Spitzer issued a statement about his letter on Lysenko. He had not, he pointed out, accepted Lysenko's theories, but rather argued that scientists ought to examine the original documents and draw their own conclusions. Even so, he had the *right* to make a judgment, as all scientists ought to do, on the basis of their own analysis of the facts. Science would be finished if scientists only looked into work that was doctrinal.

Spitzer was supported by the Progressive Party and a number of other organizations on the Left, but, as Strand's replies to them suggested, such support was already discredited. *People's World* ran an editorial about the purge at Washington and the subsequent dismissals in Oregon arguing that "once Communists are deprived of their civil liberties others of dissident or progressive opinion will be next in line for suppression" and calling for letters of protest (February 23, 1949). Strand, however, regarded such letters as further evidence that Spitzer was a fellow traveler.

Spitzer was in a rhetorical trap that made it impossible to defend himself. If he admitted he was fired for his Progressive politics, legal niceties of free speech would go unnoticed in the sensational rush to denounce, so powerful was the opprobrium already connected with communism. Nevertheless Spitzer spoke out, in meetings sponsored by the Progressives and over the radio, and he traveled to Eugene and even to the Bay Area to talk about his case. His chief topic was academic freedom.

Spitzer noted the alarming growth of anticommunist firings—at least twenty cases of dismissal that were public—and argued that his own dismissal demonstrated the strength of a dangerous trend. He pointed out that those numbers indicated many more instances of lesser intimidation that would go unknown. Quoting from the statement made by Committee A of the AAUP, Spitzer called it "prophetic," because discrimination against communists was, indeed, spreading to become discrimination against other forms of unorthodox politics, against heterodoxy in general. Furthermore, he pointed out, the cases at Oregon State were directly related to the firings at the University of Washington, as Dr. Strand's quoting from President Allen showed. Thus the case against members of the Communist Party was extended to a much vaguer notion of following the "party line." Working for Henry Wallace and seeming to support Lysenko were both evidence to President Strand of party-line thought. Spitzer pointed out that Strand treated one's "attitude toward Lysenko as a sure test of loyalty," with Lysenko "one hundred percent wrong." Strand participated in the "wide-spread movement to suppress dissenting opinion by labeling it disloyal" (Radio Address, February 24, 1949).

Spitzer drew upon Henry Steele Commager's argument that the "new loyalty" involved a demand for conformity: "It is the uncritical and unquestioning acceptance of America as it is. It rejects inquiry into the race question or socialized medicine or public housing or into the wisdom of our foreign policy." Far from thinking of such conformity as a version of postwar patriotism, Spitzer called it profoundly un-American.

The impact of the firings on the possibility of free expression was serious. Spitzer himself was responsible for making information quickly available, through newspaper stories and the radio, about the consequences of his firing. He claimed (having no idea yet of the years of pain yet to come) that those who were dismissed did not suffer so much as those who were left behind, the students and faculty who must carry on in an atmosphere of terror. He cited a number of instances showing that fear was already having its effects on academic decisions at Oregon State. The political science department refused to hold a forum discussing the problem of "party line" thinking, because the topic was too controversial. An instructor called off a scheduled showing of a film on the Soviet Union. A student who wrote a letter to be published by the *Barometer* about the dismissals found herself, with her father, in the president's office instead. The *Barometer* suppressed news and refused, among who knows how many others, to publish a letter from Linus Pauling. Students proposed to establish a new Civil Liberties Committee—which would, they agreed, *not* address the Spitzer-LaVallee case—and the Senate refused to grant them recognition.

Spitzer had no idea what he was up against, and doubtless the difficulties he endured in the next few years continued to seem surprising. The most paranoid faculty member could scarcely have imagined the powerful forces with which President Strand had become allied when he fired Ralph Spitzer. It was not mass hysteria that led both Spitzer and Pauling himself to be persecuted by investigations into "Un-American Activities." Those involved in right-wing politics who wanted to discredit left-wing academics (and not just Communist Party members) worked in concert, especially through the Committees and the FBI, to research and document their allegations.

The persecution of American scientists and intellectuals was well organized, with plenty of governmental help. President Strand made his speech about Spitzer on February 23. According to copies of letters received by Strand's office, by March 7, 1949, Oregon congressman Walter Norblad had made note of the statement in the *Congressional Record,* submitted it to the Committee on Un-American Activities, and sent a copy to J. Edgar Hoover. In response, Hoover wrote, ominously for Spitzer, "This information . . . is indeed appreciated and you may be assured that I am having it made a matter of permanent record in our files" (March 16, 1949). Spitzer was perhaps from that moment—scarcely more than a month after the dismissal—assured of his eventual appearance before the Judiciary Committee in 1953.[22]

Even the liberal president Strand had willingly put himself into the politics of anticommunism, and his records show how rapidly that changed the nature of his discourse as well. There was nothing subtle about the demonizing rhetoric he took up once he was committed. Strand pursued the Spitzer case in a number of important exchanges with individuals and institutions outside the university. Linus Pauling wrote letters to Strand as well as to the student newspaper protesting Spitzer's dismissal for Lysenkoism.[23]

Strand was far from impressed by the letter, even though Pauling was not only the president of the American Chemical Society and one of the most widely respected scientists in the country, but also an alumnus of Oregon State. He replied. "We'll have to get along without your aid" (March 4, 1949). A later letter continued: "It is indeed surprising that a man of your stature and experience would lend himself to 'the Bolshevik struggle around the campus'" (the quote is from Sidney Hook).[24] Pauling did subsequently refuse to make any appearances at Oregon State—his own alma mater—until the fifties were over and Strand was no longer president.[25]

What is most striking about Strand's position is the tone of absolute conviction that would allow him to call the entire faculty to denounce Spitzer and to insult Pauling and also others who wrote to protest or to defend Spitzer. Perhaps his vigorous reaction against Lysenkoism is understandable given his own scientific training as a geneticist. But some of the best scientists in the world did not agree with Strand about Spitzer or the firing of communists. The Federation of American Scientists brought the case before its Council for deliberation because Lysenkoism had played such a central role in Strand's argument for "party line" thinking. After a review of the scientific situation, the FAS reasoned that the political argument for the firing was not justified.[26] The statement adopted by the Council says that free scientific inquiry "is hindered when decree is substituted for the time-tested method of experiment and scientific discussion—whether this is done by exponents of the Lysenko school, or by the President of Oregon State College" (May 5, 1949).

In response, Strand wrote to accuse the Federation of American Scientists of communist leanings:

> Can it be that only the Federations, Unions of this and that, and the Society of Scientific Workers, etc., are concerned with academic freedom? I have recently talked with a man who attended one of your organization's early meetings in Chicago. His impression was that the Federation was largely in the hands of the Communists. (June 14, 1949)

In fact, the Federation, according to their telegram to Strand, had grown out of Hiroshima and the concern of atomic scientists about the social responsibility of scientists; it included Oppenheimer, Urey, Szilard, and

Shapley as advisors, with two thousand members and twenty active chapters. It seems unbelievable that men of such stature could be discredited by a university president, but Strand would not be the last to attack some of these scientists as communists.

In spite of the danger, many liberal individuals and institutions spoke up against the firings. The national AAUP took the position that institutions could not fire professors for belonging to the Communist Party so long as it was legal in the United States. (Unfortunately, the AAUP never took action on this principle to censure any institution until long after the anticommunist excess now thought of as McCarthyism was over). In the Oregon State case, the AAUP sent President Strand a series of highly critical letters that led him to believe he was going to be censured. However, the correspondence and the investigation stopped mysteriously in 1950, as it did for the Washington case and for other cases submitted to the AAUP.[27]

President Strand wrote defiantly to the AAUP associate secretary George Pope Shannon: "It is rather apparent from all your letters that you intend to censure us. . . . I suggest you go right ahead and do all the censuring you please" (June 29, 1949). Although the AAUP failed to act on this and many other cases, Strand's letter suggests that they might not have had much effect.

There was more evidence that might have increased Strand's sense of conviction and counted against Spitzer. Although Strand made several statements to the effect that the dismissals didn't have anything to do with Spitzer's activities with the Progressive Party, Strand did, apparently, think of Henry Wallace and the Progressives as "party line" thinkers. In his lengthy form-letter reply to inquiries and letters of protests about the case, Strand complained about Spitzer's wife's doctrinaire politics—she was a Young Progressive and "I was just all wrong and that was that." It is hard to imagine why the wife would play so large a role if Strand's thinking had not become thoroughly a matter of party lines and fellow traveling, where association rather than acts became the evidence. The influence of the associative and gendered logic that supported George Kennan's foreign policy statements seems, perhaps, to inhabit Strand's rhetoric as well.

Then, in an encounter on May 9, 1949, that appeared in the national press, Strand went backstage to confront Henry Wallace himself after he spoke in Portland. Strand said to Wallace, according to his own notes about the dialogue:

> "If anyone had any doubts as to the real purposes of the Progressive Party when he came into the auditorium, he certainly couldn't have left with any."
>
> . . . "Then you are against peace," said he.
>
> "I'm just as much for peace as you are," I countered, "but

I don't want a peace that has the brand of a hammer and sickle on it."[28]

This prompted reports that Strand had called Wallace a communist.[29] Strand was, in fact, inclined to label as fellow travelers all who corresponded with him to protest. He wrote to an OSC alum, "You have been reading the party line press" and the Wallace meeting "was nothing more or less than a Communist rally" (May 16, 1949); to a letter from an Oregonian, "Yours reads more like some that have come to me from Brooklyn. . . . You had been reading too much communistic propaganda that has appeared under the guise of the Progressive Party" (March 28, 1949); and to an Indiana University zoologist, "All your words sound like a bunch of Dutch Cheese to me" (March 26, 1949).[30]

If the letters begin to sound like the rhetoric of a reactionary rather than a rational decision-maker, that was not the perception of Strand's faculty, who thought he was like many liberals in the political context of 1949. President Strand found support not only from the conservative citizenry of Oregon, but also from faculty, scientists elsewhere, and liberals besides Sidney Hook. He himself was a Democrat, known to his faculty as "definitely not a reactionary conservative" but one who "has consistently promoted liberal and democratic administrative policies," zoology professor Ernst Dornfeld wrote to H. J. Muller (March 3, 1949). The great independent senator from Oregon, Wayne Morse (at that time a Republican), had recorded in the *Congressional Record* a speech he gave on "The Threat of Communism" (March 3, 1949). Morse took the Sidney Hook line of argument: "True Communists do not possess free minds but rather are indoctrinators of a philosophy which seeks to promote revolution and reduce our people to the dictates of a totalitarian form of government" (A1823). Many Americans had taken up the vocabulary of purification associated with anticommunism, and Strand received endorsements from Oregonians such as the insurance executive who wrote that there were "too many educators with leanings diametrically opposed and subversive to our form of government and I hope that your stand will lead the way for a general house cleaning" (February 17, 1949). But his own arguments were not so much about cleaning house as they were about limiting academic freedom in order to save it: "My difficulty is with the purists of academic freedom," he wrote to a member of the Arizona Board of Regents, "I suppose most of the communist organizations in the country have passed resolutions condemning me" (March 11, 1949).

Nevertheless, President Strand had moved to identify himself solidly with the forces of anticommunism, with increasing disregard for the specificities of the argument. His response notes to thank supporters did not bother to distinguish his views from those of the most extreme right wing: "Yesterday's paper said there are 850,000 communists and communist sympathizers in this country. I am now of the belief that is an understatement" (March 26, 1949).

Furthermore, the case had put him on the side of right-wing investigatory politics. An engineer from Los Angeles sent a letter copied to Senator Tenney (head of California's infamous Un-American Activities Committee): "Our nation would be much better off if we had more college presidents who had the courage to uphold Americanism in the face of public criticism from a high ranking scientist whose name and association has been linked with groups of individuals whose interests are allegedly subversive" (April 14, 1949). The letter lists reports gathered by the Tenney Committee on Linus Pauling and his affiliations and congratulates Strand for his denunciation of Pauling.

President Strand had made the argument a matter of scientific freedom, but scientists outside the university were not in agreement about the matter, and many were not so willing as Strand to say that a plea to understand Lysenko might mean a scientist was not fit to do science. Pauling and the FAS were willing to criticize Strand's decision openly, and were in their turn dismissed by him. Other scientists hoped they could avoid taking positions, even if Strand had interfered with academic freedom.[31]

However, Joseph Mayer, editor of *The Journal of Chemical Physics*, member of the National Academy of Sciences, and professor at the Institute for Nuclear Studies at Chicago, wrote to defend Spitzer as a promising young scientist whose work he had noticed: Spitzer's presence on the faculty seemed "an indication that your university was intending to build up its rather weak physical sciences."[32] After he read Spitzer's letter, Mayer wrote, he would "assume that its author . . . was strongly influenced by the 'Party Line.'" This, however, is "no reason for dismissal of a capable scientist from a free American university." Reversing the logic embraced by Strand, Mayer wrote that his "violent opposition to the Russian action in the Lysenko controversy is due to just those beliefs that prompt me to write this letter" and argues forcefully the case being made for academic freedom by many of the best scientists: "I do not believe that our freedom must be suspended in order to destroy its enemies" (March 7, 1949). As the tone of the letter suggests, Mayer, like other scientists at this time, refused to acknowledge the virulence of anticommunist politics, that any affiliation with communism might cast one on the side of the devil.[33]

Significantly, the Academic Freedom Committee of the American Civil Liberties Union took a similar stand, arguing that the search for knowledge had nothing to do with the politics of nations, a perspective one might describe as internationalist:

> In the true academic spirit any scientist should be in a position to investigate any theory he considers valid until he is

positively convinced that the theory is false. Differences of opinion have always been the bulwark of true scientific investigation, and to dismiss a man because of his interest in a scientific theory, regardless of its worth, solely because it originates in a nation whose political ideologies are at variance with those we uphold, is to be deplored. (March 11, 1949)

They urged "reconsideration" by President Strand "of so drastic a step."

Fifties banality, cheerleaders, and football soon stole public interest away from the horrors of McCarthyism at Oregon State as it seemed to do across the country. However, what happened to the case at Oregon State suggests that this banalization of public life didn't come from the passivity of ordinary people but that it was orchestrated from on high. The Spitzer controversy had only a brief life in the headlines of the student newspaper, the *Barometer*. Just weeks after the firings, the coverage suddenly disappeared and in its stead came candidates for the homecoming queen, stories of fraternity hijinks like goldfish swallowing, and arguments in the letters to the editor about what kind of girl was most desirable. One could blame the banality of the student body for this superficial news, but the suddenness of the change in the paper's content points to decisions from above. In spite of ongoing sporadic efforts, there was no revival of political discussion.

An underground paper, the *Campus Review,* began publication in the fall of 1949 under the editorial leadership of Marion Syrek, otherwise known as "Sy." Prompted by the striking change in the *Barometer*'s coverage of political issues after the Spitzer case, Syrek printed stories in his mimeographed *Campus Review* on free speech, the state of the campus, criticisms of the newspaper, and reprinted articles on academic freedom and civil rights by Bernard DeVoto, Robert Hutchins of Chicago, and others. That first year of Bernard Malamud's arrival, Spitzer was gone. The front page of the student paper announced a new faculty forum series, with speakers from the humanities engaging with ideas. Bernard Malamud was a participant. He would have agreed with Spitzer, one would think, that the firing had left behind a crisis over free speech.

Strand received virtually unanimous support on campus: the local chapter of the AAUP removed themselves from considering the issue; the Chemistry department did not complain, even though the act had been done without consultation; the Committee on Faculty Rights to which Spitzer immediately turned responded by finding nothing out of order. This uniformity of faculty opinion did not, in all appearances, falter through the years. Retired members of both the English department, where Malamud taught, and the Chemistry department, where Spitzer taught, told me after they heard my argument that Strand was a good president and he was right to dismiss Spitzer.[34] In any event, President

Strand entered the case into the wider public debate, and whatever his contribution to the suppression of academic freedom, he found wide support for his act, added the Spitzer case to the snowballing perceptions of campus subversion, and never suffered censure for it, unless we count Malamud's book.

Is the Spitzer case significant for our reading of Malamud's work? Bernard Malamud arrived at Oregon State College as Spitzer was leaving, in the summer of 1949. *A New Life* appeared twelve years later, in 1961. It was written, at least in part, in Corvallis, and it represents at least in some respect Malamud's reflections about the fate of academic freedom in the aftermath of Cold War terror. He may very well have heard about the Spitzer case when he was in New York. It was in the national press and discussed widely in the teacher's union in New York (Malamud was teaching at Erasmus High). When he arrived in Corvallis, he was probably warned, perhaps as he says Levin was warned, about the fate of Spitzer—he must have heard him mentioned in campus gossip, perhaps at first in a remark such as Gilley makes about Duffy in his novel, calling him "a sort of disagreeable radical who made a lot of trouble" (35). He might have read an increasingly banal *Barometer* and worried about a student paper so devoted to football, dating, and pictures of pretty girls, and so little to larger political issues, as faculty and students complained. He might have read also the underground newspaper published by "Sy"—and could he have thought about that writer when he later found the name for his hero, Sy Levin?

Although Malamud argued with good reason that it was a mistake to read it thusly, Malamud's book appears to be so close to local history that many critics read it as autobiographical. The faculty who worked in the department with Malamud thought the book was modeled rather specifically on themselves, with some portrayals of individuals so recognizable that everyone agrees—for example, that Professor James Groshong was the prototype of "Bucket," the sympathetic young professor who is busy building his house. Malamud's hero, Sy Levin, loses his job after agitating for change in the university. Levin feels himself to be the successor to a professor who had been fired for being a radical, one Leo Duffy. Professor Fairchild tells him about Duffy in language that could be a description of Spitzer:

> After campaigning for Wallace he embraced another lost cause; but that was after a period of radicalism during which he asked his freshmen to write on the Moscow Trials, Lenin and Trotsky, the Lysenko theory and other controversial subjects I'm sure they knew nothing about. Some of the students who complained about him said he encouraged discussions of Marxism in his classes. (44)

Unlike Spitzer, Duffy was in the English department, but he was nevertheless involved in collecting funds for a radical group, as Fairchild says to Levin, "called 'The Committee of Anti-Fascist Scientists' or some such name" (44). There are other complaints about Duffy too: he broke the windows in his office, failed too many students, was always late, didn't correct student papers on time, was constantly critical, and got himself fired because he laughed maniacally when Professor Fairchild forgot himself and ran downstairs in front of Mrs. Feeney in his birthday suit. In other words, the firing was simply unwarranted.

However, Duffy, like Spitzer, was the subject of a college-wide faculty meeting called by the president, Marion Labhart. As Fairchild recalls it: "The entire staff . . . heard the president denounce Duffy as a fellow-traveling radical. He read aloud the long list of his indiscretions—which he had had mimeographed and passed out to the audience. It was a terrible indictment" (46). Afterwards Duffy turned to the "American Association of Professors," where he was defended at first by Dr. Fabrikant, but at the end, they all agreed not to submit a complaint to the national organization. Fabrikant's part of the story seems close to the facts of Herb Child's actual participation as the chair of the AAUP chapter, where he refused to support Spitzer, and indeed sent a letter to the national organization threatening to withdraw the local chapter if it censured Oregon State College for firing Spitzer. In the book, Fabrikant appears to be the most promising intellectual and liberal in the department, so that Levin supports him for the position of department head. But Levin changes his mind and decides to run himself after he confronts Fabrikant with the question about why he would not go on defending Duffy.

Malamud's antihero, Sy Levin, does not seem most worried about his predecessor's being fired for being a communist. Indeed, although Levin is Jewish, it is not specifically the question of anti-Semitism that disturbs him either. What disturbs him is the pressure for conformity and a more general persecution of strangeness. Even though the department chair's office has a motto from Benjamin Franklin, "STRANGERS ARE WELCOME HERE BECAUSE THERE IS ROOM FOR ALL OF THEM," there is no room for the critical: "Anyone who suggested that to be too contented with one's life or society was a subtle form of death, was clearly off his rocker, alien, without doubt a Red" (318). In *A New Life*, both Duffy and Levin lose their jobs for refusing to fit in. They are, as Malamud pointed out in a 1967 lecture, two forms of the same character—a representative figure. Malamud, the more heroic Duffy, the less heroic Levin, and Spitzer were all "troublemakers" on campus, challenging the banality of an evil pragmatism with the morality of critique.

Nevertheless, there are distinctions to be made. In *A New Life*, Levin is a Chaplinesque figure, a slightly comic do-gooder who is far from a moral exemplar. He is fired not only for his efforts to change the department, but also for his adultery with the chairman's wife, Pauline. The memory of Duffy's heroic sacrifice provides a kind of ironic commentary on Levin's not-so-tragic case.[35] Similarly, the knowledge of Spitzer's firing provides a larger historical framework for the more comic and more ordinary Levin. Malamud translates a specific historical crisis about the persecution of academics for being communists into a broader cultural issue. What worries him is the widespread aftermath, the broad effects on academic freedom, constricted without any acknowledgement. For Bernard Malamud, one may suppose the Spitzer case was similarly a representative history.

The Cold War did terrible damage to the intellectual life in the colleges and universities of the United States. Bernard Malamud wrote in the middle of this onslaught, and his writing contends with the devastation, though not as a simple account or denunciation. Part of the painful truth, indeed, was that the Cold War made both complexity and the personal view impossible, reducing everything that touched the issue to the distorted mirror of the terrorizing campaign. Evidence of the violence showed in accusations, firings, and even jail sentences. But much of the violence operated on the possibilities of discourse, a vast deadening. It is this murderous effect that I think Bernard Malamud addresses.

For the twelve years when he began to make his reputation as a writer, Malamud found himself in an institution reeling from the effects of the Cold War inquisitions. The painful controversy went on and on in the years after Spitzer's dismissal, at Oregon State and in the country, exploding into headlines and paranoia as McCarthy vowed to clean the communists out of government and the crusade engulfed education. Spitzer was eventually forced to appear before the Judiciary Committee in Washington, D.C. Perhaps the extraordinary silliness of student life in the fifties and the apparent political apathy of the faculty had more to do with censorship and repression than with the mindlessness of students or professors. The headlines in the student paper, the *Barometer*, turned to football and cheerleaders but perhaps under the pressure of President Strand's resistance to discussion of the Spitzer case. If Linus Pauling's letter could be censored, what further discussion of the firing might have been suppressed? The nostalgic pastoralism and mythologized masculinity inflicted on football had less to do with the sport than with Cold War cultural narratives.

The paranoia Malamud found at Oregon State and wrote about in *A New Life* he countered with the Chaplinesque optimism that out of great defeats small victories—and victories for the powerless—might yet be won. Not that the persecution of political radicals was Malamud's chief topic, but that his chief topic was precisely the freedom for the human imagination that such persecution threatened. In *A New Life,* Malamud explicitly connects the fate of intellectual freedom to the life of individuals. Malamud's stories all have, as a function of their mythical quality, an allegorical resonance: the hero is the Jew as everyman. This locates everyman's ordinary life on the stage of world history: Diaspora, Holocaust, assimilation, discrimination become the themes. Persecution of all kinds dominated the history of Malamud's time, and he interests himself in the effects of that powerful struggle on the vernacular, at the level of individual persons without much power, caught in the larger rhetoric of politics as if in fate, with only endurance and a sense of the burlesque as a mode of resistance. Everyman is a victim of the larger struggle; everyman is a Jew.

Everyman is perhaps not everywoman. A transcendental hypermasculinity enables Malamud to overlap political and erotic transgression. Levin's pursuit of erotic adventure moves from waitress to colleague to student to colleague's wife, and he lurches from failure to failure with little understanding. He doesn't capture the narrative with his melodrama of manhood, however, because both his comic difficulties and his internal dialogues undermine expectations.

Malamud's resistance thus struggles against a logic that collapses state, religion, politics, and the emotional life of individuals, against a logic that would stop interpretation. One way of thinking about this resistance would be to say that he struggles against the logic of fascism. His work enters into the Cold War as a refusal of the categories. He had models available, certainly, for writing novels that were more overtly historical and political—for taking on the Spitzer case more directly. In 1947, Lionel Trilling had published an academic novel closely related to the Chambers-Hiss case, *In the Middle of the Journey.* In 1951, Mary McCarthy's *Groves of Academe* appeared, dealing with the search for Communists in the academy. But neither of these novels functions as a critique. Malamud is at odds with the understanding of history, imagination, and the real that supported the opinions of American anticommunists in the Cold War, and his opposition is at the level of narrative practice.

So Malamud was not a political writer in the direct sense, certainly not a writer of the Left, as his friend, Granville Hicks, once had been. Malamud counted the New York intellectuals in his critical audience— Lionel Trilling wrote an early recommendation for Malamud to receive a Guggenheim. However, the New York intellectuals who wrote about the Cold War, many of whom wrote in the *Partisan Review* were, in fact, seriously compromised. The discussion of academic freedom carried on by Sidney Hook, the career of Edmund Wilson, the critical work of Diana and Lionel Trilling all supported anticommunist positions. Even though Malamud must have felt friendly at times to their ideas, he does not make the mistake that they made, does not agree to establish boundaries to academic freedom. Malamud steadfastly refused to commit himself in interviews to supplementing his work with further interpretation. The novel is the word by which he wished to be known, and the novels undertake a long project of conscientious objection to the war of ideas. New York intellectuals—indeed most liberals—were complicit in the Cold War oppression of free thought. Willing to make the connection between communism and the Soviet Union—between the struggle of nations and the struggle of ideas—these writers acquiesced in the construction of a mythology which Bernard Malamud kept out of his books.

At its most "right-wing" extreme, Cold War rhetoric extended the paranoia to link anti-Semitism and anticommunism. It took its roots from the fascist arguments of the thirties and continued through the sixties into the present. Elmhurst's 1939 *The World Hoax,* according to the introduction of his publisher, William Pelley, "showed irrefutably that Communism was not merely a crackpot program of undermining the Christian governments of the world with unworkable socialistic theories carried into practice, . . . that Communism *is world Jewry in action!*" (2). Elmhurst thinks Jewish radicals and Jewish capitalists are in a conspiracy together against nation-states: "The international Jewish troublemakers are at present so feverishly engaged in trying to turn the world-wide turmoil into such a complete chaos that it will be impossible for any human being or group to re-establish anything resembling law and order!" (123). In 1953, Jack B. Tenney's pamphlet, "Zion's Fifth Column" argued that a conspiracy of Zionist Jews were responsible for communism, antinationalism, atheism, the new internationalism, and both world wars. This is the Jack Tenney whose famous committee was responsible for investigating communists in California, who had a special inquiry into Linus Pauling, who precipitated the loyalty oath in the University of California and the most virulent of the inquisitions. In 1965, in a pamphlet called "Cry Brotherhood!" (condensed from "The Tenney Reports on World Zionism"), he continued. Arguing that heterogeneity threatened patriotism and the nation, Tenney attacked the perpetual strangeness of Jews, attacked their "special" treatment, marking in this publication the turn from the Cold War of the fifties to the culture wars of the present, and their continuity. The discourse of anticommunism was a project of rhetorical purification, enamored of the "truth" and the "fact," and at war against rhetorical heterogeneity.

Anticommunism was not just McCarthyism, and limited to right-wing politics. The anticommunism of the Right was less immediately responsible for the assault on academic freedom than the positions staked out by the Left. Liberal voices, in other words, provided the logic according to which professors like Spitzer at Oregon State were fired. The character who represents the failure of liberals to protect academic freedom in Malamud's novel is Fabrikant, the most intellectually impressive of the faculty. If Malamud was not politically active, as his old friend Granville Hicks wrote in his 1963 *Saturday Review* essay, Malamud was sensitive to the problem of academic freedom.[36] He did, again and again, come to the aid of junior faculty who were being mistreated by the university and defended their right to raise troublesome issues. He and his family were distrusted by some as too liberal—the town was conservative, at least in the early fifties. Ann Malamud objected, in a letter to the editor, when the local newspaper suggested that the ADA was a communist organization. The editor accused her, in turn, in pages of his newspaper of being a fellow traveler. Furthermore, Ann Malamud belonged to the League of Women Voters, whose members were thought of by some in the Oregon of that time as rather pink and sometimes accused of communist leanings when they asked impertinent questions. The Portland chapter of the League had in fact written to ask President Strand about the propriety of firing Spitzer, if the case were political. So the Malamuds experienced the suspicion that they themselves were political radicals, although in fact they represented intellectual liberalism.

Malamud himself left Oregon the same year he published *A New Life*, in 1961, and left behind a college he had helped to change, with foreign films, lecture series, and new majors in the liberal arts on the way. The Young Turks he supported in the department stayed on and made sure that composition did not keep literature out and that liberal ideals rather than vocationalism informed decisions. The college became a university and hired scholars on the Left. William Appleman Williams, the distinguished Marxist historian who had known Malamud in the early fifties, when Williams was at the University of Oregon, left Wisconsin and joined the history department at Oregon State. Linus Pauling gave his papers to the Oregon State University library's Special Collections.

The story of Ralph Spitzer's firing demonstrates how science was articulated within the national realism of the Cold War. If the first step was to impose government restrictions on knowledge about nuclear energy, putting science under the jurisdiction of an expanding security state, the second step was more widespread—it was the disciplining of scientists. Although Linus Pauling won the Nobel Peace Prize as well as the Nobel Prize for chemistry, few remember that he also was harassed and denied a passport. Robert Oppenheimer was the most well-known scientist to be accused of disloyalty, but there were many others: Harold Urey and Edward Condon, as Spitzer pointed out, were forced to resign from governmental service.[37] In consequence, although science achieved a decisive victory over religion and other "ideological" perspectives as the discourse of truth and realism, science was also subsumed to national interests. The intellectual class split into the "two cultures" of science and the humanities, as Snow described it, and the social sciences split into the two strands of realists and symbolists, as Michael Paul Rogin suggested. But Cold War intellectuals in science, social science, and the humanities were all implicated in ideological pressure and all the victims of political surveillance and the censorship of academic freedom.

In his testimony before the Senate Judiciary Committee in 1953, Ralph Spitzer submitted a courageous statement in support of academic freedom, before he was forced to cite Fifth Amendment protection. He argued that science depended upon freedom of communication and that "the present atmosphere is such as to weaken scientific freedom and creativity, to inhibit scientific communication, and even to discourage young people from entering the scientific professions" (1123).

Finally, what about the storyteller? Bernard Malamud told his Corvallis friend, artist Nelson Sandgren, that one learns truth through fantasy (Panel, May 26, 1996). He talked to another Corvallis friend, professor of religion and philosophy Warren Hovland, about how truth may be embodied but not known. The storyteller was never meant to pass on cautionary tales about how men in administrative positions really persecuted left-wing scientists, or was he? In his 1967 talk to the faculty of Oregon State University, Malamud warned them against looking at *A New Life* as a roman à clef and explained how realism might be mythological:

> I try, in a sense, to write what appears often to be a realistic story with a mythological cast or structure. For instance, in *A New Life,* Duffy and S. Levin have pretty much the same meaning as characters. . . . They are outsiders who come to disturb the static inside. In a sense they are both academic knights errant—in both senses of the word—Don Quixotes, once removed. They are the mythological stranger from one part of the same country, who comes as an ambassador to another part, from the East to West. . . . Nowadays the West affects the East in interesting ways, especially politically. Think, for example, of Reagan, Goldwater, Nixon as products of the West. . . . Another theme would be almost political in nature: how does one produce change in an institution or community that is bottlenecked by small minds? By change I mean taking the next necessary step. By small minds I mean the minds of men without vision, imagination for social improvement, or courage.
>
> . . . Don't forget the book is set in the 1950's—in 1950, to be exact, during the early intense part of the Cold War that

was to burst into flame in Korea. The times produced Senator McCarthy and Senator McCarthy intensified the fear and cowardice of the times, the fear and cowardice of the academic community. You would never, in those days, at least not in institutions such as Cascadia College, have got the kind of protests from the academic community as have become commonplace nowadays against the Viet Nam War.

. . . This "political theme" was not directed only to Corvallis and the then Oregon State College, but to every college like it in the United States, and there were hundreds like it, if not thousands. The letters I got from various places in the United States told me that that particular message was being received. "Have you taught here?' I was asked over and over again. (Corvallis, 1967)

Here the Cold Warrior (President A. L. Strand? Senator McCarthy?) encounters the troublemaker (Spitzer, Malamud?), and even the storyteller may cause trouble as well as deliver counsel in his truthful fantasy.

5

Mari Sandoz's Heartland: The Abusive Frontier Father and the Indian Warrior as Counterhistory

> It is one of the salutary features of postmodern theory to suggest that it is the disjunctive, fragmented, displaced agency of those who have suffered the sentence of history—subjugation, domination, diaspora, displacement—that forces one to think outside the certainty of the sententious. It is from the affective experience of social marginality that we must conceive of a political strategy of empowerment and articulation, a strategy outside the liberatory rhetoric of idealism and beyond the sovereign subject that haunts the "civil" sentence of the law.
>
> —Homi K. Bhabha, "Postcolonial Authority and Postmodern Guilt"

Her style shattered the paratactic narration of Westerns and dissolved the perspective of distance taken by historians. She carefully put together, as if assembling the shards of a broken mirror, the fragments of differently voiced memories that might image the settler father—her own, *Old Jules*—or the Native American warrior/mystic, *Crazy Horse,* or the both doomed and victorious followers of Dull Knife in *Cheyenne Autumn,* and in her other stories of the West. Inserting the voices of the survivors into the story, Mari Sandoz put them into a conflictive dialogue with other, more dominant narratives.[1] In this respect, she was attentive to a Native American perspective in a way that was all too unusual in the forties. White history in her perspective came to look unreal.[2] She used the "displaced agency" of the Lakota and the Cheyenne to write alternate histories that provided an angle of critique on the objectivity of history. In book after book about the Great Plains during the Cold War, Sandoz promoted a revulsion against assimilating national high-handedness, questioned the recording of Western history, and promoted sympathy for the alternate histories of the American Indian. Wallace Stegner said of her "she thought she was Sioux." I don't believe he meant that as a compliment, but the mixed nature of her writing at every level is precisely what interests me. The mixed nature of her writing intersects with the mixed nature of her project. Identifications with the native have long been a questionable strategy for advocates of the frontier, and Sandoz perpetuates the violence of her father's ambitions even as she opposes them, caught in the logic of a violent hierarchy, displacing her resistance to her own genealogy onto the resistance of Crazy Horse.

The nineteenth-century consensus was colonialist: that the American Indians had to submit to a national imperative. The debate was whether to use force or more gentle and civilized means. The debate was gendered. Eastern abolitionists such as Lydia Maria Child and the activist Helen Hunt Jackson (author of the sentimental novel *Ramona*) opposed the wars against Native Americans and influenced the Indian Reform movement and the Friends of the Indian, yet their "good works" proved at times devastating to Native American culture. Neither force nor gentleness left space for un-American difference. That colonialist view would be reiterated in the twentieth century, particularly in conjunction with Westernized discourses, and not only as mythology. The Cold War language of "hawks" and "doves" arguing over the fate of the (barbarian) "Reds" (like the "Redskins" of old) linked the historical moments together at the level of the signifier. The analogy, implicit rather than explicit, avoided any interrogation. It may be argued that the drastic reductions of aid to Indians in the late forties had to do with the way they had become associated with the increasingly feminized, demonized socialism and the "welfare state." Sandoz, however, did not confront this association of Indians and "Reds." Perhaps that accounts for some of the difficulties she had making an effective argument on behalf of the Indians. On the other hand, the climate of "realism" enforced around the representation of Reds as un-American effectively prevented such critical analysis.

Mari Sandoz was among the few, in the late forties, to protest the government's Cold War treatment of Native Americans. When President Truman expressed admiration for Sandoz's *Crazy Horse* in 1949, she wrote a letter: "I have just returned from an extensive cover of the old Plains Indian country . . . where the calamities of the present compelled me to shift my interest from the old buffalo hunting days to the problems of the present" (October 18, 1949, *Letters* 230). In her view, the government's cuts in appropriations were at fault, as she said in a letter to Thomas Balmer:

> Then came the economy congress of 1947 and like all such congresses since 1854, they drew a line through the Cheyenne appropriations and with that one stroke of the pen closed the agency, the hospital and the health and home economics and agricultural advisory services, with coming curtailments in education. (November 26, 1950, *Letters* 238)

Sandoz understood, as her writing reveals, that she needed to rewrite the way the real frontier had been imagined, and her biographies interweave fictional and historical writing styles in order to address this space of American mythology. The nineteenth-century homesteading act proposed the literal colonization of an imaginary space, not of territory thought of as belonging to the Native Americans, but of wilderness, a biblical desert, where abjection, sacrifice, and horror might accompany the imposition of the Word. The imaginary space also was portrayed as what the American deserved, the land that would make him a yeoman farmer and a proper citizen: just deserts, not desert. The "American Adam," R. W. B. Lewis argued in 1957, was the chief figure in the American myth as it coalesced in the nineteenth century. The American individual thought himself new and innocent:

> a radically new personality, the hero of the new adventure: an individual emancipated from history, happily bereft of ancestry, untouched and undefiled by the usual inheritances of family and race; an individual standing alone, self-reliant and self-propelling, ready to confront whatever awaited him with the aid of his own unique and inherent resources . . . His moral position was prior to experience, and in his very newness he was fundamentally innocent. (5)

This individual, Lewis claimed, furthermore, belonged to the "party of Hope," in sharp contrast to the Cold War disillusionment Lewis saw around him, a picture of hopelessness "frozen in outline" and "anything but dialectical" (195). Patricia Limerick has pointed out in *The Legacy of Conquest* how the enduring claim of innocence has distorted the multiple, colliding interests of western subjects. Limerick argues persuasively that moving West was associated with innocent motives even in the case of a killer outlaw such as John Wesley Hardin, whose autobiography emphasized "the gunfighter as Western injured innocent, with a strong Southern accent" (37). The "innocent victim" killed by Indians made a powerful image, but even Narcissa Whitman, "who would not have imagined that there was anything to understand," risked the death that came by seeing vacancy where there was, for the Cayuse Indians, a complex and rising threat to survival from white disease, religion, and trade (41). The individual so conceived would be always innocent in his dislocation, projecting evil, abjection, and the origin of violence out of a coalescing subjectivity onto some other externalized cause—mother nature, other strangers, the government, the cultural past. The homestead anchored this innocent individual in property. The act of searching for the defining symbol of proper self and nation, the word that will locate home in the owner, as proprietor, also locates national existence in a narcissistic crisis of identity that is at once due to capitalism and yet covers it over with the propriety of the self.

Mari Sandoz wrote from within that crisis, unblinking. She relies not only upon the scaffolding of historical document and oral history, but also upon the rhetoric of the real, a careful descriptive mapping of the landscape, to keep her on her feet as she confronts the prototypical "innocent," her father, with his guilt. As a woman writing, she does not respond to the crisis in the fathers' law by simple denunciation or accusation. She represents, in writing, the subject, so to speak, on trial—herself, her father—and represents, through writing, the process of testimony and acknowledgment that could ground an ethical position.[3] She writes to address the doubleness of aspiration and violence in frontier subjects. She does this by doubling her male heroes—locating them in the narcissistic crisis that puts identity under question, leading to violence and abjection and psychosis, but also delineating forms of community and reconciliation, momentary sublimations of the death drive extremity. Like Thomas Hardy, whom she much admired, she pushes novelistic realism to naturalistic excess and to dark episodes that trouble the conscience.

Sandoz's aesthetic thus revisits the trauma of modernism as history. The modernist in history is cut off from the patriarchal order represented by older institutions of church, state, art, and economy—an alien or an outlaw. For example, her biographical novel of New York artist Robert Henri's childhood in Cozad, Nebraska traces the story not of God-fearing farmers, but of the *Son of a Gamblin' Man*.[4]

The Cold War struggle to capture the frontier story took place at many levels: while historians put the American West into a more global context, the movies seemed to rewrite the Cold War into an explosion of nativist Westerns.[5] But far from using frontier stories as a way to shore up ideology, Mari Sandoz described how the narratives of the West threatened symbolic order, and she used western storytelling to rewrite western realism. Her writing is within the traditions of Western discourses, both the folkloric storytelling and the realism I have been connecting to natural history writing. The attention to detail, to sensory experience, to the plot of discovery but also to the experience of work—these characteristics make her writing familiar and convincing. They are, as Jane Tompkins has speculated, part of the attraction of "Westerns."[6] Yet her use of poetic language in a nonfiction work, even though it helped to fragment the sentence of western adventure, also dislocated her project. The reader's report on *Old Jules* first made the observation that haunted her career: "It is a novel, yet not a novel" (*Letters* 93).

As Walter Prescott Webb was defining the West in his 1931 *The Great Plains,* Mari Sandoz was working on a parallel project, beginning with the biography of her father, *Old Jules,* which finally appeared after many rejections and revisions in 1935. Webb's influential description has certain commonalities with her narratives, even though Webb seemed to like the new man produced by the western encounter, and Sandoz has serious reservations about him. Both portray an ecology that thwarts the traditions of European culture and even the politics of European capital investments. However, Webb argued that the plains made the people unique; Mari Sandoz thought the plains offered a perspective on the abuses of civilization. And abuse for her began at home.

In Sandoz's hands, the Great Plains that produces cowboys, six guns, cattle, outlaws, and trouble for the farmer comes to seem less a natural fate than a cultural system that could have been otherwise. American Indian history provides her with other narratives occupying the Great Plains. A man like her father, Jules Sandoz, who immigrated in a gesture of willful freedom, could not rely on individualism for law or justice, nor could he be relied upon. But that gesture of freedom and that individualism was not like the weather, a natural event, nor was it the invention of a singular personality, though Jules was certainly that.

Jules was related to the extended Sandoz family whose Swiss pharmaceutical company has a plant today in Lincoln, Nebraska. He came from a liberal, Calvinist European bourgeoisie; he himself had studied medicine at the university. He mastered the modern European confidence that he could revolt against his people and find his own, free way. But even Jules, who defied his Swiss father to settle in the sandhills of northwestern Nebraska, Jules of an abusive and fierce willpower, could not master the inhumane weather; the cattle that were herded north like a natural disaster; the manic-depressive cycles of success and despair, boom and bust; the supplanting not only of the Indians, but of the knowledge they taught him about surviving where agricultural man, the man of cultivation, had too little rain. Nevertheless he persisted. He represented the response to the language of free land:

> Men with some Old Julesian traits lived in every pioneer community—even as far away as Australia and New Zealand—men with the vision of the community builder, the stubbornness to stick against every defeat, the grim ruthlessness required to hold both themselves and their neighbors to the unwelcoming virgin land. (291)

No one was more affected by the imaginary frontier than those who worked to live there, and Sandoz uses the resources of nonfiction to examine the painful intimacies of story and experience. Webb pointed out, famously, that the 98th meridian demarcated a line through the middle of the Dakotas, Nebraska, Kansas, Oklahoma, and Texas. West of that line, in North Platte, for example, where the wagons lined up to start off on the Oregon trail, the annual rainfall was not great enough to raise crops dependably. But the settlers believed boomer propaganda and the pseudoscientific arguments, for example, that "rain follows the plow."[7]

Webb argued that the arid environment shaped cultural history, but, as Sandoz shows, cultural narratives distorted the encounter with the environment. The vast grasslands that were thickly sodded by buffalo grass were plowed up, and years of drought killed corn and wheat, while the winds took away the topsoil (and still do). The big cattle enterprises ran into trouble too. In the North Dakota badlands, Theodore Roosevelt regained his health running his Elkhorn and Maltese Cross ranches along the Little Missouri, but he downplayed the economic disaster of his and other cattle enterprises that moved in at the badlands town called Medora. The Marquis de Mores, a French aristocrat, constructed a large abattoir there near the railroad, to butcher the cattle and send the beef, in refrigerated cars, to eastern markets. But the Marquis was not a good businessman and furthermore earned the enmity of Dakota locals for fencing in the range, and Roosevelt himself suffered cattle losses in the cold winter of 1886.[8]

The political economy of "natural resources"—not only of grasslands, but also of coal gas, oil, and even of gold—resembled the weather. Cold, wind, drought, flood, blizzards, and tornadoes blew across the Great Plains with regular disregard for anything built on a human scale. This is part of what Roosevelt meant when he advocated the "strenuous life." In contrast to Victorian individuals with their cults of masculinity, the manly American would respond to such conditions of economy and landscape. Both Roosevelt and Webb imagined that a strenuous response was only natural. Manliness did not appear as a set of conventions that might itself be more connected to Anglo-European civilization than to the soil. Sandoz, however, needed to separate her father from the plains, and the pain he caused her from her appreciation of the land. She puts the natural authority of the father in question.

Far from imbuing the hero of conquest with a sense of reality, as is sometimes claimed, the rigor of the plains insured disasters that reproduced the logic of desire. That is what Sandoz exposed. The Great Plains "West" was represented as empty space ("wide open spaces"), an emblem of opportunity for innovation and acquisition. The hero of settling and conquest was the subject of a desire produced by canceling out what was there: a blankness, or lack, was superimposed on top of the articulated space of Native Americans and a dream of empty fields waiting to be planted masked the fullness of the grasslands. Anarchy was the chief figure of modernist literary form, but in the United States, anarchy appears as the uncanny principal of history. Anarchy is the wilderness produced by the frontier. The desolating West required one to "make it new," as Pound's slogan held forth for poetic frontiers. On the Great Plains, the constant sweeping away of human construction, by nature or by humans in uncanny empathy with a kind of death drive, produced unbounded negativity—and psychosis.

The contact of European/American men and European/American capital with the Great Plains reinforced desire while it opened up a logic of contagion and catastrophe. What marked the plains as empty for a European immigrant such as Jules Sandoz was the absence of a cultural Symbolic, of law, in its historical, scientific, and communal hierarchies. As Mari Sandoz portrays it, the law is not a powerful stability, but the interim product of these violent struggles: in a town where the big ranchers have established a hold on the government and the court, there will be a rough justice in conformity with ranching interests (*Old Jules* 75). The response to the democratizing revelation that the law was not absolute was a struggle for dominance that Jules entered into not only with excellent marksmanship and his Vetterli, but also by his experiments with new kinds of seeds developed and imported from Europe and fruit trees that might produce well in the dry Nebraska sandhills. Jules was not of the older agricultural communities; he was the new man of a capitalist order.

Old Jules

The American West prodded by Sandoz in *Old Jules* does not earn salvation through settlement. Her "heartland" is not redeemed by an eventual success of the desire for land or gold or civilization. It is tragic or banal decline, ironic success—or the eventual victory of the environment's sublime terror. Nevertheless, ironically, her father established himself as one of the first settlers of the western Nebraska sandhills, and Mari herself succeeds by insuring that her father's reputation will live on (for worse but also for better). Jules said: "There is nobody to carry on my work. . . . If the Marie was a man she might—as a woman she is not worth a damn" (418). The daughter responds to his last request, that she write about his life, with her own many edged representation. She writes a biography that keeps his innocence under suspicion.

When Jules Sandoz drove into Nebraska to find freedom, he also found lawlessness. He was plunged from the reasoned conduct of Switzerland's order into one abjection after another, culminating in the practical joke that broke his ankle and made him a cripple. His identity was always in crisis. Accumulating horror and paranoid suspicion, he nonetheless asserted a free self in the face of ubiquitous opposition. The freedom produced, in fact, both horror and paranoia. His assertions functioned to ward off the threat of abjection. It was the dialectic of extremity that Julia Kristeva describes in *Powers of Horror*, and I use *abjection* in her sense. A subject becomes abject as the law fails and as the borders of the proper self give way.

Sandoz describes Jules's dramatic entry with considerable irony: "And out of the East came a lone man in an open wagon, driving hard" (3). Then she adds, "But there was really no hurry" (4). He enters his first frontier town, the saloon and gambling house in Valentine, on the lookout for thieves. The atmosphere is far from the advertised healthy sunshine of open prairies: "Despite the blaze of the lamp reflectors along the walls, the interior was murky, heavy with the stench of stale alcohol and winter-long unbathed humanity" (6). Jules extends his wariness about vigilantes and thieves to loose women: "He pushed away a girl who put her arm about his shoulders. There was no telling—probably diseased" (11). The human communities in *Old Jules* all seem more or less diseased, and human enclosures, in rank contrast with the outside, are like prisons, with the unwelcome intimacies of dirty bodies, anger, and inadequate shelter. But Jules himself becomes part of the abject too.

From the bourgeois point of view, his identity is precarious; he is not "free," he is disgusting. Jules has fallen out of his class. "He wore his shirts until they fell off, bathed when the river was tepid, washed his hands before and after dressing his foot, and his face practically never" (61–62). Sandoz describes his greasy cap, his rags, his crutch. Even a prostitute tells him his feet stink (96). Jules's life shocks visitors who are used to better. But his notion of his own importance and identity has to do with his activities as a builder of communities. He serves as a "locator" for homesteaders, fights to keep his post office, makes his wife do the hard work while he attends to his letter writing, and makes a name for himself with his orchard plantings. It is his wives and his children who are reduced to peasants.

In *Old Jules,* Mari Sandoz explores not only the biography of her father, but also, she says, the biography of a community. It is a story of overlapping violences. We know about the Indian wars and the range wars between homesteaders and ranchers, but we learn as well of ubiquitous violent encounters, as neighbors struggle over property, and men like Jules govern wives and children by the same explosive energy that keeps them working to develop the frontier. The admirable and the terrible are two sides of the same coin, the same impulse. There is no domestic space reserved for privacy, leisure, or the sentiments, no separate place for children. For Sandoz, the pioneer family contains the father's anarchic prerogative within. The expression of temper and self-interest (not law) governs Old Jules and those around him. He is the one who writes letters and locates claims, trying to gather a settlement together, but Jules sometimes seems as simply driven by profit as the cattlemen, so the shootings and threats are as impersonal as the market economy. He is the hero of the homesteading family, a mixed blessing, one man struggling against the big outfits as well as against the weather, but also against his own.

The biography encompasses two autobiographical layers, the self-representations of father and of daughter. In her portrayal of her father, Sandoz relies on stories he told and his boxes of notes and letters as well as on her own memories and on archival research. The daughter's perspective appears as a form of attention rather than a voice: she may have been a silent listener, but she was not uncritical. The first half of the narrative, before the birth of Marie, gives freer rein to Jules's point of view, featuring several heroic stories I will turn to later. But from the beginning Jules is associated with abjection, and his abjection is of a piece with his vituperative style. The style, I want to emphasize, becomes a necessity rather than a habit disconnected from the other necessities of his character.

Vituperation is not something that might be corrected by good manners, cleanliness, and thinking of others. Rather, the very freedom that Jules asserts—against his mother, family, the Swiss home life, and against his wives, family and neighbors in Nebraska—situates him in a claim of independence he can not sustain. He must blame someone else for the misery that follows: if he fails to castrate the bull calf before it gets too big, it must be his wife's fault—"the balky woman"—that she can not hold the calf still when he finally does the job.

When his hired hands drop him sixty-five feet into the well they are digging, Jules breaks his ankle so badly it never heals. He is finally taken to Fort Robinson, the place where Crazy Horse had been killed eight years earlier. Dr. Walter Reed, later famous for his discovery of yellow fever vaccine, was post surgeon: he recommends amputation, but Jules refuses to part with his rotting flesh. "The man was covered with dark bruises, but everything was overshadowed by the crushed left ankle, swollen the size of a water bucket, black and green with infection, the leg to the loin swelled to a shininess and lividly streaked" (43). "And it would be just like your particular brand of damn fool to pull through," Dr. Reed tells Jules, and of course Jules, who must have told this story to his daughter himself, survives, though his leg keeps running pus for years and never is right again (49). Jules, trained in medicine and an educated man, keeps in letter contact with Dr. Reed and later takes great pride in knowing him. But Jules acknowledges the cost of his injury in his later attitude toward breaking horses. He always stays away: "I can't stand to see anybody get crippled" (286). The strenuous life that Theodore Roosevelt so enthusiastically described in *Ranch Life and the Hunting Trail* may have helped produce a president and movie-star heroes, but perhaps it produced more often men with bodies wrecked, who lived in rage.

What happened when the free frontiersman must exist under the same roof with a family? The birth of Jules's daughter, Marie, the author herself, corresponds to another level of judgment that enters the book. Jules's impatient, paranoid style erupts into abuse. He whips his daughter from babyhood, the daughter reports: "When the little Marie was three months old and ill with summer complaint, her cries awakened Jules. Towering dark and bearded in the lamplight, he whipped the child until she lay blue and trembling as a terrorized small animal" (215). The author, Mari, would have been too little to remember, and her mother was not very sympathetic to her, usually. Could her mother have relayed the memory? The scene is dramatized, impossible: a symbol of trauma. The episode appears like a recovered memory, as if the child's eye saw the "towering" figure of Jules from the position of innocence he can no longer claim, and the sympathetic other (mother? grandmother? the self in protective recoil?) saw the innocent baby "blue and trembling." Innocence transfers here from Jules to the baby, and it also moves to the side of the subject made nonhuman: "as a terrorized small animal."

The violent struggles required to maintain the position of innocence are framed by the daughter's disillusioned report. Jules's abusive self-assertion depends upon blaming others for threats to his own identity: children/wife/neighbors/animals/environment. When there are three children, they watch with his wife's mother, frightened, as Jules cuts his wife's face open with a barbed wire whip for letting the bull calf kick: "I learn the goddamn balky woman to obey me when I say 'hold him'" (230). Again, the traumatic event is dramatized by its effects on the women and children, for the mother runs away to kill herself with poison:

> Then Mary ran through the door, past the children, and straight to the poison drawer. It stuck, came free, the bottles flying over the floor. Her face furrowed in despair, blood dripping from her face and her hand where she had been struck with the wire whip, the woman snatched up a bottle, struggled with the cork, pulling at it with her teeth. The grandmother was upon her, begging, pleading, clutching at the red bottle with the crossbones. (230)

Thus moments of terror and outrage interrupt the sequence of seasons. The history of frontier settlement written by Sandoz reveals the fatal unpredictability of the struggle on every level. History and Jules Sandoz share the same difficult, threatening character. Jules taught his kids useful things, but he whipped them. The grandmother cries to Jules, "For you there is a place in hell!" (230). The judgment does not come, however, from the context of an ethical community around them that might have offered agreement and sanctions, and Sandoz writes as if there were no communal supports, no counter among the white settlers to personal and general abuse. The capitalist motif of development underscores ruthlessness. The religious communities that in fact structured many homestead settlements are not there, nor are the strong women that had very different kinds of influences. It is the secular economic landscape of modernity.

Sandoz thought the uncontrolled vicissitudes of settler's lives tended to encourage storytelling. Old Jules is redeemed by storytelling, not only his own, but by the stories he attracted and the community those stories represented. In her later *Love Song to the Plains,* she specifies that truth-telling is not the most likely motive of story. The tall tales of Pecos Bill and outlaws, the stories of blizzards and prairie fires and tornadoes and rattlesnakes, join with visions and strange beliefs. The sandhills of Nebraska are the country of UFO sightings. Stories could express the longing for explanation, but they might also have a persuasive angle. Newspapers "booming" their town could be counted on to enlarge the good and repress the bad. This rhetoric of story extends out into the sermons of the "sky pilots" on the one side and advertising on the other. As the economic base underwent massive and constant shifts of power, this cultural imaginary had to lie to reproduce a narrative of stability or of realism.

The ecology of stories around Jules rested upon a conviction of innocence. What emerges, then, are uncanny inversions of good guy/bad guy. Sandoz tries to resist, interrupt, and fragment imaginary consolidations of good and evil. What she must resist most strenuously is perhaps the obvious temptation to paint Jules as a very devil, but there is also the strong pressure of frontier mythology toward heroics. No matter how abusive the hero might seem for this moment or that with his family, removing the figure from the social context frees him for renewed innocence. The solitariness of the Western hero is thus protective abstraction. Sandoz's method is to reinsert that isolated figure into the rich, conflictual detail of everyday life. Similarly, the isolation provided by print allows stories to seem representative in ways that the rhetorical situation within the homestead, with its specific cast of characters, would not allow. Sandoz's method is to reinsert the oral storytelling into the social situation that precipitates its ethical project.

Jules is scornful of women, and careless. The pretty neighbor, Victoria, apparently bought the poison from him that she used to kill herself: "She asked me if strychnine works on people like on dogs. . . . I told her all I know was wait on nature," Jules says carelessly after she dies. His long-suffering wife, Mary, who had tried and failed to use the poison for her own death, says "Poor, poor girl. . . . But it's good with her now." Jules "dismissed it as woman's grumbling. Already his mind was on other things. Deep down in the hills . . . was a large block of good land." (288). Here gender appears quite clearly, as Sandoz juxtaposes the woman's story against Jules' dreams of land. Also clear is the way the two stories modify one another: Jules makes destructive intrusions into women's lives—can it be said, then, that he makes up for that with productive intrusions into the land? Or might these be more like parallel abuses?

Images of a better world and a better woman belong to the configuration of the innocent self, from whose perspective the rest of the world seems fallen. Jules maintains his illusions, his desires split between the purified ideal and animal lust. He is the very subject of the frontier, always starting again, no matter how belatedly. If none of his settlements ever really succeed, he is to the end ready to start another, a renewal of the first look he had at the Niobrara:

> There, close enough to the river for game and wood, on the hard land that must be black and fertile, where corn and fruit trees would surely grow well, Jules saw his home and around him a community of his countrymen and other homeseekers, refugees from oppression and poverty, intermingled in peace and contentment. There would grow up a place of orderliness, with sturdy women and strong children to swing the hay fork and the hoe. (19)

Similarly, he maintains the vision of the girl he loved, Rosalie, who stayed in Switzerland and would never come to be his wife in Nebraska. The process both keeps the crisis open and makes the boundaries (between the idealizing self and the abjected other) need constant reaffirmation.

The fracturing of Jules's selfhood into irreconcilable pieces—these ideals and the disorder of everyday life—plunged those around him, especially his four wives, into horror. The women, in Sandoz's account, bore the suicides, deaths by beating, and psychoses that this history of violation, shock, and male innocence produced. The women must remain under the domain of reproduction, have babies even if unwanted, and therefore obey not only the manic demands of particular husbands but adjudicate these with the larger, perhaps more protective, domestic culture, with its schools, its laws, and its demands for standards of conduct. The women were always already guilty. But the boom and bust economy and the manic-depressive hero were at odds with the orderly vision of progress developed through the nineteenth century. What kind of personal/national history did the frontier imply? Many women and men turned to the religious meetings run by itinerant preachers. If Methodism, for example, was itself a call to remove oneself from history, it provided a shelter against anarchic extremity by its claims to renew the older Christian grounds for guilt and innocence. Even the men were sinners before they were saved; even the women could be innocent. It's not surprising that Jules rejects religion and women together. Jules prefers to identify with an outlaw such as Gentleman Jim, or with the Indians, but when he went to Chicago in his dirty clothes, a well-known photographer stopped him and took his picture. He thought Jules was a bum (416).

The frontier in Nebraska acted out the historical condition of nineteenth-century European culture, with the old regimes no longer in control and the new order in contest. Hence for the educated man, Jules, the lawlessness of the frontier mirrored clearly how the rights of man might be conceived, not guaranteed by a family or a government, but won by the anarchic individual who was a good shot: "The law was remote; the nearest sheriff almost at the Wyoming border, west of Fort Robinson, a good three days' ride away. A man made his own rights here or had none" (55). The reproduction of culture is denied, perhaps displaced onto women.

Both the outlaw and the Indians that Jules told about were men who extended help to him—these were encounters that acknowledged his feminized, helpless position. Freedom, in other words, required an unacknowledged new father who would make no demands. Jules told Mari the story of Gentleman Jim when she was seven, and he had not told it to anyone else in the family. That, and its resonance with other Robin Hood stories, suggests the story was a tall tale. But she records it, together with his other stories, as part of the biography, with the same narrative suspension of disbelief.

The story of an outlaw recapitulates, perhaps, the relationship her father imagined he had with her. On a hunting trip, Jules's pinto bolts when he tries to load up the skin of a grizzly he had shot, but a stranger takes him to shelter, on a horse with blood on its saddle. Later he heard, "Don't you know the habits of Gentleman Jim? Holds up the hold-ups, and if anybody ever gets the drop on him there'll be one man jack deader'n a doughnut, unless it'd happen to be some a them he's helped out of a hole" (159). With his usual sense of beleaguered persecution, Jules tells her that "He saved my life—when everybody else endangers it" (229). The outlaw is the impossible good/bad man, the only possible guardian.

Native Americans provide the only enduring model of a fruitful relationship to the land, not subject to the cycles of boom and bust. They also show how the frontier lays siege to ethical community. Sandoz never portrays the Indian characters as unfriendly to the settlers. She does include them as victims of a fatal history that seems unfriendly to the settlers as well. The Indians appear in Jules's biography from the beginning. A party of Oglala Sioux camped across the river, at the foot of Indian Hill, makes friends with Jules during his first week on the Niobrara. "They spoke slowly, sadly, of the buffalo days . . . as Jules's father spoke of the age of Pericles" (27). He learns from them how to guide his horse with his knees, leaving his hands free to shoot. He learns weather and game sign and goes on a hunt with them. They show him to the east, "the land of the Gone-Before-Ones, with many hundred elk in the winter, antelope the year round, deer in every brush patch, clear lakes for the washing of the hides, and sand cherries, plums, and chokecherries for the women. But it was not good to go there before the death song" (28). This land has much in common with Jules's recurrent vision of the good place, but like the other American pioneers before him, he is looking for heaven on earth. "Strange things happened to those who went" to that place while still alive, the Oglalas tell him. The Native American understanding of a certain spiritual restraint frames, then, the subsequent story of Jules's dreams of settlement, with its multiple violations of land and spirit.

Lakota Sioux appear again in the narrative in the traumatic turn from heroism to survival, when Jules is crippled. At Fort Robinson, the soldiers told ghost stories of an Indian "with a buffalo robe, a knife hidden in his hand, stalking before the guardhouse, his head down, his one feather pointing into the sky: the ghost of Crazy Horse, the greatest Sioux war chief of them all." Jules heard there from Little Bat, Baptiste Garnier, what happened at the death—that Crazy Horse was "tricked into the guardhouse and bayoneted through the kidney" (51). Sandoz says that Crazy Horse reminded her father of Gentleman Jim, "Lone men, both of them, self-reliant" (51). Jules conflated the outlaw and the Indian. Sandoz tries to remedy the conflation by providing the contextualizing differences in cultural history, but at the same time, her project continues his identifications with Crazy Horse, as if she were supplementing her father's story even as she resists it.

Estrangement from the old country and from the traditions seen now as matriarchal characterized modernity. Jules was a modern rebel against women and religion, but his daughter's writing situates the father's rebellion in another context, not that of radical discovery or radical critique, but of a utopian search for alternatives to European history and the rebellion against it—that is, another ground for cultural community. Therefore, as she tells it, Jules's life story does not follow the narrative line of his triumphs or "works," as he would have liked it, but rather the boom and bust cycles of his psychic economy. The cyclic narrative is punctuated by the parallel history of the American Indians, themselves in crisis over the catastrophic invasion of a linear (army, railroad, frontiersmen) progress into a time written as place and community. It is as if Jules dreams of the order that the Oglala had already founded, and himself participates in the destruction of such a dream. Is it an example of what Renato Rosaldo, in *Culture and Truth,* called "imperialist nostalgia"? That is, does he long for the moment when progress had not yet destroyed that cultural utopia, but also cling to the idea of imperialist progress?

Mari Sandoz calls up that utopia through the better self of her father, revealed (ironically) in the empathetic identification with the Lakota and Cheyenne Indians of his stories and her childhood. On the Fourth of July, 1885, Jules meets Young Man Afraid of His Horse, at his camp across the river from Rushville. "The thing that had drawn him to the man with the Winchester at Valentine [Gentleman Jim] he found once more, here, and in an uneducated Indian" (66). The town of Chadron invites Red

Cloud and his Indians to the Fourth of July celebration. "In the silent tipis
. . . were warriors who helped scalp the men of Custer; Sioux who were
with Sitting Bull four years before; Cheyennes who had been with Dull
Knife and saw their women and children butchered only eight years before within sight of their campfires to-night" (88). The town had not
expected fifteen hundred Indians to come. They respond to Red Cloud's
message—"My young men like to make the feast—and the battle"—with
feast, but only Jules, "who camped with his friend White Eye," is comfortable, Sandoz reports without question (88). Her uncritical endorsement of her father's stories about his Indian friends points to a desire for
alternate fathering that may shape her own stories about Native American cultural history. She learned from her father to distrust the histories
provided by a dominant culture—and yet she writes, uneasily, within it.

Perhaps the false stories of Indian atrocities that John Maher of Chadron published in the East were believed by few in Nebraska, but as Sandoz tells us, the local people panic nevertheless, especially in 1890 with
the Ghost Dance being performed (122). General Miles asks Jules to be
a scout, to hunt Indians. "I have lost no Indians. You lose any, you hunt
for them," Jules replies (129). The war correspondents, even Theodore
Roosevelt writing for *Harper's,* come to Rushville. Sandoz thought the
war craze was supported by businessmen, who profited, and Jules says,
"Big government are always bulldozing somebody" (131). The father and
the daughter shared this perspective.

The trauma of Wounded Knee makes Jules pessimistic and intervenes,
like his crippling, as a decisively alienating event. It is, Sandoz writes, "a
shocking annihilation . . . of men, women, and children mowed down
by Hotchkiss guns while they and their sick chief were surrendering their
pitifully inadequate arms and asking for the peace they had not broken"
(131). Jules rides up to witness the scene.

> From a hill to the north he looked down over the desolate
> battlefield, upon the dark piles of men, women, and children
> sprawled among their goods. Dry snow trailed little ridges of
> white over them, making them look like strange-limbed ani-
> mals left for the night and the wolves. Here, in ten minutes,
> an entire community was as the buffalo that bleached on the
> plains. (131)

Sandoz apparently takes the description from a despairing letter Jules
wrote to Rosalie the next morning. "There was something loose in the
world that hated joy and happiness as it hated brightness and color, reducing everything to drab agony and gray" (131). The massacre separated Jules from the American nation, aligned him with the immigrant.
He said: "A blot on the American flag" (132).

But Jules becomes most like the innocent hero of American western adventuring paradoxically, when he is a damn foreigner running down the government. To the end he maintains his paranoid combativeness, claiming from a hospital bed that "the damned cattleman stole me my post office I worked so hard to establish. Everybody worked against me" (421). His dream of settling the fertile land he makes innocent by thinking himself in solidarity with the Indians, welcome. They come to visit him in the hospital room, "suddenly full of Indians. . . . White Eye, an old man between two graying sons" who told them, outside, "It is the land of the Gone-Before-Ones" (420). With considerable irony, then, Mari Sandoz comes to a close on Jules's final words: "The whole damn sandhills is deserted. The cattlemen are broke, the settlers about gone. I got to start all over—ship in a lot of good farmers in the spring, build up—build" (424). Jules articulates the strenuous dream of American colonizing, and it is fully compatible with hating the government. But White Eye had called the land he dreamed of "the land of the Gone-Before-Ones": death. This helps to explain the development of Mari Sandoz's writing during the Cold War. She becomes ever clearer about the deadliness of American civilization.

Crazy Horse

The crisis of modern heroism appears dramatically in Sandoz' s 1942 biography, *Crazy Horse*. It was published in the patriotic unanimity of World War II, but Sandoz mounts her attack on the ignorance and bad faith of American warfare. Her story of Crazy Horse elaborates a warrior ethic that both doubles and critiques national heroism: as if Crazy Horse were a return of the repressed, the ego ideal prodding a bad conscience. Earlier in the century, representations of the Indian had romanticized as well as vilified the lost culture: Zane Grey's *The Rainbow Trail* (1915) and *The Vanishing American* (1925) featured Indian heroes who resisted assimilation and died. But even the story of Indian genocide had not undermined the gathering conviction that American identity was exceptional. The story of the vanishing Indian could be used to reinforce a version of the hero that Walter Benn Michaels sees as nativist: "It is because the Indian's sun was perceived as setting that he could become," Michaels argues, "a kind of paradigm for increasingly powerful American notions of ethnic identity and eventually for the idea of an ethnicity that could be threatened or defended, repudiated or reclaimed" (38).

However, in Sandoz's histories, the intervention of the American Indian into cultural narratives comes like a prompt of the unconscious, strange music that she tried to suggest at the level of style and irony that erupts like a (serious) joke or a hallucination. Others have noted that the

American Indian precipitated narrative crisis—of the sort prompted by a trickster figure that seems closer to wit, joke, or philosophy—or, as Gerald Vizenor has argued, more violently in the texts of history. As the unwelcome advent of an unrepresentable Real, such encounters do not support continuities, but interrupt, threatening a national identity not only by difference, but through bad conscience. Sandoz writes to disrupt dominant stories through poetic language, and particularly the language from Native sources reproduced in her text, but also to make a place for another set of histories.

Yet the interpretive regime that Westerns imposed on a Cold War reader must have served to screen out at least some implications of Mari Sandoz's alternative project, even though her texts demonstrate resistance to that regime. Sandoz (like Mary Austin before her) was writing in a documentary genre that intersected not only with nativist discourses, but also with the national realism of the Cold War. To the extent that Westerns interpreted modern development in terms of "savage war," they reinstalled Indians as figures of the enemy in films and popular fiction, reinvoking imperial nostalgia. But representing Indians as a race, an identifiable people, they also provided figures for an American identity, feeding the overlapping nativism and nationalism. Furthermore, if the Indian warrior seemed the authentic model for a certain masculinity, that only reinforced the supposition that warrior masculinity was a biological function.

In such a context, a certain hybridity could serve to undermine the consensus-making power of frontier stories. By "hybridity," I mean to suggest the mixed or dialogic quality of her text, and I mean to invoke the discussions of postcolonial theorists such as Homi Bhabha about cultural hybridity in discourses that critique imperialism. This hybrid prose represents memory in *Crazy Horse* at many levels: the personal memories of Mari Sandoz, oral history such as the stories told by Old Cheyenne Woman when Sandoz was a child and the interviews with He Dog and other Lakota that she participated in at Pine Ridge in the thirties, as well as written primary and archival sources. The book depends on biography's assumption that a life story may provide the structure for such writing, but the single life of Crazy Horse is dispersed into the nonhistorical moments of a people's everyday life, into the monumental present Sandoz describes as Indian time, as if the warrior were at the intersections of incommensurable sites for storytelling. Her language attempts to include the rhythms of the speech she heard, inserting Indian forms into normal history—although her sense of these rhythms is also mediated by John Neihardt's writing.

Sandoz's reliance on interviews, attention to poetic language, and her interest in the mystical were all influenced by John G. Neihardt's *Black Elk Speaks* and by his controversial and strong-minded interpretations of the Indian world view.[9] There has been criticism of Neihardt's intrusions into his material, although his book is also appreciated and used by many Native Americans. Vine Deloria edited a collection of essays in his memory, writing himself in particular about the significance of the landscape. Sandoz too represents this complex and significant landscape as, in Deloria's phrase, "the most important character" (99). This also follows the lead of Mary Austin, but with a stronger historical impulse. As a debate between Daniel Littlefield and Arnold Krupat suggests, interpretations of Native American culture by white writers occupy a troubled interface, where the possibility of unwarranted appropriation is always at issue.[10] Elizabeth Cook-Lynn argues that Native American oral traditions contain an alternate cultural history that is not represented in dominant histories, except in distorted and colonizing forms. So "American liberals without regard to the nativist struggle against colonialism continue to promote their own pet interests (i.e., Kevin Costner's childhood wish to be an Indian)" (74).[11] Sandoz's *Crazy Horse* aims to critique white history, but wasn't her father also presenting himself as the author of innocent critique, on the side of the Indians? If we read *Crazy Horse* to learn about Crazy Horse, we should also read James Welch's *Killing Custer,* to learn about the history as a Native American tells it (he makes use of Sandoz to do so, by the way). I want to read Sandoz from a different angle of approach—not as if she were contributing to a dominant, establishment history, but also not as if she could escape her culture. Mari Sandoz does indeed fall into the enduring trap represented by her father's stories and in another way by John Neihardt's stories: the images of heroic warriors belong to a war-culture hegemony impossible to fully resist. At the same time, most of all through formal strategies that modify historical realism and novelistic imagining together, Sandoz's *Crazy Horse* represents and assumes a historical discourse that is not assimilated to the national project. She reiterates a colonialist tradition in ways that make it swerve.

Might I call *Crazy Horse* an anticolonialism? Homi Bhabha suggests that the colonial subject mirrors the national subject with a difference, so that even mimicry embodies critique. Crazy Horse has been the very emblem of a refusal to assimilate—one would think not a subject of mimicry, even though his light hair and skin mirrored whiteness. The question is whether Sandoz makes him seem also an emblem of the western free male individual. The question is also whether Sandoz, as the writer, can escape the position of the colonizer through her mimicry. The biography of *Crazy Horse* is a portrait of resistance, and the narrator at times seems to take sides against the Indian "accomodationists," such as Red Cloud. Such stark alternatives reinstate, of course, the either/or logic of the frontier, a logic that would be deadly to the Native Americans either way.[12] Her narrative endangers its coherence by straying from the well-understood categories, but she often risks incoherence by describing the complexities of, for example, Red Cloud's negotiations.

Her book uses memory in ways that disrupt the methods of historians, supplementing story with archive, personal recollection with research. She begins with the testimony of people who told their stories, such as her father and other old-timers who sat around their kitchen. The ghost of Crazy Horse that haunted Fort Robinson for the soldiers also haunted the old-timer's tales, his name, she says, "like a painted strip of rawhide in a braided rope" (viii). Her own subjectivity seemed, from her childhood, inhabited by the past of Crazy Horse. An old man from the Brule Sioux once showed her the place where Conquering Bear had his death scaffold, "about where our old Dyehouse cherry tree grew" (viii). It was a favorite camping ground, and Crazy Horse had often walked there. This bodied memory, itself more uncanny than historical, also characterizes her interviews with the Indians, particularly He Dog.

Sandoz writes as a contemporary of the modernism of Anglo-European culture that Lionel Trilling was teaching at Columbia, a modernism that also recuperates or assimilates resistance to civilization, as mark of the disaffected individual. However, I would like to argue for a reading of *Crazy Horse* that acknowledges how Mari Sandoz resists a modern individualism defined by alienation. The difficult inscription of the hero, Crazy Horse, in a people's history different from the Anglo-European, and not defined only by its difference, puts the Western individual under pressure. Edward Said warns in *Culture of Imperialism* about the representation of the other that replicates the colonial gesture of mastery, and the representation of Indians in American literature as in the culture of films has certainly done that. It is hard to say whether Sandoz's strategy of using the stranger as a perspective of critique, or defamiliarization, also misuses that representation. This points to a certain doubleness. She overlaps the outsider perspective of gender with that of the stranger, making a new historical temporality, "exorbitant," as Bhabha says, and producing the loss of a massified cultural identity that Julia Kristeva described in "On Women's Time."[13] I want to explore the possibility with Sandoz that a woman's writing might have provided an alternative to the prevalent discourse precisely by identifying with the perspective of the outsider, bringing disjunctive historical times together under the sign of gender.

Sandoz's book is in a difficult situation. The book does seem to provide a warrior cult/nationalism with a certain kind of endorsement for equating war with heroism. So, on the one hand, the book solicits an identification with the warrior that is all too easy to arouse, reinforcing the cover of a tribal people for the machinery organizing the modern "warrior." On the other hand, Sandoz's *Crazy Horse* can be assimilated to mass militarism only by dogmatic reading. As Sandoz tells the story, her narrative identification with the fate of the Lakota, bodied forth in a style that reproduces the stories told to her by Indian narrators such as He Dog, complicates any easy assimilations to a national subject. Though she wrote about warriors, she wrote against war. Thus *Crazy Horse* made available another way of construing the stories of frontier history and also the stories of warriors.

Sandoz revealed something significant in American narrative histories by the doubling she elaborates—that the often reticent image of American Indians within the representations of American spaces has repeatedly unsettled heroic innocence and threatened the crisis of identity she labors to reproduce. This doubling is itself resonant of Native American philosophy.[14] More than that, the laconic word transfixes authority. The Indian advisers to Old Jules, her father, gave him the counsel he needed to live with, and not against, the plains environment. It is as if Sandoz took from Jules those Indian stories, and that capacity to see the land flower, as the fatherly conscience that could judge all the other histories of violence and dismay, most particularly his own.

At the same time that the legends of Crazy Horse seemed to fascinate the frontier settlers of Jules's time, he also represents a figure who specifically and actively resisted any accommodation to the encroachments of white culture. That resistance continues to mark his history, even as it makes him an attractive commodity—witness the successful recent effort to persuade a brewer not to name his ale after Crazy Horse, as the following excerpt from a letter online exemplifies:

> Your choice of brand name, even if inadvertently, degrades the man whose name you have used, Tashunke Witko. The man whose name is translated into English as "Crazy Horse" was renowned for his bravery and for his refusal to submit to white oppression. He was a visionary man, a spiritual leader for his people and, above all, a reverential man, with a profound awareness of the spiritual world. But because he has been both romanticized and vilified by an ignorant white world, most Americans do not know of these aspects of his nature.[15] (Postema)

In the foreword to *Old Jules,* Sandoz wrote that she meant the book to be a biography not only of her father, but "in a larger sense . . . the biography of a community, the upper Niobrara country in western Nebraska" (vii). Similarly, she tried in *Crazy Horse* "to tell not only the story of the man but something of the life of his people through that crucial time" (x). In both books, the narrative serves the interest of a witnessing: it is testimony to the moral significance of these events, ethical memory.

In *Old Jules,* the narrator's witnessing provides an ironic distance that unsettles the assertiveness of her father's claims, at the same time that she gives his voice and his stories much of the book's space. In *Crazy Horse,* the narrator speaks rather as a witness who translates and records stories that might otherwise be lost, a relay and amplifier for messages from a past in danger of not being heard.

The Sioux wars marked the nadir of American Indian culture not only because the advancing homesteaders and their protective army outposts pushed the Indians off the land and killed many of them in battles. The long threat of death to Native Americans has taken place more quietly but more massively through displacement, starvation, and disease. More significantly, the Sioux wars took place not only on the battlefield, but also as a shock in the cultural imagination, represented by sensational reports in the Eastern press about the hostile Indians. Reports about the Sioux wars misrepresented history grossly as well as specifically. They served to obscure the already significant contributions of American Indian intellectual and cultural history to the history of the United States. During the years after the Civil War, they framed the "frontier" as a struggle between Americans and a nearly inhuman other, as if Indians, not lack of rain or economic struggle, were the chief obstacle facing those on the Oregon Trail. The Sioux wars worked to make acceptable what might otherwise have at least troubled the national conscience, because they focussed attention away from the government's bad faith, the series of broken treaties and the record of Indian cooperation. The wars both followed from and justified the historical land grab of the late nineteenth century mythologized not as part of global colonialism, but as the frontier. They disguised the capitalist modernity of the adventure.

The stories about the Indian warriors also offered a heroic alternative to the misery following the Civil War and the misery following homesteaders. The nation could be defined as a reunited whole in pursuit of its western adventure, united against those described as "savages" who sought to interrupt the flow of white men into the Great Plains. The practice is what Michael Paul Rogin called "demonizing," defining not the margins, but the mainstream of American cultural narratives.[16]

This use of the American Indian to provide an enemy that might help reconstruct the American patriot did not end with the alleged closing of the frontier. It figured importantly in the Cold War and constituted a subtext for the popularity of Western movies. Thus the Sioux wars helped to construct national identity after the divisiveness of the Civil War and again, in a reprise, after World War II. In a scene from the 1950 film *Winchester '73,* Jimmy Stewart takes refuge with the cavalry, a troop of soldiers who are pinned down by the Sioux shortly after the Custer battle. They discuss in loving detail the seductions of the repeating rifle. The film shows how the Indians provide the occasion for Americans to forget divisions such as North and South and to see themselves as one nation. The commander of the cavalry was at Bull Run—so was Jimmy, as he reveals, on the other side. But no longer at odds, they shake hands in mutual respect, with a common enemy in the Indians.

Mari Sandoz risks contributing to the distortions by focusing on Crazy Horse, who was not at all typical of his people's cultural history. D'Arcy McNickle, in his 1949 *They Came Here First,* summarized the history of white/Indian relations since 1832, "The Indians lost; the white men justified their actions" as the frontier overwhelmed the law (218). McNickle wrote not about the Sioux wars, and not at all about Crazy Horse, but about Indian rights and cultural survival. The very emphasis of white cultural history on warfare over land and on the fate of individual heroes locates the center of national identity away from concerns for a community and a way of life and away from the authority of law.

Sandoz writes about Crazy Horse at least in part because of white cultural history, in other words, but not to endorse it. The Sioux wars become, in her hands, epic, the story of whole peoples. Epic exaggeration is turned to support a modified, enlarged sense of the mutual past, one that acknowledges the culture inherited by Crazy Horse and carried forward in the memories and practices of his people. Those memories inhabit the story. Autobiography, ethnography, and history fall together, although not without difficulty.

Placing him in the context of his significance to a people, she separates the warrior from the killing war and the Indian warrior from the American military. Her book quarrels with the newspaper and storybook accounts of the Sioux wars: she reveals the complexities and ambiguities in the apparently clear divisions between "hostiles" and "friendlies." She shows how both assimilation and opposition were impossible necessities; if the collaborators were compromised, the resistance was tragic. She omits entirely the phobic atmosphere that permeated much of her source material, communicated not only in newspapers, but also by the communiques of the generals, who called Crazy Horse "savage" and feared that he would catch them by surprise.[17] She elaborates the kind of communal resource she believes we might draw on from these memories of Crazy Horse and his people. She offers testimony to the hybridity of the culture and the history so distorted by the polarizations of war. She wants to locate Crazy Horse in her own past. Does she violate the very resistance that he stood for? Does she fail to honor his difference by her identifications? She is precursor to contemporary multiculturalists like myself and vulnerable to the same trouble with guilty pasts and with trying to interpret a culture not our own and yet part of our selves. She worries about the position of the would-be translator.

One of the most important differences between American Indian culture and white culture, McNickle says, was the idea of property. "White men were fond of the notion that the task of civilizing would be speedily accomplished if, by some means or other, the Indians would adapt themselves to the European property sense—if they would become acquisitive and if they would develop private proprietorship" (260). If I cite Julia Kristeva's notion of the *propre*, the "clean and proper self" developed in the process of defining identity, perhaps that will underscore the way that questions of "the proper" and "one's own" property might be tied up with structures of identity that did not translate.[18] Without the idea of the private, how can one conceive of an American "individual," who owns first of all, himself? The "strangeness" of Crazy Horse is signaled, for Mari Sandoz, by his disregard for property, his lack of acquisitiveness.

Crazy Horse's story resembles those of the saints, but it also resembles those of revolutionaries. When Crazy Horse is a boy, Sandoz writes, his father tells him a story about a poor man who saved his tribe. "It is better to be a good man than to darken the hills with your ponies" (71). So, too, Crazy Horse does not adorn himself. Sandoz emphasizes Crazy Horse's not accumulating horses and honors that would help win a woman. What "his medicine allowed" are "the quiet, hard things that made no showing" (123). After the Battle of the Little Big Horn, the death of Custer, and at the peak of his reputation as a hostile leader, Crazy Horse agrees to come in to the agency. Even the white soldiers respect him for his selfless leadership: "Soon the soldier chiefs were speaking well of the hostile Crazy Horse, calling him a fine, quiet, and modest man, one much concerned with the welfare of his people" (370). Sandoz turns aside from glorifying the warrior to an ethics of community.

Crazy Horse is the "Strange Man" in a number of senses that Sandoz emphasizes for their apparent incompatibility. Most importantly, Crazy Horse is a stranger to the whites. When a child, he was called "Curly," perhaps because he had light brown, soft hair. Whites wondered if he were a captive, but Sandoz imagines that Crazy Horse himself would have resisted that idea. The captivity narrative nonetheless plays through her book. Crazy Horse resists the captivity by white culture that even Red Cloud accommodates—all affiliation, negotiation, or assimilation seems dangerous, an invitation to betrayal. The hybrid culture around Sandoz seems no viable alternative. In her narrative, the translators, mostly of mixed blood, provoke bloodletting from beginning to end. Crazy Horse dies in the struggle when he realizes he is about to be placed in the Fort Robinson guardhouse.

And yet seeing him as a warrior/martyr itself makes his image resemble that of a white man, enacting absolutism and racial purity as if prompted to the script of the captivity narrative. In that sense, the strangeness of Crazy

Horse appears as his uncanny doubling in the two histories he wished to keep separate—that of the Lakota and that of the United States. In both, he appears as the stranger. But the governance of captivity narratives extends also to the relationship between the author and her subject, by which she is captivated. What makes Mari Sandoz captive is that emptying out of the Anglo-European cultural heritage presumed to be carried by the daughter, so that it is replaced by a mixture, hybridity, and that difficult language her reviewer complained about. If Crazy Horse articulates the difference between cultures, Mari Sandoz articulates the consequent impossibility of a proper household and a proper reproduction of Anglo-American domesticity.[19] As the daughter, she testifies to the non-universality of the Anglo-European identity, with the strangeness of one who does not reproduce the abusive lessons learned in her own family life.

The strangeness of Crazy Horse is also associated with unusual things he does. Crazy Horse does not take a wife until he is much older than is usual. Sandoz speculates that it is perhaps because he loves No Water's wife, Black Buffalo Woman, but also perhaps because war is incompatible with desire. "'The bad things done by the soldiers—they geld the good man so long as the remembrance lays cold in his heart,' a Cheyenne medicine man told him" (156). Or perhaps he believes not having a woman increases a leader's power, and he practices celibacy. Roman Nose "had another medicine too that Crazy Horse knew about, the no-woman medicine that helped him guard all the people as a man does those of his own lodge, defend them as a husband and a father his helpless ones" (173). But in many ways Crazy Horse is not the usual leader, not physically, not in his habits, not in his lineage. The women, Sandoz imagines, might have gossiped about this:

> He stood slender as a young warrior, almost a boy when riding beside the seven-foot Touch the Clouds. He did not sing or dance as a Lakota should, and never made the ordeals of the sundance to give himself fortitude and courage. It was true that he was strong in the fighting, but he brought in no scalps for the women to dance and no stories of coups counted or deeds done. He was indeed a Strange Man. (190)

Does this very moment of honoring Crazy Horse's difference remind us uncomfortably of how Sandoz represented the figure of her father, Old Jules? The condensation and overlapping of figures takes place at the very site where she is describing the "Strange Man."

Does she succeed in separating a colonizing perspective from her story? Sandoz is much more interested in Crazy Horse as a visionary than as any kind of superior tactician or fighter, but does she thus diminish the significance of his leadership as a warrior? His story resonates for her with a Greek heroism, as if the later Western civilization had come in contact with the epic stories of a culture less decadent than its own, but of course that very perspective inserts Native American history into a lineage traced back to the Greeks. It is not the story she tells or the figures she describes that seem the most likely to unsettle a Western perspective. Nonetheless, she stages the scene of revealing Crazy Horse's vision carefully, first describing in several chapters how the young boy who had the dream grew up and proved himself brave, and portraying the horrors he must have seen—the people killed by soldiers, the village devastated by the sale of alcohol, the various peoples turned against one another rather than resisting the whites together. She wants to define his leadership in relationship to the people as a whole, a Lakota nation.

She does this through a dialogue with the holy man, the father, from whom Crazy Horse takes his name as an adult. Sandoz places the encounter in 1857 at an extraordinary time when all the seven councils of the Lakotas came together in great numbers at Bear Butte, in South Dakota, near the Black Hills. This is a place Sandoz herself must have visited. It rises from the flat plain, tree-covered, with the wind loud wherever on the path to the top one emerges from the trees. Visible along the way and at the top there are many raptors: eagles, hawks, falcons. And from that vantage point one can see "far over a country stretching away in the sun like the shadow-marked flank of a buckskin horse" (101). To this day Bear Butte is a sacred place for the Lakota, and the visitor is surrounded by those who have come for spiritual reasons, the trees hung with strips of cloth marking their prayers. It is not to be taken lightly that Sandoz chose this as the place where Crazy Horse might have realized the significance of his vision, since it is a place where many now remember the significance of Crazy Horse.

The father takes "this first-born . . . chosen for sacred things" up to a high point, by himself, where the future identity of Crazy Horse and his meaning for history is defined. The description of heroic convention is brought together with Crazy Horse's vision to enact the hailing of him into extremity and resistance.

> Somewhere a good man must rise from the young ones among us. . . . One who has had no part in the old troubles. . . . He must be one who does great deeds for the young to see, great deeds for the people. . . . The man must have the help of a great vision, one that drives him straight as the bowstring sends the arrow, one that brings together in him all the powers that are in the people. . . . It is true that it will take a great man to save the people now . . . a very great man, and many will hate him, and many try to get him killed. (103)

Then, at last, Sandoz describes Crazy Horse remembering his vision. The long narrative delay, emphasized by the father's speech, but taking place through a time of several years between the occasion of the vision and the telling of it (through several chapters that include his first acts as a warrior) builds dramatic tension, but it also constructs a field of memory within which such a vision might be claimed. The vision both defines the warrior and explains the characteristic way he appeared in battle. This mode of dramatic presentation sacrifices historical chronology for significance; it is a moment in the construction of the book that might be considered novelistic, and that serves—perhaps one might say "empathetically," since the narrator's dominant genre is not novel but biography—to help persuade the readers of the idea that the power of Crazy Horse was visionary. More importantly, it demonstrates how the resistant hero appears through the father's word. His vision "was not like the world the boy knew but the real world behind this one, the sky and the trees in it, the grass waving, but all in a strange and sacred way" (105). The vision contains the elements of Crazy Horse's legend, "only one feather," "a small brown stone . . . tied behind his ear," a man riding straight into enemies "always disappearing before they struck him," "on the man's cheek a little zigzag that seemed of lightning, and a few hail spots on his body" (105). Narrating the vision in novelized free indirect style rather than from the distant, informed, and critical perspective of a historian, Sandoz tries to give it the immediacy of experience. The strangest quality of Crazy Horse, the strength of his vision, connects the individual to the nation. It is the people, in the person of his father, who give a name to his vision and himself, though it is also the people, as in the vision, who grab and restrain him as well.

The story of Crazy Horse as Sandoz sees it is an uncanny reminder of the heroism that modern Anglo-European civilization has lost, its capacity for the tragic.[20] It becomes a critique of modernity in the name of the most familiar, the classic, as well as in the name of the stranger. Her editor, Paul Hoffman, wrote that he worried about extending the heroic dilemma through a formal structure that was cyclic and repetitive rather than Aristotelian: "After all, in essence yours is a story with the intensity of an American *Iliad* and although I know it's a bromide, intensity can't be sustained unduly" (qtd. in Stauffer 155). However, the nearly unworkable hybridity of her narrative strategies aims to bring together an unrecuperated strangeness—that which provides the critique—with the honored and familiar but nostalgic categories of heroism available to Anglo-European readers.

What is the relationship between this warrior and the politics of warriors in 1942, the soldiers fighting for and against fascism—Hitler's war, with its abstractions and its exploitation of the aesthetic to control the people? Sandoz does not entirely discard the anarchistic, libertarian values of her father, Jules. But she imagines the possibility of a more democratic and communal ideal of freedom. Crazy Horse represents the power of a visionary style to reinforce voluntary assent—an alternative not only to the American military, but also to totalitarian demagoguery. Compared to the well-organized absolutism of a Hitler, Stalin, or Mussolini, such a warrior might seem indeed strange. At the same time, Sandoz writes the book as critique of the modern hero of laissez faire, a certain highly individual style of manhood, uncaring about the responsibilities to a people, particularly to "the helpless ones." Although Sandoz's father, Jules, was motivated by his dreams of orderly community and reunion with the distant Rosalie, those dreams are distinguished from Crazy Horse's vision because they reverse the relationships of individual subject to culture. The vision of Crazy Horse takes its meaning from the way the figure of the man on the horse might take his place in the communal. It constitutes the initiation of the boy to manhood by an interpellation, a calling or sense of fate that defines him as an individual within the social, in relationship to his father's name and words. It is accompanied by a sense of recognition. This is not a logic of desire; indeed, it may be accompanied, as Sandoz emphasizes, by a certain asceticism. Contrast this to Jules's projection of desire into a utopia, a no place, that repeated the frontier logic: it is precisely that lack that constitutes desire (the empty place, the absent Rosalie), but it is also the projection of lack onto territory perceived as wide open spaces rather than as the living spaces of Crazy Horse's people that drives horror and abuse.

That horror and abuse is the stable element across Sandoz's works, and her revulsion provides the grounds for her ethical stance. In *Crazy Horse,* the annihilation of the Cheyenne and the Lakota provokes the necessity of witness as well as of a warrior; hence Sandoz speaks her own story together with the perspective of Crazy Horse, sometimes conflating them. Sandoz uses the death of Conquering Bear, in the first chapter, and fragments of text from her father's visit to the scene of the massacre at Wounded Knee to provide a site where the stories might intersect, to locate her position as narrator. Old Jules had looked down "upon the piles of men, women, and children sprawled among their goods. Dry snow trailed little ridges of white over them, making them look like strange-limbed animals left for the night and the wolves" (*Old Jules* 131).

Crazy Horse comes upon the scene of "a bad and desperate stand" by his fleeing village early in his formative years: "Scattered along the rocky slope were lodge rolls, parfleches, robes, cradleboards, and many other village goods, all trampled and torn and burnt, and among these lay dark places that were blood and darker ones that were the dead of his people" (76). He reacts with sick nausea, "stooping over himself, his belly came up again and again" (77). These scenes of devastation, rather than scenes of individual valor, rewrite the significance of Crazy Horse's legendary courage and defiance. Later, after another scene of killing, "His heart was cold and black with an anger that could not be made good until many more of the white men died like those scattered naked up there on the ridge" (204). Sandoz explicitly attributes not the desire to be a warrior, but this other set of motives to Crazy Horse: "The warpath was a fine thing for the young warriors, Crazy Horse thought, but he would try to make it so Little Hawk need never see the women and children lying on the ground like animals butchered in the hunt" (139).

The sacrificial logic that connects such scenes with the burgeoning horror of Nazi treatment of the Jews emerges as a principle of historical ethics. The terrible sight would be repeated at Wounded Knee, after Crazy Horse's death, and inhabits Sandoz's vocabulary as a figure recurring uncannily: "like animals." The words are the scar of abuse; little Marie trembled as a baby "like a terrorized small animal." The abusive figure predicts Crazy Horse's inability despite all to protect the bodies of women and children. The corpses lying like animal carcasses plunge the witness into the nausea of abjection. Crazy Horse himself is sacrificed. He is killed when he struggles with his betrayors: "Between them the Indian, like a trapped animal, was heaving, plunging to get free, growling: 'Let me go! Let me go!' as the angry bear growls, the knife flashing in the late sun" (408).

Mari Sandoz as witness and translator reads the palimpsest of trails crossing the place beside the Niobrara or Running Water where she grew up, where Conquering Bear had his death scaffold and where Crazy Horse himself may have had his vision up on a hill while the old chief was dying. Far from trying to expel the bodied affect from her story and make it more objective history, she tries to call up its uncanny resonances, even to the point of writing what Crazy Horse himself might have been thinking, an imaginative breach that contains elements of possession and elements of violation. She uses Lakota names and Lakota locutions. Furthermore, the narrative itself is strung out along the seasons, punctuated by events significant to the tribal cultural history and only sometimes to the white histories—the battles and the hunts that might have been recorded in pictures for tribal history, loyalties, misunderstandings, and traditional warfare with the Crow, struggles for food and for equity, broken promises, efforts for peace, personal betrayals, friendships. Sandoz's narrative form is importantly not so familiar, particularly in its use of recurrence rather than linearity. Although the battles recall the Greek epic, the story of Crazy Horse, focused as it is on his life, follows the familiar structure of a biography, and his death by betrayal evokes Christian sacrifice. But it is tragic without remedy, without the redemption of art or religion and hence requiring redemption by history. The repeated instances of courage, death, and white failures to honor peace go on, past the ending, engendering not catharsis, but outrage and frustration, and perhaps the necessity of more stories.

The hybridity of Sandoz's text has to do with her refusal of the identity-making protocols that governed the war discourse surrounding her as she wrote, as well as her refusal of the protocols of the daughter. The external divisions of warring parties were enhanced by the construction of national subjectivity on the model Hitler's anti-Semitism represented. It was an internal separation of cultures into the natural, real subjects who belong to one's own nation and the others, who have no rights and may be unrepresentable except as the abject other, as vermin, dirt, filth, fluids, corpses. The relationship between American treatment of the Indian and Nazi anti-Semitism has been noted. Crazy Horse appeared in American history at a time when the American Indian had become legally unrepresentable. As Priscilla Wald has argued, "The legal treatment of both the indigenous tribes and the slaves profoundly troubled the concept of natural law—particularly the rights to own and inherit property, including property in the self" (80). Pressing the case for Crazy Horse as a representative of a people, Sandoz resurrects that breach in the imaginary organic unity of the nation.

She brings the complexities of hybridity and assimilation into language, in her evocation of an Indian style, but also in her representation of injustice. The part-Indian, part-white go-betweens engender both understanding and betrayal. Even the white forts represent both exchange and armed suppression. Of the mixed forms, Sandoz gives us neither the plot of a novel nor the master plot of objective history to cling to. The book is more like testimony, and yet it is the storytelling of a translator. And she herself understands so well the danger of the bad translation that she foregrounds the problem of interpreters.

The necessities of survival distorted the interpretation of Indian actions again and again. In the early days, Sandoz recollects at the beginning of her book, Fort Laramie was an Indian town, but white traders married the women of the Lakotas; the Indians were "free" to come and go. There began an enduring dispute, as more whites came, between those Indians who wanted trade and peace, and those who wanted to resist the whites. The ones who would be categorized as "friendly" by the whites are called "Loaf About the Forts" by the others and accused of selling their words for trade goods. The young warriors who want to fight, on the other hand, might not only jeopardize the safety of all, but might also by their ungovernable impatience ruin even the carefully planned strategies of Indian warfare. Those known as "hostiles" by the whites include the young warriors, but also Crazy Horse, who witnesses the arbitrary killings of his people and the depravity introduced by alcohol. But this division is never stable, nor is the division between whites and Indians. The whites do not understand Indian governance and insist on a mode of hierarchical authority that distorts all their negotiations with representative "leaders." "The Lakotas were not the men to follow like pack mares as it seemed the whites did. Today they might listen to this one, tomorrow to that, or to none at all, for they were free men" (11).

Sandoz represents the Sioux wars as a series of misunderstandings and betrayals, not a contest of manliness and heroics. At his death, Crazy Horse is betrayed by an interpreter and by the lies of other Lakota. Crazy Horse says to the general, according to Bordeaux, "If the Great Father wants us to fight we will go north and fight until not a Nez Perce is left," but Grouard, known as the Grabber, translates, "We will go north and fight until not a *white man* is left" (392). Bordeaux manages to insist on his translation only after it is too late. Though it is a white soldier, as Sandoz has it, who bayonets Crazy Horse at the last, he succeeds because Little Big Man, Swift Bear, and other Brules are holding Crazy Horse—fulfilling the prophesy of his vision. Loyalty and betrayal, true and false translation, do not finally sort out according to the divisions of nation.

Neither does Sandoz organize the good and the bad along the lines of gender, although her justification of Crazy Horse's resistance and her criticism of white contact support the associations of warrior/masculinity/fighting/resistance and negotiator/femininity/peace/collaboration so strongly polarized by World War II. Layering her narrative function together with a narrative voice that identifies with what Crazy Horse witnessed; she puts the empathy for the victim that in our culture would be feminine together with the identification with power that would be masculine. The body of the story thus becomes volatile.

The body of the text takes up the disturbances of narrative form precipitated by American Indian history. Breaks in the illusion of organic form that reveal the nation, the individual, the text to be inhabited by strangeness precipitate a sense of humor that is both tragic and carnivalesque, a perspective by incongruity. The irony of the story erupts in small incidents often marked by laughter throughout the book, until the large, dark irony of the final catastrophe. The joke reveals the perspective, defamiliarized, not white. For instance, in an early description of a Lakota camp: "Many of the women, neat-haired, in their doeskin and calico working dresses, were away too, some spreading robes around ant hills to rid them of the lice and nits from long camping among the whites" (7). One of the trader's sons "had the peculiar belief of the white man that a husband has the right to knock his woman down as though she were an enemy warrior" (231). Red Cloud tries to simplify Indian religious beliefs in his speech, "to find words easy enough for the whites to understand." The term "Great Spirit," for example, is "a little white-man name used by them as though it could mean all the sacred powers for which there were no words" (236). The "hostiles" laugh at the poor goods given the Indians—"blankets that were too small to cover a man, tin kettles that mashed flat in falling or turned red and rusty" (261). The Oglalas laugh at their old enemies, the Crows, in a fight: "Come closer, Come get some Lakota women! They are much better than the Crows!" (274). The whites all laugh, as if at a great joke, at the Indian goods from the government that were stolen, counted twice, resold, diminished. Crazy Horse laughs, for the first time in a long time, at the young girl brought to be his second wife, who "ran between the lodges when she saw me coming" (357). The Indian women are surprised to learn that the wives of the whites ride sidesaddle not because they have a disease, but because they are ashamed of their legs (368).

Finally, He Dog asks in the last days of his life, when Crazy Horse has moved into the domain of the fort and suspects trouble, if that means, "you will be my enemy if I move across the creek?" Crazy Horse laughs: "I am no white man. . . . They are the only people who make rules for others and say: 'If you stay on one side of this line its is peace but if you go on the other side I will kill you all'" (390).

Sandoz has taken that exchange, together with the report that Crazy Horse laughed, word for word from the interview with He Dog himself (23). The violations of that side-taking make an ironic laughter that restructures the clear oppositions of war and the most basic logic of the white understanding, making, but also breaking, rules for others. What Crazy Horse laughed at, and He Dog worried about, was the idea that he had assimilated white ideas of peace and war.

Sandoz and the Heartland

By inserting Mari Sandoz's books about the frontier into the international history of the Cold War culture, I hope to demonstrate the ideological aptitude of a Western history that she thought lent itself to tall tales. The rise of an exceptionally American Western hero (accompanied by a world-wide inflation in the price of authentic blue jeans that continues to this day) helped to stage the global Cold War. That the West—which often meant everyone on earth not a communist—should be thought of in the image of a cowboy seems unsurprising. What is surprising is the way the resulting configuration of culture virtually eliminated critique. In part, this absence has to do with the location of middlebrow culture in the commodified domestic sphere and the intelligentsia's criticism of commodified culture. The "great divide" described by Andreas Huyssen separated modernist high culture from popular culture and feminized the masses.

But this separation that gave cultural power to a certain critical class was violated by the agents of middlebrow literature such as the Book-of-the-Month Club, and in response the intelligentsia launched a vituperative stigmatization of such efforts to reach large audiences with "serious" literature. Middlebrow commodification revealed, as Janice Radway has argued, the "scandal" of modernist claims that the critical reader making decisions about the quality of literature acted outside the political economy of capitalism. The feminization of serious middlebrow culture affected the representation of men as well as women.

Intellectuals rejected the discourses of heartland culture as stereotypical, sentimental, nostalgic, and uncritical. (They were, of course, but intellectuals do not themselves write outside ideology, as this critique allows them/us to imagine). That is why the cowboy hero that Theodore Roosevelt did so much to reinvent, that Gary Cooper and John Wayne registered as cinematic truth, could be repeated as a stereotype that layered nation and individual together in the same image. Intellectuals did not believe that cowboys were heroes and the Easterners who came west, like Bernard Malamud, found blandness and, in Malamud's words, "unearned innocence." However, their efforts to counter such imaginary effects foundered on the separation of literature from stories of conscience. Trilling's hope for a "moral realism" left him disengaged from the struggle for a moral imagination.

Mari Sandoz wrote to connect the abusive gesture with the national imaginary hero of the frontier. Her stories aim to rethink all the layers of authority associated with the sublime landscape: the Western heroic individual, family and communal relationships, the regional history of the West, the political culture of nationalism, and the claims of historical authenticity that govern this interpretive structure. The human bodies dying "like animals" become an uncanny counter-figure in the most intimate proximity.

In the years after World War II, her representation of genocide in *Cheyenne Autumn* takes on the resonance of the Holocaust. Juxtaposing *Cheyenne Autumn*, written during the Cold War, to *Crazy Horse* underscores her shift to emphasizing national guilt. Even though the military's bad faith and violation of promises appears in *Crazy Horse*, it seems less than systematic and structural. In *Cheyenne Autumn*, the Cheyenne are without recourse, because their alleged protectors disavow the problems that will kill them. The failure of the government together with the chicanery of contractors and the thefts, lies, and cheating of individuals insure that the Cheyenne are caught in the Indian territory where they cannot find food for themselves. Supplies to them are cut in government economies and stolen. So, as Sandoz relays the memory, they make a desperate flight to their old grounds in the north. The reader's attention is held by the hope of escape—the writer solicits the reader's empathic position as witness once again, but in this book not as witness in the repetitive time of ceremony and everyday life. The writer/reader see the flight from the perspective of Western history, a subversive version of it that underscores its guilt.[21] Does the book then enable the reader to exorcise guilt through identification with what is past, to reinvent innocence? Sandoz never completely escapes her position in the history of conquest, and neither do her readers, of course. But I want also to keep in view the fact that she introduces complexity to the discourses of conquest, and troubles her readers, so that the idealized West of the Cold War is not so easy to recuperate.

One can scarcely argue that Sandoz deconstructed the idealization in ways powerful enough to be widely received, or that her resistance to the configuration of a western heartland had a large impact on the entertainment industry West, as Ronald Reagan or John Wayne saw it. She could see ways that the film of *Crazy Horse* had relied on material that could have come only from her book, but they did not acknowledge it, and the film didn't tell the story she told. Her version of *Cheyenne Autumn* didn't appear on film until 1966, when sympathy for the cause of Indians was more widespread than in 1952, when she published the book. She affected the larger representation of the Western hero in neither the popular nor the intellectual classes. Her books rest uneasily, instead, in the heartland of the middlebrow. She became a "serious" writer, as she pointedly called herself in her letters, when she won the Atlantic nonfiction prize in 1935 and when *Old Jules* was chosen for the Book-of-the-Month Club. Their committee of experts, which included Dorothy Canfield Fisher, in fact promoted a number of women writers, including Willa Cather, Josephine Herbst, and even Gertrude Stein.[22] Like other women writers, Sandoz left a trail of differing perspectives that were overlooked in the later constructions of literary history.

I don't mean to say her writing was ineffectual, however—far from it. She made a record that stored up historical complexity, a legacy. As subsequent borrowings, often unacknowledged, from her histories suggest, anyone interested in Indians or the West would sooner or later confront the difficulties she posed, even if they chose to deny them. Sandoz went on to write more critical books, fiction and nonfiction precariously aligned on the borders of history and literature as a perturbation of increasingly well-defined categories: individual/society, hero/antihero, war/peace, white man/Indian, frontier past/industrial present. But she never won the widespread endorsement of eastern intellectuals. Like other "regional" writers, doubtless, and like other Book-of-the-Month Club selections, she fell under the unfair condemnation issued by Richard Chase: "The word 'middlebrow,' although suggesting centrality of vision, inevitably suggests, judging by our American literature, a view gained by no other means than passivity and the refusal of experience" (11). Thus the activism and critical awareness of a hidden American culture populated more by women writers than by men has been effectively denied.

How did this work? That the national hero could be represented by John Wayne, switching from his Western roles to his combat roles without ever needing to put away his gun—and yet the history and fiction that both opposed and complicated the Western hero would be marginal to the interests of critical intellectuals during the Cold War? Here is precisely the site for a consideration of ethics. *Old Jules* interests me in part because it existed in the domain made public enough by the *Atlantic Monthly* and the Book-of-the-Month Club to prompt such attention. Thus the lack of attention to the problems of representing male identity, the frontier, and the Indian begins to seem a blind spot in the critical audience that needs to be addressed. Sandoz's questioning of the father's authority during the years of her writing career, from the thirties to the fifties, reached a middlebrow audience large enough for commercial success. Her hybrid prose sometimes offended disciplinarity, particularly because she personalized historical narrative with dialogue and used novels as thinly veiled historical tracts. But her books challenged the dominant construction of the heartland from inside the heartland, where her readers were perhaps more willing than the critical establishment to have the underside of cultural power exposed.

In her biographies of her father, Jules, and of Crazy Horse, she situates her inquiry in the middle of abuse, betrayal, violence, and war. Although she makes frequent use of references to gender, in particular acknowledging both the strength and the vulnerabilities of women in these stories, she explodes the gender stereotype as she complicates the male figures. She simply continuously places herself in the position of listener to the stories, skeptical and curious, but female.

This nonheroic listening delineates a renewable site for the critique of the heroic propaganda, by its very empathy marked as outside the master narrative. In 1942, *Crazy Horse* challenged the continuity of frontier myths and military heroism that provided a manly history to support the war effort. This was not a new interpretation of Crazy Horse. Her father's stories had been admiring, part of a tradition of honoring the courage of Crazy Horse. In truth, the nineteenth-century story of annihilation was all along accompanied by expressions of admiration for the Indian warriors, beginning with Black Hawk. One of Sandoz's sources, E. A. Brininstool, said in 1929 that the death of Crazy Horse was a "lamentable affair," "one more blot to the record of the treatment of the American Indian at the hands of Uncle Sam." Her *Cheyenne Autumn* at times reads like the story of an escape from a concentration camp, with settlers and cowboys as well as the military helping to demonize and pursue the starving, fleeing Indians—like Germans refusing help to the Jews.

What she opposes most of all is the individualism that derives its innocence from its denial of communal obligations. The frontier hero is defined not only by his relationship to an empty space extending before him, but also by his disengagement from intruders into that space. Jules dreamed of the lovely Rosalie but mistreated his wife and children. He railed against the government even though he ordered his seeds from it. For her model of the communal, Sandoz does not return to bourgeois domesticity. Crazy Horse, on the other hand, was distinguished from the careless heroes of the army (Grattan, Custer), whom he defeated, and the careless warriors of his people, whom he brought under control, by the forms of Indian governance that kept the people and its leaders living together.

The site of writerly empathy and critique occupied by Sandoz was not destroyed by the Cold War and obviously found an audience, but it was certainly less visible than more literary-seeming books, and the testimony she hoped to pass on has not been sufficiently heard in the academy. On the one hand, the scholars of Western history and literature have found it difficult to overcome the sanctions imposed by the very centrality of the Western trope. On the other, and this interests me even more, the very effectiveness of the stories for which Sandoz has such a good ear endangered the Cold War truce of literary intellectuals. Even though stories continued, as they must, to provide a powerful rhetorical means to communicate witnessing, literary formalism pretended not to hear. If stories embodied experience and tied the individual to the history of his community, the Cold War concept of the literary denied that either experience or history was the proper object of study.

During the Cold War, Sandoz wrote the history of *Cheyenne Autumn* with a political agenda in mind. She had been working with the Cheyenne to improve conditions, and she meant to stir up sympathy for the Indian. After she sold the book to Hollywood for $1000, she agonized at John Ford's misrepresentations of events in the 1966 film but consoled herself at last with the hope that the film, too, would help create sympathy for the Indian. This political, activist valence made her historics both more popular and more critically questionable during the Cold War.

Sandoz writes about the American male hero in the American heartland in order to both produce and reproduce cultural memories. She destabilizes the gender-based polarities not to critique men, but to make masculinity heterogeneous. She inserts the American Indian into the place of the hero, in the person of Crazy Horse, not to make him or herself un-American, but to make impossible the history that leaves the whites without a cultural marker. Hence the story of Jules describes a father that is subject and abject. The story of the strange man of the Oglalas who looked like a white man, with his light hair, reveals the whites with less attractive strangenesses, from lice to women-beating.

Instead of the flat characters of formula, she gives us the well-rounded characters of fictional realism, using the techniques of the novelist to make history. She does not sacrifice the complexities of events to plot or advocacy, but she violates the illusions of linear plot and individual psyche that realism meant to install. Hers is the mixed genre of story, mixed even beyond the novelistic. Postmodernism has famously declared the end of narrative: at least of the "master narratives" that have structured history and the authority of knowledge for modernity. Jean-François Lyotard, in *The Postmodern Condition,* argued as well that postmodernism is simply more self-conscious than modernism about this uncertainty—and that "science and industry are no more free of the suspicion which concerns reality than are art and writing" (76).

I am suggesting that the defensive certainty of the Cold War, with its accompanying endorsement of modernism, has been followed by a corrective declaration and theorizing of radical uncertainty that participates as a violent polarization of a more long-term historical dialectic. This end of narrative does not mean that it is possible to escape the storymaking principle, but rather that it is possible to escape the radical claims for the true/real made by recent history, and that we should take an interest in stories that negotiate the rhetorical function of narrative. Mari Sandoz does not call attention to the narrator, but she is not protected by the conventions of ironic distance that divide fictional narrators from authors. Her unassuming posture, like that of a translator, I have suggested, as well as that of a witness, makes use of the conventions not just of writing but of listening, and secondarily, of reading. The author function in her hands becomes a relay, sending culture along with the differences and the added charge that the bodied human subject introduces into discourse. We can see that her storytelling passes memories along to us, that it makes a difference, and that the difference she makes is vulnerable to the next relay, the next reader, and the ecology of reading that receives her text. If we have to tell the stories of our history, and we do, we should read her.

6

The Warrior Is a Stage Adolescents Go Through: Ursula Le Guin's Thought Experiments

> My book *Always Coming Home* was a rash attempt to imag-
> ine . . . a world, where the Hero and the Warrior are a stage
> adolescents go through on their way to becoming responsible
> human beings, where the parent-child relationship is not for-
> ever viewed through the child's eyes but includes the reality
> of the mother's experience.
>
> —Ursula Le Guin, "The Fisherwoman's
> Daughter," *Dancing*

Ursula Le Guin inaugurated a defiance of the Cold War divide between
high literature and mass culture in the sixties with her first publications
and soon emphasized her allegiance to the wider culture, publishing her
great Earthsea trilogy for young people (and adults). She has proclaimed
it her intention to write for the ordinary audience:

> We have been taught that only poetry of extremely high qual-
> ity is poetry at all; that poetry is a big deal, and you have to
> be a pro to write it, or, in fact, to read it. This is what keeps a
> few poets and many, many English departments alive. That's
> fine, but I was after something else: the poem not as fancy
> pastry but as bread; the poem not as masterpiece but as life
> "work."[1] (*Dancing* 18)

Le Guin writes as an artist-housewife, a role, she reminds us, that violates strong cultural strictures and risks strong retribution: "Any attempt
to combine art work with housework and family responsibilities is impossible, unnatural. And the punishment for unnatural acts, among the
critics and the Canoneers, is death" (*Dancing* 222). Though she does not
use the same terminology, she is referring to the attack on domestic fiction, the sentimental, and the middlebrow developed by modernists and
taken up by Cold War intellectuals.

As I have argued, the threat of death to one's work did accompany

Cold War criticism. The critics of the fifties did, indeed, eliminate the nineteenth-century mother/writers from literature. The new suburban domesticity of the Cold War—what Betty Friedan called the "feminine mystique"—enforced a separation of child-rearing from adult activities, children's books from real literature. Cold War feminism revealed its ties to modernism by its suspicion of maternal work. Le Guin wants to talk about mothers who write, because "it is almost a taboo topic," because she herself wrote in "a fully child-filled space," without the social acknowledgement accorded to the heroic male artist (*Dancing* 225).

However, as I have discussed in previous chapters, the Cold War also closed off spaces for writing manhood, most particularly the space of the tribal "warrior" whose heroic deeds would be subordinate to a larger communal necessity. Le Guin's sense that the hero needs to be inserted in the story of childhood is the other side of a Cold War necessity.

As Le Guin points out, the ideal of the artist/hero is founded on religious traditions. That moral responsibility for tradition situates the artist in a sacrificial activity, close to taboos and perversions. It exacts a special kind of language, strange forms. What Le Guin represents is the "double consciousness" of mothers, always split between at least self and one other. Memory in its feminine form, as Le Guin represents it, has a different relationship to strangeness, is strange, and projects forward into the genre Le Guin calls future history, because reproducing the cultural home requires it. There is an interplay of gender and genre at work. Le Guin simply disregards the Cold War vilification of mothers, or "Momism," as if it did not have to be relevant to her unrealistic genres.

Speaking as a mother, Le Guin does not represent a position on the margin, but rather a position overlapping numerous margins. It is a version of the postmodern, perhaps, if largely without privileges. (Julia Kristeva has also made the mother the very model of a postmodern split subject, although her representation of the maternal has been met with considerable critical suspicion.)[2] As Homi Bhabha suggested, writing under the sign of woman's time, Le Guin can also make a place for the postcolonial narrative and alternate cultural history. The perspective of Native American and Eastern spiritualities helps define, for Le Guin, a space that will be open to the feminine. Le Guin's recent publication of a new English version of Lao Tzu's *Tao Te Ching* (a project that has engaged her since the fifties) suggests how thoroughly her thinking has been directed toward a non-Western sense of moral instruction.

What is the privilege of motherhood for Le Guin? "Motherhood . . . simply means that she does everything everybody else does plus bringing up the kids" (*Dancing* 235). Resisting the masculinized forms of science fiction and its "cozy misogyny," Le Guin mitigates the genre.[3] The unknowable overlaps with feminine authority: "Fantasy is the grandmother of all fictions" (*Norton Book of Science Fiction* 29). Home is her most paradoxical and basic term, the wedge with which Ursula Le Guin critiques an American and global culture that is increasingly filled with the homeless—refugees, but also those apparently willing victims of a market economy that demands relocation of even its most powerful figures. Such a concept of home points out how the capacity to stay home, or to keep a community intact, becomes a luxury most cannot afford. During her career she becomes more and more explicit about the significance of home and how Native American conceptions of the spirit of place have influenced her convictions. "The six directions can meet only in lived time, in the place people call home, the seventh direction, the center" (*Dancing* 82).

Le Guin's insistence on home represents something other than the extremities of Right and Left, of the propertied and those without property. She inserts the ideas of motherhood associated with the era since late eighteenth-century revolutions and the rise of the middle class—that is, with the rise of the United States as a nation—into a different history, yet to come. This recasting of home shifts family narratives from the heroic context of gendered spheres and political economy into a more local and material future history. "My intent is not reactionary, nor even conservative, but simply subversive" (*Dancing* 85).

Le Guin's "home" is nonetheless familiar because in many respects it is and it advocates a turn to narrative structures resembling Native American stories. The structure of home replaces (by a topos) the logos of history because "the Spirit of Place is a more benign one than the exclusive and aggressive Spirit of Race" (*Dancing* 84). Thus Le Guin's escape from the Cold War history takes place at the level of genre, but she takes genres once denigrated as escapist (science fiction, fantasy) as the very place for a history.

Reclaiming "home" from a Cold War foreclosure would make a different discussion of subjectivity possible, and that is the work Le Guin's texts do. If strangeness has been a particularly modern theme, the fantasy of home has been its seductive opposite. Not only has it supported regressive nostalgia, home has also served to construct and affirm the right of a certain kind of individual to have priority over every other person's claims. During the Cold War, the renewed idealization of home served to organize the working class into suburbanized and isolated heterosexual pairs, who then identified with roles defined by gender and sexuality rather than by work. The Cold War "home" disciplined the greatly expanded middle class into units of the "nuclear family."

Forms of abusive ideology—racism, sexism, and other abuses excused by politics, such as anticommunism—are inculcated and enabled at the level of the *household,* by the treatment of men and women and children in their intimate relations. But the Cold War ideology of home had such force that the political work accomplished by the nuclear family became invisible, disconnected. One could talk about the psychology of individuals, or the sociology of institutions, but the individual's relationships to institutions came to seem necessarily oppositional, even—or especially—to intellectuals. When Le Guin makes *home* more significant than *heroism*, she signals her challenge of such individualism. However, so central to Cold War ideology is the formation of the nuclear family that it is almost impossible for any imaginable return of the critic "home" to avoid traversing a terrain of sacrifice, where a failure of critique will open up an instance of exclusion, hatred, and victimization. It is difficult, I mean, to value "home" without supporting the abuses hidden there.[4]

In a reversal of logic that would be an antidote to the Cold War schisms and splitting, Le Guin defines the strange in relationship to a familiar other. If it is a form of the response to the alien that Julia Kristeva recommends, seeing the strangeness within, it is written from the place within culture (and the symbolic) occupied by one who speaks the language. Le Guin gives us always the sense not of shock or the uncanny but of recognition. Her places seem like what we are used to, as if she is describing the known, as if nothing could be easier to imagine (for example) than the idea documented in "Sur," that women discovered Antarctica first. She does not give us the strangeness of the street where we live (like David Lynch); she gives us difference as the street where we live, appropriate to what is proper to us.

She restores our memory by a future history that is an antidote to discovery. "One of our finest methods of organized forgetting is called discovery," she points out: "the non-urban peoples of the Americas had no history, properly speaking, and therefore are visible only to the anthropologist, not to the historian, except as they entered into White history" (*Dancing* 84). Her recent works in particular have revised both history and history making by using spatialized narrative forms. Her 1985 *Always Coming Home* gives us a future history borrowed from native peoples, a rescue of our endangered species imagined through a collection of cultural materials. Her 1991 *Searoad* imagines a matrilineal history for a small coastal town in Oregon through a collection of individual stories. The book reads as if this is how we understand ourselves, but this is indeed how we understand ourselves. She wins recognition of a dailiness overlooked as insignificant. The everyday story may include realistic detail and a familiar style, but it does not exist in the tragic historical time of Cold War realism. In her foreword to the diary of her husband's grandmother, Magnolia Wynn Le Guin, she argues for another aesthetic that is based on another sense of time:

> I have thought that the inevitable repetition of events and
> wordings that characterize the unselfconscious diary are more

appropriate than any device used by the conventional novel to describe the actual gait of most people's lives—in which dramatic episodes punctuate and change, but do not climax or culminate, a long, returning rhythm, or complex cycles of rhythms, or a riverlike ongoing the essence of which is its incessance. In this appropriateness is an aesthetic power—like that of the refrain or burden of a ballad or song?—which our conventional narrative forms almost entirely lack. (ix–x)

The storyteller once served an important function for culture but, as Walter Benjamin has argued in "The Storyteller," is threatened by the abstract political economy dominating modern Western literacy and infiltrating every communal experience. Le Guin shows us the response to this bleak portrayal: not quite, not in the woman's sphere and other daily places.

In other words, Le Guin turns to *communitas* to correct the unbalance caused by making structure and cognition the center of knowledge. Her project is allied to poststructuralism, but she does not see the institutions of reason (the academy, for example) as the best place to inaugurate subversion. This is not to say that she believes the academy is reasonable. From Victor Turner she has taken the set of antitheses that places *communitas* in relationship to the more abstract formations elevated by the Cold War to absolutes:

> structure . . . /*communitas*
> cognitive . . . /existential
> a model . . . /a potential
> classifies . . . /reclassifies
> legal and political institutions . . . /art and religion (*Dancing* 88)

Choosing science fiction and fantasy as her favored genres, Le Guin uses her "thought experiments" to work out the future implied not by natural sciences and technologies such as physics or chemistry or even information sciences, but by the human sciences, by anthropology in particular. She belongs to a distinguished family within the academy that she so regularly complains about. As the daughter of Theodora Kroeber and Alfred L. Kroeber, she addresses the intellectual project of anthropology from a place that is at once critical and at home.

What kind of anthropology, then, does she give us? We have many figures of the anthropologist in her Hainish novels, where they are "hilfers," a name shadowed by the notion of "helpers" but also "halfers," creatures of neither kind. Unlike other characters, these hilfers are able to see things from an alien perspective. They are, in other words, figures of the writer as well as the anthropologist, but perhaps figures for motherhood as well. Le Guin's "thought experiments" show how the study of culture implies a relationship with the alien and how the Western idea of the hero, the idea we thought we couldn't do without, might be put into dialogue with another context entirely. It is a writerly anthropology.

Future history depends upon naming in a very material way. The *Earthsea* books frequently cite a concept of "true names." The use of language as "charms" in magic, alchemy, and esoterica influenced symbolist literature from Baudelaire to Valéry, and the effective power of "voodoo" fascinated modernist poets. Descriptions of an archaic matriarchal culture have been, since Bachofen, associated with the idea of an original mother tongue, like the Indo-European posited by nineteenth-century comparative linguistics. And magical language is connected to the Celtic and to the medieval romances that much fantasy draws upon, as Tolkien drew upon the Mabinogion. However, although Earthsea seems to belong to the medievalism of fantasy traditions, it owes much to Native American world views as well. The idea of a naming that has material force resonates with Native American thought in particular. Like the California peoples—the Yurok—whose stories Le Guin's mother, Theodora Kroeber, tells in her collection, *The Inland Whale,* the people of Earthsea map their conceptions around the known "Center of the World." The young "Toàn" of the Yurok has learned the proper obligations of an aristocrat, as has Arren in *The Farthest Shore (FS)*. For the Yurok, Kroeber tells us, the "matter of the personal name is one that is left in abeyance unless its owner chooses to tell it" (161). In "Love Charm," a young woman hopes to cast a spell with a poem on the one she loves as he passes by.

Future history depends not only upon naming, but also upon place—upon a very precisely described ecology. Location has to be imagined in the six dimensions of the senses, so that the future is embodied. In *Always Coming Home,* Le Guin responds to the primary question of the Cold War: will humanity survive? Unlike postcatastrophe novels such as *On the Beach,* she gives us a heartbreakingly optimistic scenario for how human life might look in a future village culture that provides a recipe for survival, in a way that should turn us quickly to the work of protecting the village cultures that remain self-sufficient (for example, in Mexico) before international capitalism displaces them from that ecology. Her utopia might lead us to think about the obliteration of village culture in Chiapas in the wake of NAFTA, for example. Her future history, in other words, is shaped by the Cold War in a larger environmental economy and not just by the standoff of East and West, or the political economy of revolution.

Taking an anthropological perspective on future history, many of Le Guin's narratives feature revolution not as a death of the past, but (as even its eighteenth-century advocates may have taken it) as a turn in a revolving process, that might lead to return: what the earth does in its revolutions around the sun. When Le Guin writes about the 1830 pan-European revolutions in the historical novel *Malafrena*, the search for freedom includes the problem of whether or not one should leave home. The successful anarchist revolution that founded the culture represented in *The Dispossessed* is led by an old woman, Odo (like Emma Goldman, perhaps) who says "true voyage is return." In other words, political revolution in Le Guin is defined in relationship to home.

Even though this supplies a gendered revision of heroic modernist frontiers, it is not outside the intellectual history of literary modernism. Le Guin's emphasis on community and on craft resembles the radical ideas that accompanied the early formations of literary modernism, when the idea of the "beloved community" included the circles frequented by anthropologists. Furthermore, the modulations on a theme of revolution seem very different if they are not simply assimilated to the East-West conflict posited by the Cold War, but rather traced in their specific sites, in many modernist communities. The Modern School inaugurated in 1916 in New York by a wide-ranging community of radicals, artists, and intellectuals that included Emma Goldman, Ariel and Will Durant, Man Ray, John Dewey, and Leon Trotsky was based on an ideal of learning that was craft-centered and brought adults together with children. Portland, Oregon—home to radicals like C. E. S. Wood (who wrote regularly for *The Masses*) and John Reed *(Ten Days That Shook the World)* and Louise Bryant before it was home to Ursula Le Guin—was another site for a Modern School. Ursula Le Guin was undoubtedly influenced by the international movement of anarchy and the ideas of its philosophers, such as Kropotkin (Philip Smith). She is the inheritor, however, as well of a local western tradition that emerges in different shapes—as, for example, in environmentalism—a tradition without a history partly because the topological element of western American anarchist history goes largely unacknowledged as the other force in the dialectic with international history. Le Guin may sound familiar because she is writing out of a revolutionary history forgotten by being too much gendered and by being too much assimilated to the dominant stories of modernity: of the frontier, of capitalist political economy, and of heroic progress.

Thus one of Le Guin's returns is to a West that is not an abstraction, but a place. There is little doubt that Le Guin's imagination has been profoundly shaped by the forest, the northern California/Oregon/Washington landscape and its history. Those who live in the forest, according to Le Guin, are the strangers who are ourselves, who enlist our identification: green men *(The Word for the World Is Forest)*, explorers in a twilight zone *(The Beginning Place)*, isolates who know the truth *(City of Illusions)*. Her sympathies are not urban (the city houses the bad guys in *Always Coming Home*). But she lives in a city (Portland) and has collaborated on a poetic/photographic book, *On Thurman Street,* that represents the street as a peopled place and a neighborhood. She belongs with the craftsman tradition of socialism and anarchy, and the schoolteacher tradition of the frontier, daily workers having little to do with the high adventure of individual revolution, discovery, or conquest.

One comes home to the mother's perspective, the desire for perpetuating life. The depressive or melancholy aspect of this view fits well with the rainy fertility of northwestern forests: it is melancholy because death exists inside life, which becomes a cycle rather than an adventure, and future history will be, finally, if all turns out well, the same. That life goes on, however, is far from a tragic perspective.

Le Guin gives us many strong women, particularly matriarchs or crones, and not on the male model, either. In several books, she reveals the extent to which we ourselves have always been functioning under matriarchal models as well by telling their familiar stories. This is to say not that she advocates separatism or even matriarchy, but that she resists the idea that patriarchy dominates with a single story. She reveals the woman-centered genealogy of a small town in *Searoad.* The resilience of mothers defines the community of *Always Coming Home.* Even though Earthsea seems to be about the coming of age of boys, it also inserts the mother's narration as ethical teacher or storyteller into the domain of popular fiction for young people. The maternal perspective of its narrator is fully revealed in *Tehanu,* called "The Last Book of Earthsea," a book that is not really for the young. (For those of us who are crones, at least, it may be the best of all, showing wizards in old age, sexually alive, and as parental figures for the next generation.) The maternal frame changes the cultural context to renew a literary anthropology, revealing not something new, but what was there all along, concealed.

The success of the Earthsea books introduces a wobble into the categories of fiction. Theodora Kroeber wondered in her notes to *The Inland Whale* about the status of the oral tradition, with its didactic subjects—"how we came to relegate such material to juvenilia"—not only the myth and story of native California, "a literature cut off in its course," but also the "early Greek myths, the *Arabian Nights,* and Gulliver" (154). Can good fiction be about stories that children and adults might read together? Can it do without the shock of sexual violation? Without the pessimism of defeated men? Can fiction take up the ancient task of the storyteller, to instruct the community? This wobble is not like the shocking incongruities of modernist form. The Earthsea books are quietly located under the containing rubrics of adolescent fiction and fantasy. It is not their departure from literariness that raises questions, but rather their proximity to the literary.

Le Guin reproduces the heroic plot but increasingly puts it into its adolescent place, restoring the context of communal reproduction to the trajectory of individual development, adventure, and change. It is a form of schooling, and a form of ethics.

Clearly, one of the most important conditions of a postmodernism, the path out of the Cold War, assembles around the ecological movement that began as an accompaniment to sixties counterculture. What makes ecocriticism significant in this history is the new situation of discursive logics in which it participates. Literary criticism through the theorizing of language itself and the sense of rhetorical epistemology now works with rather than against science. Science fiction should be its most representative genre. That is, through storytelling we can explore the implications of knowledge, because knowledge always involves a story. Evolution, as Stephen Jay Gould has been trying to show us, must be told differently than the popular representation of man's progressive development from ape to modern citizen. The grand narratives organizing knowledge for modernity are, as Lyotard has it, no longer master. Le Guin's work has helped to develop this postmodern understanding of the relationship between literature and knowledge. Le Guin practices a narrative ecology, with a subject that is displaced from scene to scene. This instruction is topocentric instead of logocentric.[5]

What she has instructed us about has, in other words, a double valence. On the one hand, she participates in the lineage of moral instruction traced by schoolteachers and sentimental writers as well as by those who tell stories for children, a lineage that for most cultures and for most of our own history has served to define the *literary*. Horace said *"ut pictura poesis"*—poetry, like a speaking picture, instructs by giving pleasure. Contemporary uses of the speaking picture have so degraded the "instruction" that only cynicism and critique seem an appropriate response. But the institution of media/entertainment that Theodor Adorno identified with mass culture has failed to standardize reception in a way that would produce a mass movement. It has served, rather, to proliferate differences, to produce the illusion of differentiation as a substitute for knowledge, and so to reproduce the ethic of individualism (or libertarianism) as the only moral direction.

Le Guin participates in the progressive countertradition often upheld in American literary history by women, belabored as "sentimental" during important struggles for power (the American renaissance, modernism). This countertradition passes on the knowledge about how to organize a sense of mutuality and purpose that enables ethical action. Cold War rhetoric used a demand for loyalty rather than the aristocratic imposition of force, and it used liberal institutions and their techniques of surveillance and control to regularize disciplines. Le Guin's subversive teaching advances an ecofeminist ethic not through a totalizing act of persuasion that would include all her work as a single thesis, but through the proliferation of stories.

New Histories of the Hero: Earthsea

> Genre is a useful concept only when used not evaluatively but descriptively. Authors and readers of any genre form a community, with certain shared interests and expectations. Modern poetry is a good example of genre as community. So is science fiction.
>
> —Ursula Le Guin, introduction, *Norton Book of Science Fiction*

Le Guin argues that genre both reflects and defines the relationships within a community. That is, the genre interacts with questions of identity. Thus modern poetry, from her anthropological point of view, represents not the defining model of literariness, but the work of a very specific community. In her introduction to the *Norton Book of Science Fiction,* this point serves to counter the idea that some genres (such as modern poetry) have more value than others (such as science fiction). By implication, the fact that communities are different cannot serve as the basis for claiming some are better than others.

Questioning the modernist use of style to disrupt standardization and convention, Le Guin shows how powerfully literary style can function in the service of communal values and in the exploration of communal identity. Issues of genre that appeared solely as questions of form reappear, then, as questions of morality. In particular, the rupture of conventions appears with a double valence that requires judgment. On the one hand, there is the classic view of rhetorical knowledge: convention reproduces communal wisdom and individual revolts against convention run the risk of unforeseen consequences, of damage to the community, of a destructiveness that is evil. On the other hand, in the romantic view displaced by modernism from personality to language, convention mindlessly repeats the forms appropriate to another time and denies individuality and the possibility of change.

In Le Guin's revisions, convention seems neither "nature" nor the arbitrariness of culture but rather obligation. Le Guin's male heroes encounter ethical dilemmas that make them acknowledge the claims of community. But her female heroes move us past the modernist dilemma to a postmodern sense of how communal discourse might form gendered subjectivity. In the Earthsea trilogy, the boy wizard, Ged, must learn the evil of excessive individuality and self-interest—the temptations of the poet—but the girl, Tenar, must break free from the deathlike constraints of old ritual and ego loss—the dangers of womanhood. *The Dispossessed,* like *The Left Hand of Darkness,* juxtaposes two radically different views of cultural identity and value to raise questions about our most naturalized assumptions about gender and about loyalty. In *Always Coming Home* and *Searoad,* conventions of genre are disrupted to reveal how closely cultural convention is attached to its representation. The disruption of genre shows how our cultural narratives of adventure, purpose, conflict, community, and history are masculinized and arbitrary.

In Earthsea, the overlapping of fantasy and coming-of-age narratives places the question of personal identity within the province of romance, a tradition deeply implicated in the formation of American heroic ideals, at least from the perspective of the Cold War. Richard Chase's *The American Novel and Its Tradition* argued that "Americanness" in fiction is marked by "the element of romance" that incorporates the virtue of what Thoreau called "wildness" in the national imagination (viii). Romance, with its freedom from novelistic realism and its internalizing of conflict, suited Cold War tendencies to locate national history in the psychology of heroes.

In other words, the use of fantasy in the Earthsea trilogy provides continuity rather than challenge to Cold War narratives and the boy's adventure seems well within the parameters of American literary traditions. Bending the imaginary to the service of a comic impulse (as did Mark Twain), Le Guin uses the old stories of feudalism and aristocracy to promote a more democratic, accessible heroism. Earthsea feels like a classic book series for the young in part because the conflicts are familiar and their resolutions seem so exactly what ought to be taught—even, or especially, that the lessons learned are the result of hard experience and not of following the instructions of the elders. Familiar values are confirmed, and that marks the wizard's hard-won wisdom as both elevated and common sense. The use of fantasy, the emphasis on self-discovery—these would appear to combine nostalgia and liberal humanism into something humanistic psychology could endorse, without opening the idea of individuation to critique. Earthsea allegorizes psychic life. It risks falling into the stasis elaborated by a Jungian sense of archetypal forms. (And Le Guin tells us Jung has been an influence.)

However, the Earthsea trilogy also mounts a critique of the dominant Cold War representations, a critique that extends questions about identity and individuation into the larger ecology. Scenes of apprenticeship mark the dominant structure of the Earthsea books and portray Le Guin's understanding of craft knowledge, which she substitutes for harsher economies of truth. Here is the young hero in *A Wizard of Earthsea (WE)* at the beginning of the series, impatient to learn power: "'I haven't learned anything yet!' 'Because you haven't found out what I am teaching,' replied the mage" (*WE* 17). Let the reader be instructed: if the point is to learn something, it will require finding out what Le Guin is teaching. The making of the hero/heroine is analogous to writing a book or creating a work of art, with tropes of mirroring, watching, the imaged self, and wizardry calling attention to the craft. On the one hand, this self-making faces into the Emersonian reflection of American thought; but this making is doubled by craft. The magic requires (like discourse) community. Diction and style call attention to themselves, with slight archaisms of word and syntax. The trilogy opens and ends with the *Deed of Ged,* the "official" legend not written there, a reference to epic high seriousness that makes us understand Ged is a figure in a people's history. This story, however, is the vernacular, the story behind the history—"this is a tale of the time before his fame, before the songs were made" (*WE* 1). At the end, this reminds us that his has been a story unrecorded in legendary history: "In the *Deed of Ged* nothing is told of that voyage nor of Ged's meeting with the shadow, before ever he sailed the Dragon's Run unscathed" (*FS* 183). In accordance with the maternal, domestic space inhabited by the narrator, the books will tell the private story.

A *Wizard of Earthsea* is a tale of how the hero had to give up on fame to do the deed that would bring fame to him. Hubris in this story is not tragic, but a function of adolescence, a stage, a psychology familiar to the most ordinary American reader. Le Guin does not fix identity to a relationship with the Freudian father or the Lacanian phallus in an Oedipal narrative.[6] The woman also could appear—as she does for Kristeva— as a critical witness, a split subject. The point of identity in the Earthsea trilogy is to represent a process that recurs. The relationship between the narrative function and the character of the wizard, Ged, articulates the subject in process. The mother abjected as "shadow" is subsumed by naming, by a version of the psychoanalytic cure. It is not a matter just of putting the male and the female or the semiotic and the symbolic into balance, because that would jettison history and the action of fantasy upon cultural discourse or, to put it another way, claim that the cure stops uncertainty.

The shadow of death rather than the shadow of sexuality appears to represent the most potent unconscious force. The trilogy unfolds under a depressive threat. Twentieth-century writers have associated this problematic of melancholia with the situation of the artist, but also in particular after World War II with the unmourned and unresolved deadliness not only of the war, but also of the Holocaust and the nuclear bomb. The problem of identity has to do not so much with the Oedipal configuration of rivalry and contest over the objects of desire, but with the developmentally earlier crisis of loss and sublimation, of good and bad, attending entry into language. On the level of the individual, of course, the problems of melancholia have been psychoanalytically associated with feminine issues. Freud thought that girls were especially liable to suffer from an inability to separate from the mother or to mourn.

In Le Guin's trilogy, the inability to accept death becomes the source of an evil that threatens to destroy everyone. Ged pursues the figure of the shadow, hunts dragons along the way—but the pursuit of danger is only a distraction from the larger enemy. "At least he sought this danger of his own free will; and the nearer he came to it the more sure he was that, for this time at least, for this hour perhaps before his death, he was free. The shadow dared not follow him into a dragon's jaws" (*WE* 85).

Shape-changing is the danger for the artist, whose openness to the unconscious and capacity for mimicry, masquerade, and impersonation may overwhelm the ego's ability to maintain integrity within a social context— the wizard can turn himself into a hawk, but he nearly loses the human: "The price of the game . . . is the peril of losing one's self, playing away the truth. The longer a man stays in a form not his own, the greater this peril" (*WE* 125). Ged calls the fatal shadow by his own name, curing the alienation and projection. "Ged had neither lost nor won but, naming the shadow of his death with his own name, had made himself whole: a man" (*WE* 180–81). The recognition scene that in tragedy leads to death opens out here, as in the psychoanalytic project, into life.

The difficulty of writing about a girl's development seems evident in the split plot of the second volume in the trilogy, *The Tombs of Atuan* (*TA*). Ged appears in a heroic mode to help Tenar escape her fate as the so-called resurrection of a no-name priestess, the "Eaten One." Tenar eventually rebels, not because she wants adventure and independence, but because her duties underground are like being buried alive. "Her boredom rose so strong in her sometimes that it felt like terror: it took her by the throat" (*TA* 31). Far from enabling her to become a stronger person, her position as the priestess of the ancient powers implicates her in something impersonal and dark. Her servant, Manan, says, "You're mistress of all that. . . . The silence, and the dark," and her duties include death— "the sacrifice of certain prisoners." A bizarre calculus enables Tenar to find her way in the dark of the labyrinth and caves by counting turns. It is like the underground knowledge of prisoners. Representing that deeply conservative—and deadly—force that is earth itself, she ought to sacrifice Ged when he comes to the Tombs searching for the Ring. But when Ged arrives in her caves, he enlists her empathy and her help in finding the Ring, and thereby brings down ruin on all the Tombs of Atuan and the ancient rituals she has been conscripted to perpetuate. What kind of story is this?

This is not the story of a prince of fairy tales liberating the heroine into sexuality. Ged appears in the guise, rather, of the asexual hero of Westerns whose mission serves a larger cause. He binds the young Tenar to help him and then abandons her to her own freedom. His words might have come out of a cowboy film in the fifties:

> I go where I am sent. I follow my calling. It has not yet let me stay in any land for long. . . . I do what I must do. Where I go, I must go alone. So long as you need me, I'll be with you in Havnor. And if you ever need me again, call me. I will come. I would come from my grave if you called me, Tenar! But I cannot stay with you. (*TA* 151)

Tenar feels abandoned: "Now he didn't need her. . . . He would not stay with her. He had fooled her, and would leave her desolate" (*TA* 155). Even though Ged helps free Tenar from an extremely claustrophobic situation, a living death as the "Eaten One" serving the old gods, he does not replace that institutional apparatus with what would amount to an alternative mastery. (We learn in *Tehanu* that Tenar finally marries a rather patriarchal farmer, has children, and only gets together with Ged after her husband has died and Ged has lost his powers.) The male hero must find himself within a maternal narrative. Indeed, Ged himself gets to participate in a heroic venture here only with the aid of Tenar's empathy. However, the problem of the hero in the Cold War appears here as this awkward lack of empathy for Tenar on the part of Ged—and her typical, adolescent response that she has been abandoned.

The gap between individual and community called alienation during the Cold War is felt by the girl, Tenar, but not by Ged. Does the narrator believe Tenar ought to use her freedom to become more fully individual? What about the fact that girls could not be wizards? Or does the narrator believe the reader ought to notice how unsatisfactory is the resolution for Tenar, although the volume ends with the triumphant return of the Ring to Havnor? Is Tenar a representative of the ordinary person, caught up in heroic narratives but not identified by them? Tolkien's Frodo did not improve his life by his involvement with the fate of a ring and a people. *The Tombs of Atuan* occupies a middle ground between a story that seems to be about heroic individuals and the third volume, where the triumph is for Earthsea and not for Ged.

The Tombs of Atuan appeared at a time (1971) when humanistic psychology, influenced by Jung, argued that growth and individuation were the primary issues for individuals—taking responsibility for one's own life, realizing one's potential, and so forth. The assumption that the individual was free and responsible was central, institutional authority seemed not only fallible (both sides wrong in Vietnam), but open to individual challenge, and some therapies took the idea of personal choice to great—one might say hyperbolic—extremes. "Existentialist" therapists might demand of those who were crippled why they chose to cripple themselves, or of those who had suffered from an abusive childhood, why they chose such parents.

The Earthsea trilogy in general resists humanistic and existential versions of a psychic life. The narrator of this book does not hold Tenar entirely responsible for her own fate, nor for the fate of the two men who died in the caverns while she was ostensibly in charge of such sacrifices. When Tenar sees a chance, she makes the ethical decision to help her next prisoner, Ged, go free. She becomes amnesiac when she is taken by the priestesses and trained to become the nameless one. The decisive moment in her willingness to violate that training and help Ged is accompanied dramatically by his calling her "Tenar" (*TA* 108). She remembers, then, her identity, her name. The scene enforces the presumption that names have significance. It is by becoming the nameless one that Tenar is allied with death. Names root a fragile identity in the order of things.

In *The Farthest Shore*, the final book of the trilogy, the relationship of identity to death becomes central. What makes people lose their names, their knowledge of the true names of things, their craft, and their magic is the hole that opens the barriers between life and death. The antagonist, the errant wizard Cob, lost his name and identity by trying to do away with death. Ged tells him at the end, "You have given everything for nothing. And so now you seek to draw the world to you, all that light and life you lost, to fill up your nothingness. But it cannot be filled" (*FS* 180). "You chose despair" (*FS* 187).

For psychoanalysis, this refusal of separation—denial—might be connected to the refusal of mourning, and its subsequent disabling of the entry into language.[7] Since speech depends upon separating from the mother and refinding her in language, a failure to separate also impairs speech. So depressive speech may be disconnected from affect, or the depressed person may lose speech altogether. The absence of a king/father accompanies the lack of separation from the mother. Ged and Arren pursue the villain into the land of death; Ged must expend the whole of his magic powers to close the hole between life and death, and the chief task for the young Arren is to help the archmage. Published in 1972, the third volume of the Earthsea trilogy is not a story designed to encourage the sixties generation in their rebellion against those over thirty: Arren is a young hero who must apprentice with his mentor to earn the kingship that his heritage points to. The restoration of "the balance" puts Arren on the legendary throne that has been vacant for eight hundred years, as well as restoring true names and wizardry. It is, in other words, a restoration of proper order and significance.

The principle of tact called "the balance" governs fitness in Le Guin's

Earthsea. Survival depends not upon the "fitness" of competitive individuals, but fitness to the difficult challenge of social relations. One danger of strangeness is the possibility of violating propriety. Ged says to Tenar: "I am a stranger, and a trespasser. I do not know your ways, nor the courtesies due the Priestess of the Tomb. I am at your mercy, and I ask your pardon if I offend you" (*TA* 88). Bringing together the heroic narrative represented by Ged and the more archaic female coming-of-age story is like overlapping two cultures. Tenar is the "Eaten One," and in thrall to the "nameless ones," even though she is a priestess. The metaphor provokes. She has been consumed by the institution and its ritual, in an enclosure without men or sex, with the ceremony in the dark. Ged brings light, freedom, and another kind of violation. This juxtaposition of strangers enables Le Guin to complicate what a "balance" might look like, unsettling the conventional hierarchy of male over female by an anthropological comparativism. She will use the analogy of culture and gender again, in *The Left Hand of Darkness,* to help her inquiry, which I take to be this: given that human solidarity and moral relationship depend upon the maintenance of balance and fitness—an intuitive restraint—how to take into account the radical strangeness of other people and other cultures?

Even though it seems that Le Guin has given the spotlight in Earthsea to her male heroes, the fact that the heroic quest turns back upon the problem of propriety feminizes that trajectory, placing the narrative largely before the Oedipal moment of competition. What is proper to oneself and to others? In French, *propre* means both "one's own" and "clean": Kristeva writes, in *Powers of Horror,* of the way the "clean and proper self" emerges out of struggles with abjection, prior to identity. As the infant begins to make the first distinctions between self and mother, the ambiguous material associated with the mother/child—belonging clearly neither to the one nor the other such as excrement, milk, sweat—becomes abjected, dirty, horrifying, and separate from the clean and proper self that comes into view by that very separation. Ged's struggles with the "shadow" are filled with the kind of indistinct horror associated with the abject. In English, the overlapping categories of "property" and "propriety" suggest how ownership is implicated with good manners. These define proper relationship by casting away strangeness and/or by hardening the boundaries to reify identity, even to make it marketable. The propriety that circulates in Earthsea, however, depends upon reconciliation through naming. The performance of naming regulates social order through every encounter.

Finally, the question of balance and propriety is writerly. Ged says the mage philosophy with respect to acts requires a sense of the proper nature of things: "On every act the balance of the whole depends . . . insofar as we have power over the world and over one another, we must *learn* to do what the leaf and the whale and the wind do of their own nature" (*FS* 66). And as mentor to the future king, he advises:

> If there were a king over us all again and he sought counsel of a mage, as in the days of old, and I were that mage, I would say to him: My lord, do nothing because it is righteous or praiseworthy or noble to do so; do nothing because it seems good to do so; do only that which you must do and which you cannot do in any other way. (*FS* 67)

This counsel is to behave like this writer—to prolong the moment of contemplation and the distance between decisions, to refuse the sensationalism of a climactic plot.

Le Guin's most signal opposition to our culture is this resistance to invention. It is a resistance to modernity and a resistance to seeing change as the necessary resolution to conflict. A revisionary attitude to stories informs her writing, even of fantasy, but it is far from the well-known gambits of the avant-garde because it does not have "make it new" as its goal. At the level of story, it depends upon the primacy of recurrence rather than conflict/resolution. Her science fiction writing as future history even inscribes this resistance within the very genre of modern invention, and her restraint about the power of magic also goes against the grain of fantasy. The mage as the wizard who refuses to invent would refuse to participate in the innovative extremities of capitalism. To read the notion of the "true name" correctly, then, we must refer it to the sense of appropriateness to one's proper self but not to anything that escapes mortality or uncertainty. Meaning is propped on nothing but returns. As it is said in *The Farthest Shore:* "There is no safety, and there is no end. The word must be heard in silence; there must be darkness to see the stars. The dance is always danced above the hollow place, above the terrible abyss" (*FS* 121).

The Earthsea trilogy enters into dialogue—as does literature itself, and psychoanalysis in the twentieth century—with a theological project. Taking up the roles of writer, therapist, and critic together, the narrator's desire to explore moral instruction accompanies the story at every moment, and with the binaries of good and evil, light and dark at play at every level, from plot to scene to metaphor. Eastern ideas of yin and yang have deeply influenced Le Guin's thinking. The binaries of light/dark have such strong attachments to Judeo-Christian traditions of interpretation that the binarism may throw readers into familiar dilemmas. Sacvan Bercovitch argued, in *The American Jeremiad,* that a claim to reconcile opposition symbolically defined the nationalistic ideology of American individualism. The narrator's ongoing refusal of conventional resolutions drives the plot—where will the evil be located? "There's a center to this bad luck," says the mage in *The Farthest Shore* (83), and he will find it at last in the one who desires immortality. However, at the same time that a spiritual valence informs the writing, affirming distinctions, the fantasy of effective instruction battles absolutism—and the Western reliance upon a religious intuition that would deny how moral distinctions depend upon teaching, upon specific historical conformations, and upon culture. These dependencies are resolved not through attachments to the set of good and evil contraries embodied in mythical conventions, but through the act of naming. The performative function of writing therefore modifies imaginary absolutes, including the absolutism of national reconciliation.

Although Le Guin provides us with an ecological fiction that has benefited ecofeminism, she does not allegorize through symbols. The earth itself provides an image not only of natural propriety, but also of evil absolutism in its very stones and rocks, especially in the story of Tenar, the young priestess.

> "The Earth is beautiful, and bright, and kindly, but that is not all. The Earth is also terrible, and dark, and cruel." There are sharks in the sea, and there is cruelty in men's eyes. And where men worship these things and abase themselves before them, there evil breeds; there places are made in the world where darkness gathers, places given over wholly to the Ones whom we call Nameless, the ancient and holy Powers of the Earth before the light, the powers of the dark, of ruin, of madness. (*TA* 118)

This indictment of the amorality of the earth, or of nature, repeats some of the negative conventions associated with the ancient matriarchies. It might seem unexpected in an author often connected with ecofeminism— it seems to critique some of the principles of ecocriticism in the name of "the light," to privilege a masculine sanity over a feminine dark madness: to privilege an ideal of humanism that Robinson Jeffers, for example, specifically countered. Nietzsche made use of such collections of binary images when he distinguished the Apollonian from the Dionysiac (the earth would be Dionysiac and also feminine); Hélène Cixous returned to binary structures in "The Laugh of the Medusa" to point out how strongly the paradigms mark gendered hierarchies, particularly a masculine reason and a feminine irrationality.

In her later considerations about the idea of utopia, Le Guin said, "Our civilization is now so intensely yang that any imagination of bettering its injustices or eluding its self-destructiveness must involve a reversal"—"go yinward" (*Dancing* 90). A yin utopia would, like Atuan's awful tombs, favor the dark and cold, but seeing this other side of the "light" would not involve a simple capitulation to the "Old Powers": "It would be dark, wet, obscure, weak, yielding, passive, participatory, circular, cyclical, peaceful, nurturant, retreating, contracting, and cold" (*Dancing* 90). The later statement resonates with radical feminist arguments for peace, such as Helen Caldicott's *Missile Envy: The Arms Race and Nuclear War*, and with friendlier representations of matriarchal religions.

The Earthsea trilogy balances on the hope for renewal beyond the Cold War. At critical moments it seems to resolve Cold War antimonies in the Cold War manner. Earthsea echoes the gesture of internalization that Thomas Schaub points out. Evil is read in its effects, or traces—disease, depression, or despair. Le Guin's acknowledged interest in Jungian theories must have influenced the way she uses the term "shadow." What Ged conjures in his pride as the aftermath of a spell, like the aftermath of a terrible accident, is a lump of shadow "the size of a young child" (*WE* 61). "It is the shadow of your arrogance, the shadow of your ignorance, the shadow you cast" (66). In a larger sense, the very quality of the human produces evil as well as good, precisely by the tendency to extremity that threatens balance: "When we crave power over life—endless wealth, unassailable safety, immortality—then desire becomes greed. And if knowledge allies itself to that greed, then comes evil" (*FS* 35). And it seems as if the three books are stories about individuals who learn to mitigate extremity, without much reference to the late sixties–early seventies environment of polarization and struggle around Vietnam, equal rights, and the development of new lifestyles. This retreat from extremity does not separate Earthsea from the inheritors of Cold War criticism. For example, Murray Krieger, in *The Tragic Vision*, proposed that an ethics provided the only response to post-Nietzschean heroics of inhuman belief. More recently, Wayne Booth has advocated a resistance to dogma through humanist rhetoric.

The Earthsea books, however, imagine a different coming-of-age, another means of bringing a new generation to power. Shifting the center of gravity from the (Oedipal) scene of rebellion so familiar in the sixties to the scene of reciprocity that grounds sociality, they elaborate a fantasy that the young need the older generation and the knowledge of wizardry to come into power. They write postmodernism as a continuity, not a break. The journey ends in return, a return in part like the restoration of craft knowledge through apprenticeship. Le Guin's imaginative generational continuity and the conduct of respect contrast with isolated individuation.

Knowledge and truth in the Earthsea trilogy must be crafted and the beautiful trick of the books themselves prove the power of such fantasy. The wizards depend upon knowing the "true names" of things. Such power resurrects the literary dreams handed down from symbolist poets and evokes the curative medicine of psychoanalysts, with their assertion of the material magic of words sounded to musicate thought. The words produce *anamnesis,* unforgetting. Ferdinand de Saussure believed that there was word magic—"paragrammes"—in Old Latin texts. As Le Guin wrote in the sixties, French poststructuralists such as Barthes, Derrida, and Kristeva were taking up the inheritance from the symbolists and Saussure and rethinking the power of material language to destabilize the logical absolutism of structural linguistics and metaphysics.

The chaste awakening into knowledge, creativity, and power associated with the art magic of Earthsea turns out to have a startling omission: it leaves out sex. Perhaps that is what allows it to maintain the maternal quality of the teacher/student apprenticeship. In *The Tombs of Atuan,* however, Ged's incursion into the caves governed by Tenar sometimes makes sorcery sound like the power of sexual attraction: "She was afraid of his power, the arts he had used to enter the Undertomb, the sorcery that kept that light burning" (*TA* 79). The power struggle between Tenar and Ged puts his fate into her hands, meant to make sacrifices. He is saved not by wizardry, but by her boredom and sense of "the grinding meanness of their common life" (*TA* 93). He is "the prisoner: the dark man, practicer of dark arts, bound in iron and locked in stone, waiting for her to come or not to come, to bring him water and bread and life, or a knife and a butcher's bowl and death, just as the whim took her" (*TA* 93). There is a kind of Gothic sexual seduction in the opportunity to act out upon the hero the sadism that has been taught to her. She chooses restraint, chastity, or submission, depending on how you see it, and she also thereby chooses to escape from the erotic structures of the Gothic.

Earthsea presents several kinds of endings. They suggest the intertwining of genre and gender identity in Le Guin's development. *A Wizard of Earthsea* returns to the question of the legendary hero. The story of Ged's encounter with the shadow is a story prior to heroism that will define the heroic without scapegoating, not a public story, not—we are told—preserved in *The Deed of Ged* or any other song. The story of Ged becomes more and more like the story of Tenar because it leaves the heroism of the adolescent to go on to a life beyond the heroic. This is true even though the Ged of *The Farthest Shore* has apparently grown up and become archmage. When he expended his power in the struggle to close the hole in the world, his chaste singlemindedness and adventuring became a prelude to ordinary life. *The Farthest Shore* ends with Ged's retreat to his home. In *Tehanu,* the last book of Earthsea (not part of the trilogy, but published eighteen years after *The Farthest Shore,* in 1990, and meant for adult audiences), the exhausted hero and the too-domestic heroine at last come together to make a more modest, a sexually mature kind of life, with its continuing requirement for heroic effort. Now the capacity for starting all over again that was required of the young girl, Tenar, becomes a capacity for renewal that characterizes Ged, Tenar, Tehanu, and the changing writer herself, Le Guin. After they rescue the abused child who turns out to be Tehanu, the child of the dragon, the ex-celebrities Ged and Tenar retreat to their garden—like Thoreau and after him the Yeats of "Innisfree"—to "rows of beans and the scent of the bean flowers" (252). It's another genre.

Intellectual History and *The Dispossessed*

> "You cannot buy the Revolution. You cannot make the Revolution. You can only be the Revolution. It is in your spirit, or it is nowhere."
> —Shevek's speech, Ursula Le Guin, *The Dispossessed*

The Dispossessed evokes the Cold War antagonism of East and West, and it focuses on the crisis for scientists that the history produced. It is of particular interest for my purposes here because it takes up the themes of the Cold War and alters them radically by plunging them into the solvent of a home perspective. It is the story of a scientist, Shevek, on the postrevolutionary anarchist planet of Anarres, who must go into exile on the rival (capitalist) planet, Urras, to gain the freedom to pursue his scientific discovery, the Theory of Simultaneity. The anarchist scientist seems not a representative Russian, finally, after all, but rather someone more like those persecuted in the United States. One thinks of Robert Oppenheimer or Linus Pauling.

In *The Dispossessed*, Le Guin makes a critique of American Cold War culture through a science fiction not only about two different political systems on two separate planets, but also about the nature of home. A comparison of two worlds in the future lets her put the ideological values into a dialectical relationship. After an uprising, anarchists had left the planet Urras—which resembles the Earth of the Cold War—to establish a colony on a moon, Anarres. They live under marginal conditions, with scarcity and the threat of famine, but with strong commitments they have been successful through several generations. Anarres resembles Israel more than the Soviet Union in certain respects: the colonists have had to start with empty hands in a desert, with a new language, and have arranged their lives like the communal kibbutz. Furthermore, the suffering they have endured has brought them together and made work for the good of all a strong communal value.

Although the original world is corrupt with power struggles, the anarchist community is not ideal: it imposes onerous constraints on intellectual freedom. We cannot put Le Guin on the side of Cold War communism. Her utopia/dystopia is located, and limited, precisely by somewhere. "The rationalist utopia is a power trip," she has said (*Dancing* 87). In this book, the anarchist utopia escapes the worst problems of Soviet nationalism but falls victim to the unacknowledged power of social opinion.

The Dispossessed locates *home* not in opposition to exile, not on any kind of native soil, but within a diaspora. The anarchist world that is the home of the scientist, Shevek, is where the anarchists built their community in exile. In *The Dispossessed,* the cycle of exile and return does not simply continue the dialectic of private and public, domestic and economic spheres: it replicates neither the nuclear family nor the institutions of nuclear defense. Shevek is not a capitalist. He is not, as a "creative spirit," in solidarity with other workers either. The modernist intellectual—expatriate, exiled—occupies a place like Anarres, here literally a place of estrangement. Even the sexual mores, with their easy acceptance of free love, are modernist: Shevek and Takver become unusual for wishing to live as man and wife, entering into a familial "bond" promising monogamy. Anarres resists the erotic consumerism of a mass culture. It is more like a wasteland than like the fertile landscapes of the romantic poets; enforcing asceticism, it is also purer, without excess. It is a mental landscape, sparely furnished not only by necessity, but also by preference. A modernist architectural ideal defines this place and this social web and this culture, produced out of critique, scarcity, alienation, and estrangement but—precisely because of that suffering—the more beloved for it. Home in this book neither possesses nor is possessed; it is precisely the topos of the dispossessed.

"Home" in *The Dispossessed* is a return to the beloved community of modernism. Instead of reading *The Dispossessed* as an allegory of the two worlds of communism and capitalism, therefore, I am going to examine what it implies about the dilemma of intellectuals, as the Cold War solidified it. The anarchist world of Anarres embodies not only the desert landscape of T. S. Eliot's *The Waste Land*, but also a version of the modernist utopia imagined by a certain significant intellectual community throughout the twentieth century. Elsewhere, in *Sentimental Modernism*, I have argued that the political figure implied by modernist style, and embodied by Emma Goldman, was *anarchy,* the rupture of conventions. The modernist community associated with Greenwich Village before World War I (and before the Revolution linked communism to the Soviet system) endorsed a politics and a cultural life very much like that described by Le Guin for Anarres. Modernism specifically reacted against the rise of middle class excess and consumerist values, anchored in a domestic life that normalized and restricted sexuality. If the "beloved community" never succeeded in the wider culture, nevertheless the formation of intellectuals as part of the rising professional-managerial class

some of its nineteenth-cen-
ges. When the adult Shevek
it "rebirth," and Rulag is
"touched and struck some-
ce, a place walled in, where
ss," and he refuses her and
ation of why she was gone
ything about the culture de-
have kept Shevek with her
contact is essential" and an
e children move away into
re four—Shevek's own little
Shevek's rejection of Rulag
ss sympathetic, as a power-
ffers no support for the po-
therhood, much debated in
as published.

agments shared by intellec-
all-too-familiar markers of
nd uniformity of Cold War
f the very scientific inquiry
d realignment of Cold War
ce of a postmodernity, but
nues many elements of the
t necessarily to enforce dif-
is characterized by a dual-
ons to dissolve the either/or
ialectical structure of chap-
rn frame such a reading.
ar icon of a wall, a symbol
narres is the only free place
hich side you are on. Later
ms of a wall and that the
appears as the key to dis-
olved when Shevek solves
(225). The wall had been
ty. Shevek's project is not
an, perhaps in a sense ex-
oubleness of time as both

e arrow, the running
o progress, or direc-
r the cycle, without

was associated with certain repetitions of that anarchic culture: its advocacy of sexual and intellectual freedom, its critique of capitalism and support of exploited groups, its preference for an ascetic, spare decor, its association with "Modern School" models of progressive education.

Shevek, I take it, is not just a figure for science; he also represents the writer. Indeed, he represents the way, for Le Guin, that the scientist and the writer might do the same thing. Scientific discovery is in certain respects like writing. Shevek's greatest insight about his Theory of Simultaneity is that he does not need to assure its certainty in order to theorize it. He can write it, as one would write fiction, *assuming* its truth before proving it. In this he follows the "stochastic method" devised by Linus Pauling, who pioneered the method of building hypothetical models of the chemical bonds and then using empirical methods to verify the correctness of the models. Francis Crick recently said he and James Watson adopted the method from Pauling to theorize the double-helix structure of DNA (Pauling's own model of DNA was a triple helix at that time). Furthermore, Tom Hager, biographer of Pauling, said he himself used this "stochastic method" to write the life.[8]

Like the writer, the scientist needs more freedom than law or social convention will easily allow. Shevek works in a state of isolated concentration and intensity that is at least asocial, if not entirely antisocial. Like Jo of *Little Women* and Le Guin herself, he gives himself over to what—if it were not feminized—would be the claims of "genius." Le Guin quotes Louisa May Alcott:

> When the writing fit came on, she gave herself up to it with entire abandon. . . . Sleep forsook her eyes, meals stood untasted, day and night were all too short. . . . The divine afflatus usually lasted a week or two, and then she emerged from her vortex, hungry, sleepy, cross, or despondent. (*Dancing* 215)

This description of the artist working is, Le Guin asserts, "the real thing—domesticated. . . . This passion of work and this happiness . . . are fitted without fuss into a girl's commonplace life at home" (215). As she goes on to point out, asserting that a woman can write *and* participate in a family life makes the whole question of artistic work more complex.

Le Guin's scientist, Shevek, also participates in a family life, though with terrible yearlong gaps inflicted by the Anarres system of work. That participation in another life is just what rescues Shevek from the dangers of becoming a figure of romantic genius like the libertarian heroes of Ayn Rand. Even though Shevek comes close to asserting the right to selfishness of creative spirits (and the narrator comes close to agreeing), his social ties to family and loyalties to community remain another kind of motive, which both interrupts and validates his work. *The Dispossessed*

raises the question of intellectuals together with a certain (
roic individualism, particularly as it can be turned into a p
ture, supporting capitalism. When Shevek finds himself a
on the other planet, Urras, he worries about his theories |

The most painful conflict in the book as in the life of c
tuals, however, comes from challenging received wisdom.
associated itself with the "new" and with "change," of c
avowed the ways that the new depends upon a continua
The Dispossessed is full of passages that fervently support
argues that Anarres is a utopia, in fact, only to the exte
tains its society as a "permanent revolution" (142). How
talist and communist versions of revolution turn out to
The narrative engine of the book contrasts two versions
a critique of the way Shevek is treated as abnormal, dis
on Anarres—as too individualist for the collective—and
disease of individualist consumerist excess on Urras.

The discourse of purification comes and goes in the tex
with an intensity that does not continue and may, in sc
later contradicted or disavowed. Shevek wants to tell th
out loud about their "shit," but we later hear from the
Terra that Urras is Paradise. The modernist desire for cl
trajectory of Shevek away from Anarres, but the desire f
for social justice, for family, and for home shapes the ;
as narrative intervals. Instead of learning what is wro
for change, the reader learns, through repetition, that
lates and wanes. The desire for change is not allowed t

It comes particularly close, however, in the conflict
research and communal dogma. While the anarchist p
position from which to see the flaws in Western civil
emerge as a utopia in the chapters devoted to descr
life there, and the barriers (walls) to his work and h
to his departure. Shevek makes a complicated hero
the conditions of the Cold War. Like a woman, he is
he goes. This is partly because his extreme scientif
social order, especially one that forbids hierarchy. M
can be counted on to see episodes dramatized from
ticularly when his desire for scientific discovery is
sympathetic audience from the planet Urras might.
spective, the anarchist world looks more like a dy
community. Annares is not sympathetic to inventio
himself does not finally agree with our perspective
reader will be to understand why.

The anarchist society on Anarres operates acco
tices that impose considerable suffering on the inve

comes first" (100)—motherhood takes bac
tury religious connotations in several passa
comes back to life after an illness, he call
there—but realizing who she is evokes pain
thing very deep in Shevek's being, a dark pl
it reverberated back and back in the darkn
her offer of friendship (97). Rulag's explar
during his childhood does not contradict an
scribed on Anarres, and she claims indeed t
during the early years, "when the individual
"affectional beginning" is established. All t
the communal dormitories by the time they
daughter, for instance. Still, Le Guin present
very persuasively and later makes her even l
ful figure who opposes his work. The text o
sition of feminists who chose work over mo
the sensational press at the time the book w

This book collects not only the utopian fr
tuals and artists, but also, as fragments, the
the Cold War. The hypermasculine certainty
knowledge breaks apart under the pressure (
it pretended to support. This fragmenting ar
categories may be thought of as the appearar
like the postmodern everywhere it also cont
Cold War modern. The effect of pastiche is n
ferent ways of reading. If the Cold War logic
ism that refuses dialectic, then the textual acti
into a both/and are especially significant. The
ters and the doubled plot of absence and retu

The book opens with exile and the Cold W
repeated then throughout the book. Whether A
in the universe or a prison camp depends on w
we find that Shevek has grown up with drea
primal number, written on a stone at its base
solve it. The recurring puzzle of the wall is s
his theoretical inquiry: "The wall was down"
the scientific absolutism that required certair
only like quantum physics, it is also Nietzsche
cluded by Cold War modernity. It asserts the
sequence and simultaneity:

So then time has two aspects. There is th
river, without which there is no change,
tion, or creation. And there is the circle

which there is chaos, meaningless succession of instants, a world without clocks or seasons or promises. (*Dispossessed* 180)

The characteristics of Le Guin's "Simultaneity" suggest, of course, quantum theory: the contradiction of seeing light simultaneously as particle and as wave. It might also remind us of the description Julia Kristeva, drawing on Nietzsche, would elaborate several years later in "On Women's Time": "As for time, female subjectivity would seem to provide a specific measure that essentially retains repetition and eternity from among the multiple modalities of time known through the history of civilizations" (191).

In Le Guin's text, Shevek addresses a businessman who objects to such doubleness: "'You can't assert two contradictory statements about the same thing' . . . 'one of these "aspects" is real, the other's simply an illusion'" (180). Rather than acknowledge the postmodern both/and of Sequentiality and Simultaneity, the businessman reaffirms the either/or logic of Cold War knowledge. Kristeva's discussion, showing how Sequentiality or linear time, together with the linearity of language, has been "men's" time, and Simultaneity "women's" time, clarifies the way this objection might use gendered categories as a way to stabilize a hierarchical foundationalism.

This foundationalism exists on both worlds in *The Dispossessed*, and so Shevek is a kind of hero of postmodernity who does battle with the intellectual oppression of the Cold War. Le Guin knows the usual dismissals of any attempt to challenge the either/or binary. Shevek has to fight for intellectual freedom, and it is the freedom to assert a new idea. Academics must shudder with familiarity reading Sabul's critique rejecting Shevek's book—a rejection that effectively prevents its publication:

> That Sequency Physics is the highroad of chronosophical thought in the Odonian Society has been a mutually agreed principle since the Settlement of Anarres. Egoistic divagation from this solidarity of principle can result only in sterile spinning of impractical hypotheses without social organic utility, or repetition of the superstitious-religious speculations of the irresponsible hired scientists of the Profit States of Urras. (192)

This sounds at first like the kind of ideological censorship practiced only by the Soviet Union (the insistence on political correctness that marked Lysenkoism). However, the connection with nationalism, the insistence on principle that is in fact just consensus, the charge of impracticality, and the dismissal of a rival idea as "superstitious-religious" all characterize elements of American intellectual life as well—and in the book, they also show up on Urras, where it is a businessman who makes these objections to Shevek. Le Guin knows the phrases well: "the fact is," "fun for you theorists, maybe, but it has no practical application, no relevance to real life," "we're not babies, we're rational men." "Is your Simultaneity some kind of mystical regressivism?" (*Dispossessed* 178–79). Shevek encounters the kind of resistance to his science that women writers have experienced. If modernists tried to silence women writers by calling them "sentimental," the agents of a modernist economy try to silence Shevek by calling him mystical.

The most important conflict in the book is over this censorship of intellectual life. The representation of the conflict is both modern and postmodern, because it is narrated in the agonistic mode, with a male hero encountering and defeating his opposition, at the same time that it promotes a postmodern double consciousness. Furthermore, the kind of opposition and censorship that Shevek encounters presents itself as the good and the true; it is he who is isolated as an exceptional child, who feels out of step, guilty. The processes of ideology only gradually appear as normalizations, conventions, custom, and public opinion. Le Guin is willing to be critical of Soviet communism in this book, but it is on these grounds, that it doesn't see itself. Shevek finds socialism on the other world, and Chifoilisk, like a good Marxist, tells him "your habit of approaching everybody as a person, an individual, won't do here, it won't work! You have got to understand the powers behind the individuals." Shevek replies: "You fear we might bring back the revolution, the old one, the real one, the revolution for justice which you began and then stopped halfway" (*Dispossessed* 111). The real enemy here is the reification of a revolutionary process. And the real hero is not just Shevek, but the community he—however odd—feels himself to represent. The individual and the society function analogically as subjects. So the solution to the conflict comes about when the individual and the society put this subject on trial, making it function as a "subject in process."

The Dispossessed returns to the intellectual environment of Greenwich Village before World War I and Wood's Hole before the atomic bomb. It renews the utopian aspiration to combine solidarity and community with a technological avant-garde. Perhaps it is also reminiscent of the days in the thirties when a group of intellectuals that included Alfred and Theodora Kroeber gathered for "Stammtisch" in the hills of Berkeley:

> Among the Saturday night regulars were Arthur Ryder the Sanskritist and Robert Oppenheimer the physicist. . . . He became Oppenheimer's "guru," and he taught him Sanskrit— the language, its poetry, and its ancient wisdom. Obviously, these early discussions of cultural evolution were slanted steeply Eastward. . . . Those were the years when we dreamed of a

world at peace, when the Eastern contemplative way seemed to some of us a possible twentieth-century way. We were, I suppose, the doves of the depression in our Innocent Bohemia. (*Alfred Kroeber* 236)

The Dispossessed advocates a "permanent revolution" that ought to encourage new thought, "the power of change, the essential function of life" (267). Reading the anarchic culture of Anarres as a representation of the intellectual class, I see that Le Guin's critique of the academy here goes beyond a critique of its aristocratic egotisms. She demonstrates how the censorship of ideas arises from the operations of power in institutions, no matter how liberal or anarchic or socialist. The banality and cowardice of the average and of public opinion can be found in the heart of the intellectual community. Modernism constructed itself in part in opposition to mass culture, which was accused of philistinism and banality. What Shevek must fight on Anarres, however, is not the excremental excess of the other world, but philistinism and banality within the highest circles of science. If the adolescent hero of *The Wizard of Earthsea* found his shadow within, the anarchic society on Anarres similarly finds itself shadowed by the worst kind of intellectual oppression, from within.

More subtle than a simple reprise of the arguments about the two sides of the Cold War, *The Dispossessed* takes account of the dispossessed history of anarchy, progressivism, civil rights, feminism, and peace activism as well as communism in the United States. The American Left might well see its own painful history in the mirror of Anarres—its exile and its internal struggles. The heroism of Shevek turns out to depend not only on defying the constraints of his own community on Anarres, but also on returning: he risks being stoned to death by his neighbors at each crossing of the wall. Shevek may remind us of Robert Oppenheimer and more widely of other Cold War scientists such as Linus Pauling who played unexpectedly heroic roles pursuing the free exchange of knowledge. What does not enter into the book is the tragedy of nuclear physics. Shevek never has to think about his theory being used to invent destructive weapons. Instead, the time theory will lead to the production of the *ansible,* a tool for universal communication. Since the ansible is not inherently destructive, unlike the bomb, Shevek has only to worry about not giving one side undue advantage.

According to Victor Turner's antitheses, as a scientist and a man of reason, Shevek might be expected to be attracted to a culture with its legal and political institutions claiming to be based on cognition, structure, and classification. However, this narrative shows why liberal intellectuals should not have resolved the antitheses by choosing the hypermasculinity of Cold War institutions. The alternating chapters' juxtaposition of memory and critique enlists the rhetorical powers of literary language to persuade us that *communitas* ought to have a strong hold on Shevek. The storytelling function passes on the communal wisdom as personal experience. *Enargeia*, or description, embodies Shevek's nonlinguistic, sensuous attachments to his past. This nostalgia also makes claims about the significance of the embodied, existential life framed by art and religion. Nostalgia in this book makes connections between community and a politics that is not reactionary. At a time when the American Left was splitting radically over the difference between lifestyle politics (the counterculture) and political action, and feminism was emerging out of and in reaction to the rationalized sexism of the Left, Le Guin's book assumes what poststructuralist theorists from Foucault to Judith Butler would eventually argue: that ideology works in the words *and* in the body to articulate cultural possibilities. There is no outside to ideology. A visit to another planet offers the advantage of estrangement but not—as the portrait of Urras makes impressively clear—any access to pure reason. Le Guin is arguing for the critical effectiveness of literature.

The Body in History

> Are my images all body, then? Are they soul at all? What are these words to which I have entrusted my hope of being? Will they save me, any more than I can save my child? Will they guide me in my search, or do they confuse and mislead me, the beckoning arms, the glinting eyes, laughter in the fog, a line of footprints leading down to the edge of the water and into it and not back?
> I have to think they are true. I have to trust and follow them.
> —Ursula Le Guin, *Searoad*

Heroic narratives may involve leaving home to test maturity, but in Ursula Le Guin's rewrite of life stories, exile itself may be only a stage we must go through. Would any woman living in the watery dominions of the coastal West feel, as I felt, the renewal of the very concept of "uncanny," reading *Searoad*? The narrative style cuts the slightest possible deviation from the utterly familiar. Nothing shocks. After a page that sets the metaphor of foam women and rain women, as if to evoke atmosphere, the narrative begins in the ordinary language of small-town Oregon. There is, apparently, no figuration. There is no ironic distance between author and narrator, or narrator and subjects either, after that evident contrast of poetic language and the vernacular.

Without dialect, this vernacular does not call attention to itself. It is the language of characters who are the opposite of exceptional. The apparent narrators in each chapter change empathetically to correspond to the characters. These narrators do not detach themselves from the reader by mistakes or misunderstandings or other evidence of unreliability. Fiction making has left no trace. Or rather, fiction appears as a tracing, such as children learn to do when they practice sureness of hand, using the nearly transparent paper that allows them to follow the drawing underneath. However, the masterful claim of a realism to represent the world transmutes into a speculative claim that this world portrayed here might be real—the claim of science fiction. This history about the lives of women with its cyclic plot of life and death arising from a woman's time is a story that might be told and revealed as already here.

I am not ignoring the major figure that appears in the book in my claim of zero figuration: the figure that Marleen S. Barr cites for her argument that *Searoad* is feminist science fiction because it practices "fabulation." If it is a story about "foam women and rain women," however, it is not the poetry written by the author of the metaphor; the narrative style does not foreground its poetics through other striking metaphors or symbols. Who, then, is speaking/writing? Why, the answer must be: the members of the community of Klatsand. If the book were located on Mars, the sense in which this is the representation of an imagined community would be more marked, as in "Chronicles of Mars." More clearly than *The Dispossessed,* the book has a community as its hero, and it steps back more firmly from heroic plots. Like *Always Coming Home,* it describes possible culture on the site of familiar landscapes. Nevertheless, in particular, it is a story that surrounds the writing woman who tells the story of foam women and rain women and her place in the generations of women. Her name in the final chapter appears as Virginia Herne, a poet who has written a Pulitzer Prize–winning book of poetry called *Persephone Turning.* Her relationship to the author is/is not figurative.

Her name is not Ursula Le Guin, yet "We have the same name, I said" is the final line of the book, set off by a wide white space from the text of Virginia's story so that it is not clear if this line belongs to Virginia's text or to the author's. Who has the same name, then? Virginia Herne and Virginia Woolf? Women writers? Women? Is the name written in the body? It is Virginia who asks, "Are my images all body, then? Are they soul at all? " (175–76). But it is Ursula Le Guin who writes stories that take bodies literally. The issue reaches into theology, for the literal figure will confuse and reconfigure the culturally defined lineaments of soul. In French one could use the word "face" or "visage" for face, but the most current usage for the form of the face, its character, is the word "figure." It could appear in a sentence such as "I recognize that face" ("Je connais cette figure-là"—*Petit Robert*), or "I know that face," or "I know that expression." Ursula Le Guin is writing the kind of knowledge that recognizes a face, a *figure* that is embodied and that, called up, will be what is always already known.

When Mary Catherine Bateson tries to write about such knowing, she emphasizes that school does not usually teach to it. She falls back on the experience of mother-child bonding. She argues that learning in such a situation feels like recognizing something one has always known. Learning then seems not a change in oneself, not alien, but more like returning home. As Bateson points out, such knowledge relies on the experience of unforgetting, anamnesis. Figure in Le Guin is like recognizing a familiar face.

Indeed, the figure of the familiar visage revisits the unhomeliness of the Freudian uncanny by revealing the familiarity of the strange. What is above all unknown, she shows us, is the *figure* so close it is home. In our culture, this unspeakable knowledge would reveal the *figure* of mother, her face hidden in plain view, under the veil of banality. Lost with mother is not the individual, not poetic genius, but *communitas*. The figure is learned and lost with the mother tongue in the gesture of exile that characterizes individuation. But should human time be counted only in this chronicle of estrangement? Is there no direction other than diaspora? Yes, Freud tells us, the drive presses most finally to death; the human narrative finishes not with the fetishized object of desire, but with the return to no desire, death. Is returning home a figure of melancholy?

The setting of the Oregon coast community, Klatsand, resists the genius of progress with the weapons that resist real estate development, even if not altogether successfully: weather—fog, salty wind, rain—and water—river, creeks, rivulets, waves, breakers, spray, sandy foam. (Every decade, I would testify, a new wave of outsiders with money discovers the beautiful coast of Oregon again, only to retreat, worn down by the elements as they replace cars that rust, wash windows encrusted with salty spray, or pull out nearly-forgotten swim suits and sleeveless dresses for the few days of sun. Some people suffer from depression because of the insufficient sunlight.) The landscape promotes not ambition but perhaps reflection. Is it womblike in its moist darkness? A scene for melancholy, with its movements of repetition? It is certainly yinward.

Or can Le Guin simply rewrite the story, so that home becomes not a dead end or a trap, but the place one in search of knowledge might return to? The seacoast is the embodiment of yin, a corrective. In this story, it is a matter of paying such careful attention to the too familiar that a figure-ground reversal takes place, and home becomes the figure. By the same logic, the chronicle becomes a genealogy, and the genealogy is matrilineal. Virginia Woolf committed suicide, but the death of the artist takes place in two times, as an end of language and as part of the monumental. Thus the crisis of melancholy (which is the death of the individual, a literal or figurative suicide) is inserted into a linked chain of stories that does not end with death. The individual becomes ground; the community provides figure.

The stylistic daring of this book takes risks with postmodern hybridity. It does not emerge into catachresis, although it mixes genres (science fiction, the novel, the diary, poetry). It is mainstream fiction but, then, in an American version of rhetoric learned from Virginia Woolf. That is the rhetoric of everyday epiphany. It takes up the subtle gambit of Woolf, enlarging not stream of consciousness or an experimental rupturing of the ordinary, but rather her defining the ordinary as woman. Here, then, is a chronicle of a very ordinary community organized to convince the reader of a science fiction assumption: that it makes sense to chronicle community according to a matrilineal order. The convincing is done not at the level of argument, but (as literature can do, and science fiction points out) at the level of the commonplace, to name a truth you will recognize (home, the matrilineal).

How does the metaphor of rain and foam women function in this book? Not, I think, to turn the whole back to literature after an excursion in the vernacular. Like Raymond Carver, Le Guin in this book makes survival ironic. Perhaps I should say that Raymond Carver, like Le Guin, practiced what I call "maternal irony," that life goes on, babies are still born, women write books. "This continuity of existence, neither benevolent nor cruel itself, is fundamental to whatever morality may be built upon it. Only Civilization builds its morality by denying its foundation" (*Buffalo Gals* 11). That ironic knowledge touches the resistance to civilization and human mastery through naming that Le Guin shares with Robinson Jeffers. The text here is written on the sand—by the lacy foam—and in a lace collar, "handmade, handwritten," that the writer, Johanna, finds in a secondhand clothing store: "'My soul must go,' was the border, repeated many times, 'my soul must go, my soul must go,' and the fragile webs leading inward read, 'sister, sister, sister, light the light.' And she did not know what she was to do, or how she was to do it" (121). The book reads the writing of the soul, not of exchange. Does Le Guin hope to escape capitalism and commodified relationships? Perhaps. If so, it is not by imposing the symbolism of an archaic mother, to replace the ciphers of economism, violence, and hierarchy with another order of civilized namings, after all, but rather by an act of writing as not knowing (resistance to climax, resistance to conclusion) that makes understanding come and go, foam and lace tracings that may or may not be hieroglyphs of a true naming, that may indeed be instead a way of unnaming. "My words now must be as slow, as new, as single, as tentative as the steps I took going down the path away from the house, between the dark-branched, tall dancers motionless against the winter shining" (*Buffalo Gals* 196).

Le Guin's writing appears at the turning point of the Cold War, in the sixties, when the fragmentation and struggle submerged beneath a hypermasculine consensus would explosively emerge, and when feminism would be reborn. The postmodern break resembles the modern most decisively in the conviction that the break is new. What I have argued in this chapter, however, is that Le Guin reveals continuities with a life that already existed in the thirties, and with progressive communities whose values were obscured by the Cold War but never ceased to operate. Her understanding of how it could be impossible to name the history she wanted to tell, because the very shape of history had centered on the Western warrior, led her to science fiction as alternate history, a way of unnaming. Thus, Le Guin situates the trial of manliness outside apocalypse, in histories that come and go.

Conclusion: The Whiteness of the Cold War and the Absence of Women

The Cold War in its early years, until the advent of postmodern fragmentation in the late sixties, propped an illusory coherent subject—of national and individual identity—upon gendered identities that were, in fact, on trial. The nuclear bomb exploded any possibility of maintaining the old heroic nationalism that Teddy Roosevelt had mythologized: the American manliness of the frontier. But the initial response to the fragmentation of a masculinized identity reasserted warrior culture. Americans getting their postwar bearings turned to American myths of the West for ideological help (even Vannevar Bush spoke of the "new frontier" of postwar science). This illusory coherence was all the more powerfully invoked precisely because it was on trial, under threat of disintegration. Cold War culture looked as if it glorified the masculine, but at the same time, manliness was displaced onto the supposed objectivity of "national realism." The situation was ambiguous, but there was no tolerance for epistemological ambiguity.

The historical subject of manliness identified with the warrior and his war-culture split, along lines that were suggestively connected to class. Working-class veterans found class identifications with unions called "communist" increasingly untenable and turned to identify with gender roles that were exaggerated, a masculine individuality that was less urban, more western. The professional and managerial classes and intellectuals denied that ruling class ("rational" or "economic") subjects were marked by any gender, race, or class at all. They asserted, rather, the universal coherence of rationality in the face of chaos. The male subject split in literary representations as well; highbrow literature featured not the hero, but the vulnerable antihero. Intellectuals from Lionel Trilling to Sidney Hook and anticommunist policymakers from George Kennan to J. Edgar Hoover shared a tragic vision that nonetheless kept reason—and its gendering repudiation of feminized excess—as its chief source of coherence. Hemingway came to seem all too masculine, and highbrow critics savaged his work. Malamud wrote ironically about an antihero who cannot survive in the middlebrow West. Is it because he is subversive? because he commits adultery? because he is Jewish? The hero and the antihero alike represented manliness on trial. Thus, Hemingway and Malamud suggest the range of heroic and antiheroic masculinities and the cultural constraints upon them.

As the warrior subject threatened either to come apart or to assert its unity by violence, alternate representations appeared—not as the cultural dominant, but nevertheless in plain view. The confused terrain of culture included "middlebrow" feminine writing that neither reproduced the subject of manliness nor destroyed it. The domestic middlebrow was, in the academic culture of the fifties and sixties, simply invisible. In the nonfiction of Mari Sandoz and the fantasy/science fiction of Ursula Le Guin, we can see growing indications of what will develop into the post-modern critique of male culture, but these works were written and ought therefore to be read in the shadow of the struggle over a unifying masculinity that controlled the field of interpretation and kept it within the history of a national mythology that can be traced back in history, importantly to Teddy Roosevelt. These women writers both turned to and exposed the cultural otherness supposed by the project of national manliness. Their works violated the categories of nationalism, realism, and gender to help put manliness on trial, with the critical help of an appeal to Native American sources. They exposed the unreal, imaginary excess of the warrior and challenged its reality at the level of form. The fact that they were in a sense "contained" by the middlebrow—that is, by class—suggests how Cold War culture regulated national identity by making all divisions except the trials of the warrior invisible, unmentionable.

The trauma and violence of war shaped the Cold War imagination even during the peaceful stasis between Korea and Vietnam, or Vietnam and the war on Iraq. It gave rise to the terms of debate, so that literature could not argue what could not be discussed. Those limits, far from appearing as the borders where outsiders might be made scapegoats, appeared as realism about the enemy, giving rise to counsels of wariness and defense. In such an arena, Ernest Hemingway appeared to be writing not about gender and sexuality as part of a heterogeneous human condition, but about the manliness that Cold War codes enforced as a stereotype. Bernard Malamud made a public success as a Jewish writer but appeared precariously situated between assimilation and sentimental ethnicity. Malamud's antihero made critique ironic and internalized political struggle. Mari Sandoz wrote friendly history about that long-term familiar enemy, the "hostile," and criticized frontier imperialism. But she too might appear as a familiar type, the overly sentimental female writer/reformer who had always tried to domesticate the West and thwarted liberalism as she practiced it. Ursula Le Guin's books seem closer and closer to a coyote realism that unsettles the very ideas of home, gender, and ethnic identity that warranted the nuclear family in the Cold War. Against a demonology of the center, what are the effects of such consistent reproach?

What is the remedy to a mechanism that obliterates detail and context, that promotes writing by severing it from its ecology? Public intellectuals of the Cold War made it difficult to think clearly about how economic relations determined the contents of public memory by demonizing Marxist analysis. Cultural history is not simply what a culture remembers about itself, but has everything to do with how the stories are told, how distributed, how reproduced, how enabled or disabled. This economy of historical memory was suppressed; like Ralph Spitzer's proposed history of science and culture, such research had no support.

This book has considered questions of ideology, which becomes visible only as it loses its convincing aura of reality, as an effect of estrangement. Cold War ideology coalesced swiftly as a new domestic conformity, heavily dependent on denying the significance of gender and projecting the threatening unreality of ideology onto Soviet plots. Thus the claims to speak the Real took on special ideological significance in the Cold War. How did it happen that the very voice of the Left, Sidney Hook, the most famous of academic Marxists, in the name of science, realism, and objectivity, could denounce communist professors? Hook could not admit that scientific discourse might be influenced by the political. The powerful claim to be representing the real demonstrates how rhetoric inhabits ideology.

The history of Cold War ideology might also lead us to ask: what are the effects of war and violence in the experience of survivors, and what may be said in the presence of pain? It becomes at once that which cannot be spoken and that reality to which all speech refers. After World War II, the United States was unusual among nations for the extreme contrast between the war experience of civilians and of combatants. Discussions of Vietnam have pointed to the differences between the reception of World War II veterans and of Vietnam veterans. Yet one similarity is striking: in spite of the presence of women in the military and the difficulties women also experienced with the reception of veterans, those who served in the military during World War II, in Korea, and in Vietnam made up a large male-dominated cohort whose unitary identity contrasted sharply with the confusing panoply of domestic lives and leant its distinctive preoccupations to the national imagination. The gendered distinction between a militarized national civic life and the domestic life of consumers both constructed and abjected the (consuming) feminine, at times equated with the enemy. The male subject of Cold War nationalism was both dominant and beset. The consequence of post-traumatic stress is that the woman disappears.

Nothing a woman can say will be heard because everything she might say will recall the intimate conflict that is to be avoided, the conflict at the center and not on the margins, covered over by the demeaning representations of banality. The Cold War constructed as a national subject the American who functioned by projecting difficulties onto the communists, an autonomous, isolated, alienated, and objectified identity that did not, precisely, put itself on trial or into history, but tried to maintain itself as continuous and independent. The denial of social constructions of reality entered into family life from Levittown to Anaheim. That peculiar formation of the free individual conditioned the rebellions of the Beats and shaped the eventual responses of feminists. It imposed a reductive hyper masculinity on representations of gender of all kinds, including that of Ernest Hemingway. It polarized representations of race and ethnicity for and against nativist genealogies. It rewrote Western narratives as the narrative of the West, exporting the American cowboy to our allies. It denied the reality of other coexisting narratives, of the dialogic, of the undefined, of the pre-Oedipal. The national realism of the Cold War denied the relevance of fantasy, most especially its own.

This preoccupation with stabilizing identity might be thought of as adolescent, just as (Le Guin would persuade us) the warrior is a stage adolescents go through. However, national realism appeared not as extremity but as the rational middle and the banal. It appeared without color. Thus, the governing metaphor of the 1998 film *Pleasantville* takes the black and white of the fifties sitcom to represent the Cold War repression of everything threatening—a repressive style that makes the world colorless.

Styles that pretend to be technologically objective eliminate the elements that Freud described in *The Interpretation of Dreams* as characteristic of primary process thinking (or dreaming): displacement, condensation (or metaphor, metonymy), fantasy. The realisms in Hemingway, Malamud, Sandoz, and Le Guin are diverse, but they have in common that they include more fantasy than anything the Cold War could admit. This is especially significant because all four writers have been influenced by the very discourses of the West that would be invoked to construct Cold War realism: nature writing, natural history, the arena of conquest, the metaphor of the frontier. But theirs is realism with a difference. Sandoz, Malamud, and Le Guin have in common their calling up of story telling from a less literal-minded past. Hemingway too uses the storyteller's secret, which he renamed the iceberg theory of construction, cutting away the circumstantial detail and deferring the obvious point. In their various ways, they all use poetic language within realism, introducing primary process and the fantastic into the imaginary sobriety of American nationalism. In this, they are not un-American. But they are all doubtless somewhat subversive.

During the Cold War, Freudian intellectuals thought of civilization as a necessary mitigation of irrational extremity. In *Civilization and Its Discontents,* Freud meant to argue for the significance of the death drive and its aggressive expression in relationship to the libido, or Eros: "Besides the instinct to preserve living substance and to join it into ever larger units, there must exist another, contrary instinct seeking to dissolve those units and to bring them back to their primaeval inorganic state" (65–66). A civilization might be judged, then, by its capacity to bring them both into the arena. In 1931, Freud added a final sentence, as Hitler's rise to power became clearer:

> Men have gained control over the forces of nature to such an extent that with their help they would have no difficulty in exterminating one another to the last man. They know this, and hence comes a large part of their current unrest, their unhappiness and their mood of anxiety. And now it is to be expected that the other of the two "Heavenly powers", eternal Eros, will make an effort to assert himself in the struggle with his equally immortal adversary. But who can foresee with what success and with what result? (92)

The phobic response of American culture to the evident capacity of civilization to destroy itself manifested by World War II had the effect of enclosing reason within the violence of aggressivity. The aggression always seemed to happen elsewhere, dissociated from the American landscape and the naturalized terrain of home. Thus manhood was dislocated from place.

In other words, scapegoats were damaged by the Cold War rhetoric of paranoia and blame, and voids appeared in place of manliness. The logic of projection and a linearity of historical narrative imposed a rigid framework that put manhood into crisis. The remedy to such estrangement is to admit the stranger (woman, Native), who is in fact already within the harshly drawn borders of national/personal identity. The reiterative structures of mixed, recovered, and translated stories may help us to relocate the warrior—within. A return to Theodore Roosevelt or Ernest Hemingway or John Wayne does not necessarily portend a renewal of the old Cold War fables of manliness, I hope I have shown, but rather acknowledgment and recognition. Garry Wills argues something similar in his book on Wayne: "The less we advert to what he did to us, the less we can cope with it. . . . Down the street of the twentieth-century imagination, that figure is still walking toward us—graceful, menacing, inescapable" (49).

Notes

Works Cited and Consulted

Index

Notes

Introduction: The Frontier Rhetoric of
the Cold War and the Crisis of Manliness

1. Judith Butler's theory of gender and sexuality emerges from a theory of language; related to but critical of poststructuralist theorists such as Julia Kristeva and Michel Foucault, as well as to speech act theory. Her definition of the performative is not the same as a performance: gender is performative because language and culture must be articulated in specific and local situations, and the meanings of language are thus not lodged abstractly in definition but reestablished through the performance of discourses. There is a rhetoricity about gender, although we are not free simply to redefine it through a new performance. See especially her *Gender Trouble* and *Bodies That Matter*.

2. The problematic status of the masculine has interested a number of feminist critics in the past decade, as well as other theorists convinced that gender inflects discourses and social practices on many levels and that the gendered male body enters into the cultural stakes as well as the female body. The collection called *Engendering Men*, edited by Joseph Boone and Michael Cadden, takes as its starting point the feminist insight that part of the gender problem is that only women are marked as "gendered." Michael Cadden's chapter discusses the "two F.O. Matthiessens" (as Jonathan Arac recalled to us) that the Cold War had put into deadly crisis: the founding critic of American Studies and the author of the letters to his lover, Russell Cheney. Kaja Silverman's *Male Subjectivity at the Margins* analyzes male subjectivity as a function of history, ideology, and politics as well as of psychoanalytic categories. In her chapter on "Historical Trauma and Male Subjectivity," Silverman examines in particular the period just after World War II and the physical and psychic mutilation of men represented in film. Elisabeth Badinter has written about masculinity with a view to showing the psychoanalytic difficulties gender presents for men, psychic mutilation as well as recovery through androgyny, in *XY: On Masculine Identity*.

3. For this observation, as for a larger understanding, I am indebted

to David Caute, Cold War Conference; Toledo, Ohio, April 21–24, 1996. I also learned a great deal from others there: Russell Reising, Donald Pease, Ellen Schrecker, Alan Nadel, Thomas Schaub, Victor Rabinowitz, Maurice Rapf, Barbara Foley, Frank Costigliola, Molly Hite, Ward Churchill, Katie Kodat, Peter Rabinowitz, and Richard Ohmann.

4. For a discussion of nuclear narratives, see Alan Nadel, "Appearance, Containment, Atomic Power," *Containment Culture;* William Chaloupka, *Knowing Nukes: The Politics and Culture of the Atom;* and Peter Schwenger, *Letter Bomb: Nuclear Holocaust and the Exploding Word.*

5. Trilling has been the subject, therefore, of much important critical work on Cold War culture, including, notably, Mark Krupnick's *Lionel Trilling and the Fate of Cultural Criticism* and Daniel T. O'Hara's *Lionel Trilling: The Work of Liberation.*

6. The literature on Cold War repressions and their influence on political culture has focused centrally on McCarthyism, although the phenomenon began earlier and was far more pervasive. Ellen Schrecker's *Many Are the Crimes* is required reading. Her *The Age of McCarthyism: A Brief History with Documents,* is also a good starting point: a bibliographical excerpt is on the Internet at http://www.crocker.com/~blklst/bibliog.html. See also Daniel Bell, *The End of Ideology: On the Exhaustion of Political Ideas in the Fifties;* Howard Brick, *Daniel Bell and the Decline of Intellectual Radicalism: Social Theory and Political Reconciliation in the 1940s;* David Caute, *The Great Fear;* Russell Reising, *The Unusable Past;* Thomas Rosteck, *"See It Now" Confronts McCarthyism;* Athan G. Theoharis, ed., *Beyond the Hiss Case.*

7. Donald Pease describes the operations of the "Cold War consensus" in its construction of American literature in a number of books and articles, including *Visionary Compacts;* "New Americanists: Revisionist Interventions into the Canon"; and "National Identities, Postmodern Artifacts, and Postnational Narratives."

8. I discuss the vilification of women's writing in *Sentimental Modernism: Women Writers and the Revolution of the Word.*

9. The restoration of a lost heritage has been the work of influential scholars including Cary Nelson, *Repression and Recovery;* Paul Lauter, *Canons and Contexts;* Paula Rabinowitz, *Labor & Desire: Women's Revolutionary Fiction in Depression America;* and Bonnie Kime Scott, *The Gender of Modernism* and *Refiguring Modernism.*

10. And Philip Fisher, in *Hard Facts,* thought that "The male conflict between archaic, but heroic, childhood and the uninteresting and subordinate toil of the pastoral ideal once it is completely in place, blinds the adventure novel to what was the deeper problem in the American setting" (91).

11. In addition to Jeffords's books, several other books have traced

the connections—and disarticulations—of gender, sexuality, and national narratives. Gail Bederman, in *Manliness & Civilization,* argues that the turn of the century marked a change from concern with moral manliness to a more bodied "masculinity." George L. Mosse's *Nationalism and Sexuality* discusses manliness, homosexuality, the body, race, nationalism, and fascism; he asks whether the bourgeois need for social coherence exercised through respectability, through the othering of homosexuality, facilitated the fascist persecution of Jews. In the collection *Nationalisms and Sexualities,* postcolonial theory appears together with feminist and "queer" theory in articles that define national politics in relationship to sexual politics. Gayatri Spivak underscores the significance of multiplying difference: postcoloniality defines the identity of a new nation by a reversal from the logic of the old colony, but "there is always a space that cannot share in the energy of this reversal," a space outside the logic of capital as well—the "space of the displacement of the colonization-decolonization reversal" in Mahasweta Devi's fiction (97).

12. See Sandra Gilbert and Susan Gubar's important sense of this framework for the history of modern literature as they develop it in their three-volume work, *No Man's Land.* Vol. I: *The War of the Words;* Vol. II: *Sexchanges;* Vol. III: *Letters from the Front.*

13. It is a commonplace of stories about survivors who now come forward to speak that they spent many years without saying anything about their experiences. See, for example, the story "Legacy of the Living," which appeared on the front page of the *Eugene Register-Guard,* May 5, 1996. The three witnesses include a survivor, a man who was sent with other children to England, and a pilot who discovered the camps, but all "share an important trait: They only recently became able to speak openly about the events that so drastically altered their lives" (8A).

14. Fredric Jameson argues in an essay on Kenneth Burke, "The Symbolic Inference," that using the notion of "ideology" in connection with literary or interpretation works to "reproblematize the entire artistic discourse or formal analysis thereby so designated," that the very word, "ideology," carries a "kind of Brechtian estrangement effect."

15. See Julia Kristeva, "On Women's Time," trans. Alice Jardine and Harry Blake, *The Kristeva Reader.* Kristeva, following Nietzsche's thinking, contrasts the linear time of history and a spatialized or even monumental time that belongs to reproduction—to a different kind of plot entirely.

1. The Un-American and the Unreal: Modern Bodies and New Frontiers

1. The text of George F. Kennan's "long telegram" is printed in Barton J. Bernstein and Allen J. Matusow, ed., *The Truman Administration: A*

Documentary History, 198–212. This analysis of Soviet ambitions, sent from Moscow in 1946 as a telegram when the State Department requested his evaluation, began its influential life as policy in that form, but Kennan went on to write it up as an anonymous article, "The Sources of Soviet Conduct," that appeared in *Foreign Affairs* for July 1947. Since he had sent Washington a number of warnings about the Soviet Union's desires for expansion, dating from before the war, Kennan was surprised that this one finally drew so much attention: it was widely read in the government even before it was published.

2. For an analysis of Kennan's rhetoric that connects "containment" to the fluidity of the adversary, which he sees as threatening because "seminal," see Alan Nadel, *Containment Culture*, 16.

3. In *The Cold War as Rhetoric,* Lynn Boyd Hinds and Theodore Otto Windt Jr. have written a very suggestive and helpful analysis of the several key rhetorical moments that helped to construct Cold War discourse during the period from 1945 to 1950, including Churchill's "Iron Curtain" speech, the "long telegram," Truman's loyalty program, and the Marshall plan. They also review the critics of what they label the "new realism" and show how the "Babel" produced by their various perspectives diminished their voices: Henry Wallace, Walter Lippman, Robert A. Taft.

4. The factual real would, then, not necessarily be well formed—in form, these writings could be fragmentary and improper and still serve the purpose of recording observations. The narrative of such a realism depended, then, not on the closures of plot, and not on referentiality or representation in a secondary sense, but even more upon the larger narrative of exploration, colonialism, progress, discovery, and science. That is, such a discourse depends not on mimesis or the verisimilar imitation of reality, but on the reality itself. And in *The Real Thing*, Miles Orvell argued that "in no other culture is the notion of "the real thing" so open a window into understanding" (xxvi).

5. Michael Davitt Bell, in *The Problem of American Realism*, points out the connection of William Dean Howells's realism to an assertion of normalcy against the critics that has been a conservative tradition in the United States, a "rational orthodoxy" stemming from the Common Sense philosophers of the eighteenth century (34). The "problem" Bell sees is the contradiction of realism's anti-art perspective with the necessity of stylistic mediation.

6. See Greg Mitchell, *The Campaign of the Century: Upton Sinclair's Race for Governor of California and the Birth of Media Politics.* Maurice Rapf told me that the entertainment industry was very much involved in that campaign (personal communication, April 1996).

7. For the idea of a spectral history, see also Jacques Derrida, *Specters of Marx.*

2. Cold War Modernism and the Crisis of Story

1. Nadel divides the Cold War culture into two periods: the first, from 1945 to the sixties, when the logic of containment prevailed, and the second, from the sixties on, when containment culture began to break down and postmodernism began to assert itself, partly under the influence of narratives counter to the logic of containment, such as *Catch-22*. "Containment was the name of a privileged American narrative during the Cold War. Although technically referring to U.S. foreign policy from 1948 until at least the mid-sixties, it also describes American life in numerous venues and under sundry rubrics during that period" (2–3).

2. The flood of rereadings has reached such proportions that some have said "modernism" no longer means anything. However, the challenge has come largely on two fronts: first, as a postmodern critique of modernism as a reactionary movement. Among these must be included Fredric Jameson's *Fables of Aggression: Wyndham Lewis, the Modernist as Fascist*. And second, as a revisiting of the canon in order to establish the new modernisms, the traditions represented by women, African American, and working-class writers first, and now others.

3. Theodore Roosevelt and the Postheroic Arena: Reading Hemingway Again

1. Perloff explained her reading of Stein—and her rejection of Hemingway—in a lecture at the University of Oregon on Gertrude Stein and Wittgenstein, April 25, 1995.

2. For a careful discussion of the modernist appropriation of dialect and the relationship of primitivism to modernist claims of authenticity, see Michael North, *The Dialect of Modernism: Race, Language, and Twentieth Century Literature*.

3. For a study of Indians in Hemingway, see Robert Lewis, "'Long Time Ago Good, Now No Good:' Hemingway's Indian Stories."

4. See Ellen Schrecker's *Many Are the Crimes* for the use of membership lists and subversive organizations by the FBI (105, 112–14).

5. Rose Marie Burwell, *Hemingway: The Postwar Years and the Posthumous Novels*, has conducted an extensive review of the late manuscripts. She argues that they all are concerned with the writer's dilemma, but she does not see this dilemma in terms of a cultural politics.

6. Roosevelt, Wister, and Remington had varying experiences and interpretations of the West, of course, but they shared the view that inserted the west into a larger history—the progressive, evolutionary development of civilization. Thus they were responsible for interpreting the West in a way that made it politically responsive to the concerns of the eastern establishment, at the same time that it reinforced a certain version of capitalism's story—particularly the version that dramatized the

role of the United States. They "saw the West as a stage in the history of American civilization" (78), as G. Edward White writes in his description of the translation, *The Eastern Establishment and the Western Experience*. Roosevelt and Wister were also formed by the construction of manhood at Harvard, a subject treated at length by Kim Townsend in *Manhood at Harvard*.

7. Haraway's analysis of the Natural History Museum and its confluence of interests leads her to characterize the institution as a "Teddy Bear Patriarchy," the title of the chapter included in *Cultures of United States Imperialism*. The "central moral truth" is "the effective truth of manhood, the state conferred on the visitor who successfully passes through the trial of the museum. The body can be transcended" (241).

8. For the story of Roosevelt's early years and his extraordinary involvement in natural history, I draw from David McCullough, *Mornings on Horseback*.

9. Items #1805 and #1806 in the Appendix VI, "Inventory of Hemingway's Reading," Michael Reynolds, *Hemingway's Reading, 1910–1940*. James D. Brasch and Joseph Sigman, *Hemingway's Library: A Composite Record* list the same volumes, p. 318.

10. James David Teller gives an account drawn on Shaler and cites the others in *Louis Agassiz, Scientist and Teacher* (74ff); the stories have been widely published.

11. See Louise Hall Tharp, *Adventurous Alliance: The Story of the Agassiz Family of Boston*.

12. This and other Hemingway stories I consider in this chapter are in *The Complete Short Stories of Ernest Hemingway: The Finca Vigía Edition*. Subsequent page numbers are cited parenthetically.

13. See Michael Reynolds, *Hemingway's Reading, 1901–1940: An Inventory*.

14. For an example of a contemporary view, see Lisa Tyler, "Ernest Hemingway's Date Rape Story: Sexual Trauma in 'Up in Michigan.'" Marylyn A. Lupton responded with a defense of Jim in "The Seduction of Jim Gilmore." But Robert W. Lewis Jr. characterized the story within the larger context of Hemingway's lifelong discussion of love, as an example of initiation and disillusionment suffered by a woman but similar to that suffered by male characters who are romantic. See his *Hemingway on Love*, 4–5.

15. Ronald Weber, in *Hemingway's Art of Non-Fiction*, makes the comparison with the doubleness in Thoreau that, according to F. O. Matthiessen, gave him a literary dimension beyond the reportage of other naturalists and travelers.

16. For an insightful discussion of "The Natural History of the Dead," see Susan F. Beegel, *Hemingway's Craft of Omission: Four Manuscript Examples* (Ann Arbor: UMI Research, 1988). She examines in particu-

lar the ramifications of Hemingway's cutting four manuscript pages that ended the story with a return to satire.

17. "Censored Books" cites Anne Lyon Hight and Chandler B. Grannis, *Banned Books 387 B.C. to 1978 A.D.* (New York: R. R. Bowker, 1978).

4. Unsettling the West: The Persecution of Science and Bernard Malamud's *A New Life*

1. For information related to the Spitzer case, I am very much indebted to the Oregon State University Archives, Corvallis, Oregon, which made the files available to me on microfilm. They occupy a section all their own in the President's Office Records for A. L. Strand, labeled "LaVallee and Spitzer Case, 1949–1952: Correspondence, 1949–1952." I am equally indebted to Cliff Mead for his important help with my research in the Oregon State University Library's Special Collections: the Linus Pauling papers include a number of files on the Spitzer case and on the question of academic freedom as well. Future references in the notes will identity these archives as "President's Office: Strand's file" and "Pauling Collection."

2. See Alan Nadel's discussion of *Hiroshima* in *Containment Culture*, 53–67.

3. See Elizabeth Young-Bruehl, *Hannah Arendt*.

4. This history of the Left is discussed in Alan Wald, *The New York Intellectuals: The Rise and Decline of the Anti-Stalinist Left from the 1930s to the 1980s*. See also Hugh Wilford, *The New York Intellectuals: From Vanguard to Institution*, and Stanley Aronowitz, *Roll Over, Beethoven*.

5. See Alan Nadel, *Containment Culture*, for a discussion of the way that *Playboy* represented progressive politics during the Cold War.

6. "Bernie said that he used to sometimes start stories and the kids would flock around and he'd tell stories to the other kids and they took a lot of interest in his ability to tell stories. He was good at it. And he kind of made a little reputation in the neighborhood, he was the storyteller. He recalled that with quite a bit of pleasure I believe. Because I know he always thought that a good novel really ought to tell an interesting tale, an interesting story." Interview with Nelson Sandgren, professor of art on the Oregon State University faculty, who was a good friend of Bernard Malamud when he taught there. May 28, 1988.

7. In my essay, "Bernard Malamud in Oregon," I described Malamud's relationships to his colleagues and neighbors, his habits of work, and his lasting contributions to the English Department at Oregon State. This information comes largely from a series of interviews that I carried out in 1988–1993 with those who had known Malamud during the years he and his family lived in Corvallis.

8. The debate over how to read *A New Life* took place at a local and a national level. In Corvallis, Professor James Groshong, in the English Department—the model, many thought, and he acquiesces, for "Bucket"—wrote a favorable review for the *Gazette-Times:* "Trouble in the West: Malamud's New Book." Groshong admits that Levin is a "difficult man," in a "complex and at times difficult book." But he understands Levin "metaphorically as the humanist intellectual in American academic life, fallible but vital and militant." Malamud's friends and colleagues argued that the book should not be read as some kind of exposé of Oregon State, though some townspeople wondered if the faculty really had such immoral sex lives. By contrast, Robert B. Frazier, a well-regarded reporter and associate editor for the paper in the rival university town, the Eugene *Register-Guard,* wrote: "In a bitter, bitter book that is sometimes funny, often unfair and sometimes perceptive, Mr. Malamud takes off on the college where he once taught" (October 10, 1961).

9. The war of Left and Right was governed by plots become dogma, making any twists to the story almost impossible. Even though Malamud offers the possibility of renewal, his readers have had difficulty rethinking the plot. And so Jessamyn West, for example, notes the radical politics in the story but excuses them: "This is by no means the usual novel of left-wing politics in a college." John Hollander's *Partisan Review* essay praises the book, its truth about the details of bureaucracy in college life, its truth about sexuality, without even mentioning its connections with the history of anticommunism.

10. Malamud reflected about his career in a lecture at Bennington College given October 30, 1984 and later published as a chapbook: *Long Work, Short Life.*

11. See Thomas Schaub, *American Fiction in the Cold War.* He emphasizes the critical consensus around a distinction between art and ideology. Trilling, he says, associated realism "not with external facts but with the dialectical form of literary ideas produced by conflicting emotions. This was moral realism, in which literature became politics recollected in anguish" (36). However, Trilling also held out for the significance of external history against the polemical formalism of the New Critics. In "The Use of the Past" (collected in *The Liberal Imagination*), Trilling argued that, while we ought to complicate our historical sense and not oversimplify the way the writer might be related to history, we cannot pretend that literature has no past; the poet is both effect and cause of his environment, and ideas are situated in the conditions of their development and transmission. Trilling recommends that we take up a Nietzschean notion of a historical sense which "speaks to the historian and to the student of art as if they were one person" (197).

12. In 1968, Sidney Hook gave a speech on academic freedom that attacked the Students for a Democratic Society for trying to make the

university an instrument of social action. He incorporated this essay into the 1971 collection he edited, *In Defense of Academic Freedom.* I cite this to argue for the continuity of the debate from the beginning of the Cold War through the sixties and on.

13. A copy of this statement was preserved in President Strand's file.

14. See, for example, Carl Bernstein's painful struggle with his parents over his decision to write about their persecution, described in *Loyalties: A Son's Memoir.* In all my conversations with those on the Left who experienced those years, I have encountered similar reluctance to revive the past—often accompanied by enduring fears of suffering again.

15. See the list, for example, on the letterhead of a letter to Pauling from Lou Harris, January 17, 1946. Pauling Collection.

16. He continues: "I know extremely few people who are recognized as Communists; but I do belong to a number of organizations that are described as Communist-Front organizations, and I have been interested to see how well the members of these organizations find it possible to get along with one another, and in particular how well the members of the Boards of Directors get along with one another. I have been encouraged by my own experiences, to the extent that they do represent collaboration between Communists and Non-communists, to believe that the peoples of the world will ultimately find it possible to get along together, through the formation of an effective world government" (February 28, 1949).

17. Spitzer wrote: "A perusal of Lysenko's report shows that the issue is largely over matters of biological and technological fact and theory. Are vegetative hybrids possible? Mr. Lysenko has samples. Can the heredity of organisms be changed by changing the environment at an appropriate time and in an appropriate way? The Michurinists have changed 28 chromosome spring wheats to 42 chromosome winter wheats by suitable temperature treatment during several generations."

18. Information about the firing is in a letter from Ralph Spitzer to Linus Pauling (February 9, 1949) and in subsequent press reports in the Portland *Oregonian,* the *Corvallis Gazette-Times,* and more, and in the statements by Spitzer, President A. L. Strand, and other parties assembled in the archives of the Oregon State University President's Office records. Where I do not cite a specific source, I summarize from these.

19. See documents of the Appeals Committee in President Strand's files.

20. He quoted from an "official announcement of the Moscow press, Aug. 27, 1948," perhaps seeing frightening connotations to the word "eradicate." President Strand's file.

21. President Strand quoted at length from an article by OSC zoologist C. D. Darlington published in *The Journal of Heredity* (vols. 37–38, 1946–47, pp. 143ff), which traces the rise of Lysenko. Darlington argues that Lysenko's success came because his environmentalist theory suited

Marxist theory better than the empiricism of his predecessor, N. I. Vavilov, who died in the subsequent purge in 1939. President Strand's file.

22. The record of his correspondence with his mentor, Pauling, shows him frantically searching for jobs, and Pauling trying to help, writing letters of recommendation. He endured the problems with passports and the difficulty getting new positions that many American scientists of that era experienced. Finally, in the middle fifties, he trained as a physician at a medical school in Canada, opened up new lines of research, and made a new and productive life teaching medicine in British Columbia.

23. He wrote: "It seems to me from the available evidence that there has been some violation of the principles of academic freedom in Russia, in connection with this controversy. I do not believe that this can be given as the justification of a similar violation of the principles of academic freedom in the Oregon State College" (Linus Pauling to A. L. Strand, March 1, 1949, President's Office archives). Pauling also sent this letter to the student newspaper, the *Barometer*, which refused to publish it.

24. Strand's letter to Pauling concluded, somewhat recklessly: "Graduate students in chemistry here, stirred up by Spitzer, are concerned lest my correspondence with you might jeopardize their future and also the accreditation of the department. I told them that I could not imagine such a possibility, but that if they expected me to make some gesture of obseisance [*sic*] to the president of the American Chemical Society, who has acted with the audacity of a Young Progressive, their suggestion fell on deaf ears" (President's Office Archives).

25. In 1995, the Pauling Institute moved to Oregon State University, and its Special Collections have his papers. The possible ramifications for the university of Strand's willingness to offend Pauling were considerable.

26. The FAS telegram to President Strand stated:

> It does not appear justified to regard support of Lysenkoism as indication of lack of scientific competence or integrity. . . . The issue raised is whether, under the strain of the conflict with the Soviet Union, we are not becoming "soft" toward abridgement of democratic freedoms. . . . The competence and integrity of a scientist cannot be judged by his beliefs, but only by his performance as an investigator. It must be concluded, therefore, that President Strand's actions in the Spitzer case raise not only the general issue of academic freedom, but the specific issue of scientific freedom and imposed orthodoxy as well. (April 26, 1949)

27. For a review of the AAUP's less than impressive record, see Ellen Schrecker, "Academic Freedom: The Historical View."

28. Quoted from Strand's own notes about the incident, May 9, 1949. The Oregon State student paper, the *Barometer,* reported the incident on May 11, 1949: "The 'peace forum' is a Progressive-sponsored movement for 'peace in America'" (1). Do the quotation marks signal their political skepticism?

29. Strand did write, in a letter to E. O. Holland, president emeritus of the State College of Washington, that "His meeting was little more than a Communist rally" (May 16, 1949). In a letter to the *San Francisco Chronicle,* Strand charged Wallace with disloyalty to genetics as well as to his country: "Wallace knows as well as anyone in America that the teachings of this Lysenko compose merely a revival of the universally discredited inheritance of acquired characters. . . . The party line sure plays hob with a man's intelligence" (May 14, 1949).

30. Letters such as these, "for" and "against," are carefully organized in the Office of the President's Spitzer-LaVallee file.

31. For example, Spitzer's infamous letter to the *Chemical and Engineering News* was in response to an editorial by H. J. Muller, zoologist at Indiana University. Muller himself wrote to Ernst Dornfeld at Oregon State, the zoologist who provided Strand with the documentation on Lysenko, that "if the case is really as it has been reported to be, the limits of interference with academic freedom have been exceeded here" (March 3, 1949). Muller, however, was not willing to put up a public fight on Spitzer's behalf. Citing Sidney Hook's February 27 *New York Times Magazine* article, he worried that "followers of the Party Line are themselves . . . working for the revocation of academic freedom" and therefore could legitimately be dismissed. Asking for more information before he went public, Muller said that belief in Lysenko was not necessarily grounds for dismissal; a geneticist who supported Lysenko "must *upso facto* [*sic*] be incompetent" but a professor in another field might "simply be mistaken." This argument does not take the strong stand that even Communist Party members ought to have their academic freedom protected.

32. Strand might not have taken the insult to heart, however, since Mayer had mistakenly addressed the letter to OSC's archrival, the University of Oregon.

33. David Todd, chemist at Amherst, also wrote to say that he knew Spitzer and his work; agreed, having worked with him during the war, that Spitzer had "a highly emotional attitude on anything connected with Russia," but argued that his views on Lysenko did not make him incompetent—"he will never accept outside dictation in his own field, and I feel that you are making a serious error to assume that he may" (February 25, 1949).

34. Since these conversations took place after my interviews, as infor-

mal reactions to drafts and a reading of this work, I do not believe I have permission to name names. None of those I interviewed about Malamud mentioned the Spitzer case before I wrote about it.

35. Tom Hager, who is the author of *Force of Nature: The Life of Linus Pauling*, is responsible for persuading me to distinguish between the heroic Duffy and the less than admirable Levin.

36. Warren Hovland, a particularly close friend of Malamud who was on the faculty at the time, says firmly that Malamud was not political.

37. Ralph Spitzer's testimony is contained in the record of the investigation of "Subversive Influence in the Educational Process," a copy of which was sent to President Strand: "Hearings Before the Subcommittee to Investigate the Administration of the Internal Security Act and Other Internal Security Laws of the Committee on the Judiciary, United States Senate, Eighty-Third Congress," Part 12 (June 8, 9, and 11, 1953), Washington, D.C.: United States Printing Office, 1953.

5. Mari Sandoz's Heartland: The Abusive Frontier Father and the Indian Warrior as Counterhistory

1. James Welch, in his own retelling of the story, *Killing Custer: The Battle of the Little Bighorn and the Fate of the Plains Indians,* noted that "One of the common fallacies in regard to the Battle of the Little Bighorn is that there were no survivors. There were plenty of survivors— Sioux and Cheyennes" (21–22). Thus he and Paul Stekler made the movie around Native Americans telling the story. He uses Sandoz as one of his sources for the events surrounding the death of Crazy Horse (308).

2. Barbara Rippey says of *Cheyenne Autumn,* "Ultimately, Sandoz reverses our familiar historical view, and we find ourselves questioning the white way-of-being" (248).

3. By using the terminology "subject on trial," I mean not only to call attention to the judgment that is enacted in her writing, but also to evoke Julia Kristeva's formulation describing the subject revealed by psychoanalysis, a subject in process. See, for example, her *Revolution in Poetic Language.*

4. *Son of the Gamblin' Man* (1960) was a story Robert Henri's family hoped she would write; they provided her with information and papers. The doubling of a frontier hero here with the artist may have resonances, however, that Sandoz didn't know about. In any event, in 1960, when the book was published, she was presenting an artist's childhood that seemed to have almost nothing to do with the formalist avant-garde and that could only have reinforced Cold War art history in its abstract prejudices against the realisms of Henri's school. Sandoz thus ironically contributes to that other narrative, the lineage of American writers and artists scorned as romantics or mystics and all too easily recuperated into

the national symbolism of the heroic individual she was working to deconstruct.

5. Michael Paul Rogin, *Ronald Reagan, the Movie, and Other Episodes in Political Demonology,* and Richard Slotkin, *Gunfighter Nation: The Myth of the Frontier in Twentieth-Century America,* read Western films as representative of cultural developments. My reading of Sandoz may be seen as participating in this project, but in order to call attention to texts that explicitly resist the cultural narratives under construction—whose resistance may be read not only by me, in this later time, but probably was understood by many ordinary readers then.

6. In *West of Everything,* Tompkins describes the unreal experience of reading Westerns. She goes on to argue that Westerns were not about escape, but about work: "Hard work is transformed here from the necessity one wants to escape into the most desirable of human endeavors: action that totally saturates the present moment, totally absorbs the body and mind, and directs one's life to the service of an unquestioned goal" (12).

7. Robert D. Clark has traced the lives of Nebraska homesteaders in the last two decades of the century. They assumed that farming conditions in New York or Illinois could guide them, and family by family, crises of mortgage and crop failure followed the onset of drought. The settlers read the mythology of the boomers that claimed, as his book title records, *Rain Follows the Plow.* Of course it did not, but settlers acted on the belief.

8. For the story of Roosevelt's North Dakota ranch and the Marquis de Mores, see also David McCullough, *Mornings on Horseback.* The Marquis's "chateau" has been preserved and tours are given all summer: the town of Medora presents a pageant on the story, and the nearby Theodore Roosevelt National Park features Roosevelt's cabin and ranger talks on the history.

9. Helen Stauffer says in her critical biography, *Mari Sandoz: Story Catcher of the Plains,* that Neihardt alone among western writers seems to have impacted Sandoz's work, and she examines a number of ways that *Crazy Horse* reflects the association: not only in the matter of speaking as the voice representing Indian perspective, but in particular choices of locution (141).

10. For a critical exchange about the issue of white scholars' use of Native American material, see Daniel F. Littlefield Jr.'s 1992 MAASA Presidential Address, "American Indians, American Scholars, and the American Literary Canon," and Arnold Krupat's "Scholarship and Native American Studies: A Response to Daniel Littlefield, Jr."

11. Thus academic norms keep the Indian perspective out. Cook-Lynn goes on: "The non-Indian or nontribal intellectuals, then, in failing to become aware that the interests of submerged cultures have survived, and the memories of the grandmothers who were witnesses to outrage have

informed the present story, are left to confront the irreconcilable elements and philosophical matters of their own cultures, remain in ignorance and fear, or become obstructionists to rival precepts" (75).

12. Thanks to Shari Huhndorf for reminding me of how impossible this situation was: the very necessity of trying either resistance or accommodation was governed by military pressure, and both sides spelled death for the Native Americans.

13. Bhabha discusses this double temporality that the gendered sign can hold together in "DissemiNation," in *Nation and Narration*, 304. He draws from Kristeva's "On Women's Time."

14. Sidner Larson has pointed out to me how the concept of doubling is related to "the dualism, polarity, paradox, or relationship between opposites *crucial* to Native American philosophy, that is, Tricksterism." Personal correspondence, May 1996.

15. From "Crazy Horse Protest" by Jim Postema, a letter posted on the Internet, April 14, 1995. The letter was addressed to the owners of Hornell Brewing Company, producers of "Crazy Horse Malt Liquor." It is signed by many pages of supporters.

16. In *Ronald Reagan, the Movie*, Rogin analyzes the logic of abstraction that enabled Indian destruction to be national policy: "To face responsibility for specific killing might have led to efforts to stop it; to avoid individual deaths turned Indian removal into a theory of genocide" (168).

17. These source materials are stored, together with some of her notes on them, in the Mari Sandoz collection at the University of Nebraska.

18. For Kristeva's development of the concept of the "clean and proper self," see *Powers of Horror*.

19. Nancy Armstrong discusses the importance of captivity narratives for understanding the transmission of Englishness by daughters in "Purity and Daughters in American Fiction," *Oxford Companion to Women's Writing in the United States*. The ideal of womanhood realized in daughters, she argues, is crucial to group identity: the family bears the burden of cultural transmission. At the same time, "The sentimental conventions of the family actually divided a national population into racial, ethnic, and regional groups that existed in a peripheral relationship to an elite core whose values are both universalized and critiqued in canonical literature" (ms. 11).

20. Mari Sandoz herself wrote that the story of the Indians was Greek in its tragic dimensions. After the war, she would see the parallels between the treatment of the Indians by the United States government and Hitler's Holocaust.

21. In 1939, when Sandoz was preparing to write *Cheyenne Autumn*, she discovered that Howard Fast would beat her to the story—something she considered to be unethical, since it was widely known that she had

been researching those materials for several years. He published *The Last Frontier*, a fictionalized, lightly researched version of the Cheyenne's flight in 1941. Meanwhile, she turned instead to Crazy Horse. See Stauffer for the reports of this sequence of events.

22. Janice Radway has described the Book-of-the-Month Club's operations in "The Book-of-the-Month Club and the General Reader," and "Mail-Order Culture and Its Critics."

6. The Warrior Is a Stage Adolescents Go Through: Ursula Le Guin's Thought Experiments

1. Can she live by bread alone, by craft, not aesthetic, and let go of stylistic rupture as "fancy pastry"? Her recent virtuoso story, "Sunday in Summer in Seatown," demonstrates how these modernist distinctions might give way. It is written in a repetitive style that should recall Gertrude Stein, but that also shows us how Stein's significance is not only in being difficult or elite: Stein, like Le Guin, enforced forms of attention not based on a linear plot. Le Guin takes the figure from the sea (and Virginia Woolf): "The waves come in, the many waves as many as ever coming in" (*Unlocking* 88).

2. The field of shared interest between Kristeva and Le Guin may be suggested by their mutual respect for the work of Marina Warner, whose book on Mary influenced Kristeva's thinking about the place of Mary and the maternal in Western culture: *Alone of All Her Sex: The Myth and the Cult of the Virgin Mary*. Kristeva's essay, "Stabat Mater," (reprinted in *The Kristeva Reader* 161–86) juxtaposes material about her own experience of maternity with reflections about the absence of a discourse of motherhood in modern culture. Though she had not read that work by Warner, Le Guin gave her *Six Myths of Our Time* high marks in a recent review, "The Stories We Agree to Tell."

3. See her discussion in the introduction of the *Language of the Night*, where she declares that "genrification is a political tactic" (3). A critic of her anthology for Norton accused her of political correctness: this may attest to the connection of gender and genre.

4. Family bonds provide a counterpoint to the modernist (and individualist) drive toward freedom, but it's not easy, in the field of Cold War debates, to free the idea of the family from its context in a narrow moralizing heterosexuality. In spite of all that this book does to imagine a culture free of exploitation that might nonetheless be based on real human attachments, the very scene of family reproduces conventions of exclusion as well. Shevek's radical friend, Bedap, sees father and daughter together in "that one intimacy which he could not share, the hardest and deepest, the intimacy of pain" (297). He thinks, "Time's going to run

out on me, all at once, and I will never have had . . . that" (298). While "that" is not specified, as Samuel Delany has pointed out, the fact that Bedap appeared earlier in a homosexual relationship with Shevek suggests that only heterosexual bonds can make "that"—what he has not had. Or perhaps "that" is simply the bond of commitment: unlike most of the people on Anarres, Shevek and Takver have taken a pledge to bond, to a lifetime together. It does not turn out to mean that they are not separated, but rather that Shevek always returns.

5. Evidence of the instructional effect of Le Guin's texts has begun to accumulate—what the critics learned (including those who never thought they would find such lessons in such a genre); what the teachers hope to teach, using Le Guin. If it is hard to know what the young take away from their reading, the record of some quarter-century's interest in the Earthsea trilogy testifies that adolescent readers have wanted to read Le Guin's books. Kathryn Ross Wayne has written about an "ecocentric" reading of Le Guin: "Le Guin educates us . . . about the relationship between morality and language and culture and environment, through metaphor" (3). Wayne's orientation is to the pedagogy of moral value, especially Carol Gilligan's arguments for an "ethic of care" and Chet Bowers's arguments for an ecocentric theory of pedagogy. Diana Sheridan's dissertation, "Ecofeminist Strategies of Peacemaking," analyzed rhetorical strategies from *Always Coming Home* as a new model for feminist processes. She argued, for example, that Le Guin's violations of conventional forms demonstrate a political rhetoric that would help escape linear thinking and that Le Guin gives us "a teaching book of strategies" (211).

6. Bernard Selinger has argued that the question of identity is important in all of Le Guin's writing. He reads the Earthsea trilogy as an allegory of the wizard/artist who learns through an encounter with the shadow to keep the Semiotic and the Symbolic in balance. Selinger acknowledges that the book seems clearly indebted to Jungian ideas, but he nevertheless undertakes to give it a more Lacanian reading. According to Selinger, the shadow gathers together associations with women—Elfarren, the Lady of O, Serret, Yarrow—as "representatives of Ged's conflicting desire to reestablish the primary narcissistic unity of identity with the environment-mother, as against his fear of the environment-mother (frequently associated with the vulva)—fear of being drowned, sucked in, overpowered" (47). Although Selinger doesn't analyze the representation of the earth's dark "old powers" in the *Tombs of Atuan,* that would support his point.

7. In "Mourning and Melancholia" Freud advances his theory of the interconnection between language and mourning, on the one hand, and the idea, on the other, that melancholy accompanies a failure to undergo the separation from the mother. Julia Kristeva analyzes the close connec-

tion between melancholy and the artist in *Black Sun,* arguing that a depressive text such as that of Marguerite Duras can have a certain psychic danger, with its seductive but unaesthetic style.

8. Francis Crick and Thomas Hager both spoke at a Conference on Linus Pauling, held at Oregon State University in Corvallis, Oregon, March 1, 1995.

Works Cited and Consulted

Adams, James Eli. *Dandies and Desert Saints: Styles of Victorian Masculinity.* Ithaca: Cornell UP, 1995.

Aldridge, John. *After the Lost Generation: A Critical Study of the Writers of Two Wars.* New York: McGraw-Hill, 1951.

Arendt, Hannah. *The Origins of Totalitarianism.* 1951. New York: Harcourt, 1973.

Armstrong, Nancy. "Purity and Daughters in American Fiction." *Oxford Companion to Women's Writing in the United States.* Editors in chief, Cathy N. Davidson, Linda Wagner-Martin. Ed. Elizabeth Ammons et al. New York: Oxford UP, 1995.

Aronowitz, Stanley. *Roll Over, Beethoven.* Hanover: Wesleyan UP, 1993.

Badinter, Elisabeth. *XY: On Masculine Identity.* Trans. Lydia Davis. New York: Columbia UP, 1995.

Baker, Carlos. *Ernest Hemingway: A Life Story.* New York: Scribner's, 1969.

Barker, Jane Valentine. *Mari: A Novel.* Niwot: UP of Colorado, 1997.

Barr, Marleen S. *Feminist Fabulation: Space/Postmodern Fiction.* Iowa City: U of Iowa P, 1992.

Bateson, Mary Catherine. *Composing a Life.* New York: Atlantic Monthly, 1989.

Baym, Nina. "Melodramas of Beset Manhood," *American Quarterly* 33.2 (1981): 123–39.

Bederman, Gail. *Manliness & Civilization: A Cultural History of Gender and Race in the United States, 1880–1917.* Chicago: U of Chicago P, 1995.

Beegel, Susan F. *Hemingway's Craft of Omission: Four Manuscript Examples.* Ann Arbor: UMI Research, 1988.

Bell, Daniel. *The End of Ideology: On the Exhaustion of Political Ideas in the Fifties.* New York: Collier, 1961.

Bell, Michael Davitt. *The Problem of American Realism.* Chicago: U of Chicago P, 1993.

Belton, Don. *Speak My Name: Black Men on Masculinity and the American Dream.* Boston: Beacon, 1995.

Beneke, Timothy. *Proving Manhood: Reflections on Men and Sexism.* Berkeley: U of California P, 1997.

Benjamin, Walter. *Illuminations.* New York: Schocken, 1969.

Bercovitch, Sacvan. *The American Jeremiad.* Madison: U of Wisconsin P, 1978.

Berger, Maurice, et al. *Constructing Masculinity.* New York: Routledge, 1995.

Bernstein, Barton J., and Allen J. Matusow, eds. *The Truman Administration: A Documentary History.* New York: Harper Colophon, 1966.

Bernstein, Carl. *Loyalties: A Son's Memoir.* New York: Simon, 1989.

Betcher, R. William, and William S. Pallack. *In a Time of Fallen Heroes: The Recreation of Masculinity.* New York: Guilford, 1994.

Bhabha, Homi K. "DissemiNation." *Nation and Narration.* New York: Routledge, 1990: 291–322.

———. *The Location of Culture.* New York: Routledge, 1994.

———. "Postcolonial Authority and Postmodern Guilt." *Cultural Studies.* Ed. Lawrence Grossberg, Cary Nelson, and Paula Treichler. New York: Routledge, 1992.

Bissell, Richard M., Jonathan E. Lewis, and Frances T. Pudlo. *Reflections of a Cold Warrior: From Yalta to the Bay of Pigs.* New Haven: Yale UP, 1996.

Bittner, James W. *Approaches to the Fiction of Ursula K. Le Guin.* Ann Arbor: UMI Research, 1984.

Bloom, Harold. *Ursula K. Le Guin: Modern Critical Views.* New York: Chelsea, 1986.

———. *Ursula K. Le Guin's "The Left Hand of Darkness."* New York: Chelsea, 1987.

Boone, Joseph, and Michael Cadden. *Engendering Men.* New York: Routledge, 1990.

Bowers, C. A. *The Culture of Denial: Why the Environmental Movement Needs a Strategy for Reforming Universities and Public Schools.* Albany: State U of New York P, 1997.

Braidotti, Rosa. *Patterns of Dissonance.* Oxford: Polity, 1991.

Brasch, James D., and Joseph Sigman. *Hemingway's Library: A Composite Record.* New York: Garland, 1981.

Breen, Dana. *The Gender Conundrum: Contemporary Psychoanalytic Perspectives on Femininity and Masculinity.* New York: Routledge, 1993.

Brick, Howard. *Daniel Bell and the Decline of Intellectual Radicalism: Social Theory and Political Reconciliation in the 1940s.* Madison: U of Wisconsin P, 1986.

Brininstool, E. A. "How 'Crazy Horse' Died: Thrilling Details of the Foul Murder of One of the Greatest Fighting Chiefs of the Sioux Nation." *Nebraska History Magazine* (December 1929): 4.

Brittan, Arthur. *Masculinity and Power.* Oxford: Blackwell, 1989.

Brooks, Cleanth. *The Well-Wrought Urn: Studies in the Structure of Poetry.* New York: Harcourt, 1947.

Brown, Ian. *Man Medium Rare: Sex, Guns, and Other Perversions of Masculinity.* New York: Dutton, 1994.

Bucknall, Barbara J. *Ursula K. Le Guin.* New York: Ungar, 1981.

Burwell, Rose Marie. *Hemingway: The Postwar Years and the Posthumous Novels.* New York: Cambridge UP, 1996.

Bush, Vannevar. "Science, the Endless Frontier." A report to the President. July 1945. United States Office of Scientific Research and Development. Washington: U.S. Govt. Printing Office, 1945.

Butler, Judith. *Bodies That Matter: On the Discursive Limits of "Sex."* New York: Routledge, 1993.

———. *Gender Trouble: Feminism and the Subversion of Identity.* New York: Routledge, 1990.

Cain, William E. *F. O. Matthiessen and the Politics of Criticism.* Madison: U of Wisconsin P, 1988.

Caldicott, Helen. *Missile Envy: The Arms Race and Nuclear War.* New York: Bantam, 1986.

Cannon, Kelly. *Henry James and Masculinity: The Man at the Margins.* New York: St. Martin's, 1994.

Carpenter, Ted Galen. *The Captive Press: Foreign Policy Crises and the First Amendment.* Washington, D.C.: Cato Institute, 1995.

Caute, David. *The Great Fear: The Anti-Communist Purge under Truman and Eisenhower.* New York: Simon, 1978.

"Censored Books." Internet site. <http://simr02.si.chu.es/FileRoom/documents/Cases/266 hemingway.html>.

Chaloupka, William. *Knowing Nukes: The Politics and Culture of the Atom.* Minneapolis: U of Minnesota P, 1992.

Chase, Richard. *The American Novel and Its Tradition.* Garden City: Doubleday, 1957.

Cixous, Hélène. "The Laugh of the Medusa." 1975. Trans. Keith Cohen and Paula Cohen. *New French Feminisms: An Anthology.* Eds. Elaine Marks and Isabelle de Courtivron. New York: Schocken, 1981.

Clark, Laverne Harrell. *Re-visiting the Plains Indian Country of Mari Sandoz: A Pictorial Essay with Captions and Photographs.* Marvin: Blue Cloud Quarterly, 1977.

Clark, Robert D. *Rain Follows the Plow.* Lincoln: Foundation, 1996.

Clark, Suzanne. *Sentimental Modernism: Women Writers and the Revolution of the Word.* Bloomington: Indiana UP, 1991.

Clifford, Stephen P. *Beyond the Heroic "I": Reading Lawrence, Hemingway, and "Masculinity."* Lewisburg: Bucknell UP, 1999.

Cohan, Steven. *Masked Men: Masculinity and the Movies in the Fifties.* Bloomington: Indiana UP, 1997.

Comley, Nancy, and Robert Scholes. *Hemingway's Genders: Rereading the Hemingway Text.* New Haven: Yale UP, 1994.

Cook-Lynn, Elizabeth. *Why I Can't Read Wallace Stegner: A Tribal Voice.* Madison: U of Wisconsin P, 1996.

Cooney, Terry A. *The Rise of the New York Intellectuals: Partisan Review and Its Circle, 1934–1945.* Madison: U of Wisconsin P, 1986.

Corber, Robert J. *Homosexuality in Cold War America: Resistance and the Crisis of Masculinity.* Durham: Duke UP, 1997.

Craig, Steve. *Men, Masculinity, and the Media.* Newbury Park: Sage, 1992.

Crossman, Richard, ed. *The God That Failed: Six Studies in Communism.* New York: Harper, 1949.

Cummins, Elizabeth. *Understanding Ursula K. Le Guin.* Rev. ed. Columbia: U of South Carolina P, 1993.

Cutright, Paul Russell. *Theodore Roosevelt, the Making of a Conservationist.* Urbana: U of Illinois P, 1985.

Davidson, Michael. *The San Francisco Renaissance: Poetics and Community at Mid-century.* Cambridge: Cambridge UP, 1989.

De Bolt, Joe. *Ursula K. Le Guin, Voyager to Inner Lands and to Outer Space.* Port Washington: Kennikat, 1979.

Deloria, Vine, Jr. "Neihardt and the Western Landscape." *A Sender of Words:*

Essays in Memory of John G. Neihardt. Ed. Vine Deloria Jr. Salt Lake City: Howe Brothers, 1984. 85–99.

Derrida, Jacques. *Specters of Marx: The State of the Debt, the Work of Mourning and the New International.* Trans. Peggy Kamuf. Introd. Bernard Magnus and Stephen Cullenberg. New York: Routledge, 1994.

Diller, Jerry Victor. *Freud's Jewish Identity: A Case Study in the Impact of Ethnicity.* Rutherford: Fairleigh Dickinson UP, 1991.

Di Stefano, Christine. *Configurations of Masculinity: A Feminist Perspective on Modern Political Theory.* Ithaca: Cornell UP, 1991.

Easlea, Brian. *Fathering the Unthinkable: Masculinity, Scientists, and the Nuclear Arms Race.* London: Pluto, 1983.

Ehrenreich, Barbara. "The Warrior Culture." *Time* 15 Oct. 1990: 100.

Eliot, Thomas Stearns. "Hamlet and His Problems." *The Sacred Wood.* London: Methuen, 1920. 95–103.

Elmhurst, Ernest. *The World Hoax.* Introd. William Dudley Pelley. Asheville: Pelley, 1938.

Engelhardt, Tom. *The End of Victory Culture: Cold War America and the Disillusioning of a Generation.* New York: Basic, 1995.

Enloe, Cynthia. *The Morning After: Sexual Politics at the End of the Cold War.* Berkeley: U of California P, 1993.

Fast, Howard. *The Last Frontier.* New York: Duell, 1941.

Feidelson, Charles, Jr. *Symbolism and American Literature.* Chicago: U of Chicago P, 1953.

Felman, Shoshana, and Dori Laub. *Testimony: Crises of Witnessing in Literature, Psychoanalysis and History.* New York: Routledge, 1991.

Fisher, Philip. *Hard Facts: Setting and Form in the American Novel.* New York: Oxford UP, 1985.

Foucault, Michel. *The History of Sexuality.* Vol. 1. Trans. Robert Hurley. New York: Vintage, 1980.

Frazier, Robert B. Rev. of *A New Life.* [Eugene] *Register-Guard*, 10 Oct. 1961.

Freud, Sigmund. *Civilization and Its Discontents.* Trans. and ed. James Strachey. New York: Norton, 1962.

———. "Mourning and Melancholia." *The Freud Reader.* Ed. Peter Gay. New York: Norton, 1982. 584–88.

Gibson, James William. *Paramilitary Dreams in Post-Vietnam America.* New York: Hill, 1994.

Gilbert, Sandra M., and Susan Gubar. *No Man's Land: The Place of the Woman Writer in the Twentieth Century.* 3 vols. New Haven: Yale UP, 1988–94.

Gilmore, David D. *Manhood in the Making: Cultural Concepts of Masculinity.* New Haven: Yale UP, 1990.

Greenwell, Scott. L. *Descriptive Guide to the Mari Sandoz Collection.* Lincoln: U of Nebraska P, 1980.

Groshong, James. "Trouble in the West: Malamud's New Book." Clipping from *Corvallis Gazette-Times.* Malamud Collection. Valley Library. Oregon State U, Corvallis.

Grosz, Elizabeth. *Volatile Bodies: Toward a Corporeal Feminism.* Bloomington: Indiana UP, 1994.

Hager, Thomas. *Force of Nature: The Life of Linus Pauling.* New York: Simon and Schuster, 1995.

Halberstam, David. *The Fifties.* New York: Villard, 1993.

Haraway, Donna. "Teddy Bear Patriarchy: Taxidermy in the Garden of Eden, New York City, 1908–1936." *Cultures of United States Imperialism.* Ed. Amy Kaplan and Donald E. Pease. Durham: Duke UP, 1993. 237–91.

Hearn, Jeff. *The Gender of Oppression: Men, Masculinity, and the Critique of Marxism.* New York: St. Martin's, 1987.

He Dog. Interview with Eleanor Hinman and Mari Sandoz. Oglala, South Dakota, July 13, 1930. "Oglala Sources on the Life of Crazy Horse." Eleanor Hinman. *Nebraska History* 57.1 (1976): 23.

Hemingway, Ernest. *Across the River and into the Trees.* New York: Scribner's, 1950.

———. *The Complete Short Stories of Ernest Hemingway: The Finca Vigia Edition.* New York: Scribner's, 1987.

———. *The Dangerous Summer.* New York: Scribner's, 1960.

———. *Death in the Afternoon.* New York: Scribner's, 1932.

———. *For Whom the Bell Tolls.* New York: Scribner's, 1940.

———. *The Garden of Eden.* New York: Scribner's, 1986.

———. *Green Hills of Africa.* New York: Scribner's, 1935.

———. *Islands in the Stream.* New York: Scribner's, 1970.

———. *A Moveable Feast.* New York: Scribner's, 1964.

———. *The Old Man and the Sea.* New York: Scribner's, 1952.

———. "On the American Dead in Spain." Cassette recording. *Remembering Spain: Hemingway's Civil War Eulogy and the Veterans of the Abraham Lincoln Brigade.* Ed. Cary Nelson. Urbana: U of Illinois P, 1994.

———."Roosevelt." *Poetry* 21.4 (1923): 193–94.

———. *Selected Letters, 1917–1961.* Ed. Carlos Baker. New York: Scribner's, 1981.

———. *The Sun Also Rises.* New York: Scribner's, 1926.

———. *The Torrents of Spring.* New York: Scribner's, 1926.

Hicks, Granville. "Hard Road to the Good Life." Clipping. Malamud Collection. Valley Library, Oregon State U, Corvallis.

Hinds, Lynn Boyd, and Theodore Otto Windt Jr. *The Cold War as Rhetoric.* New York: Praeger, 1991.

Hollander, John. "To Find the Westward Path." *Partisan Review* (Winter 1962): 137–39.

Hook, Sidney. "Academic Freedom." *New York Times Magazine* (27 Feb. 1949).

———. *The Hero in History: A Study in Limitation and Possibility.* Boston: Beacon, 1943.

———, ed. *In Defense of Academic Freedom.* New York: Pegasus, 1971.

———. *Psychoanalysis, Scientific Method, and Philosophy.* New York: New York UP, 1959.

———. "Should Communists Be Permitted to Teach?" *New York Times Magazine* (27 Feb. 1949): 23–24, 26–28.

Horrocks, Roger. *Male Myths and Icons: Masculinity in Popular Culture.* New York: St. Martin's, 1995.

Horrocks, Roger, and Jo Campling. *Masculinity in Crisis: Myths, Fantasies, and Realities.* New York: St. Martin's, 1994.

Hulme, T. E. "Romanticism and Classicism." *Speculations.* Ed. Herbert Read. New York: Harcourt, 1924. 113–40.

Huyssen, Andreas. *After the Great Divide: Modernism, Mass Culture, Postmodernism.* Bloomington: Indiana UP, 1986.

Jameson, Fredric. *Fables of Aggression: Wyndham Lewis, the Modernist as Fascist.* Berkeley: U of California P, 1979.

———. "The Symbolic Inference." *Representing Kenneth Burke.* Ed. Hayden White and Margaret Brose. Baltimore: Johns Hopkins UP, 1982.

Jeffords, Susan. *Hard Bodies: Hollywood Masculinity in the Reagan Era.* New Brunswick: Rutgers UP, 1994.

———. *The Remasculinization of America.* Bloomington: Indiana UP, 1989.

Johnson, Sally A., and Ulrike Hanna Meinhof. *Language and Masculinity.* Oxford: Blackwell, 1997.

Jonsson, Christer. "The Ideology of Foreign Policy." *Foreign Policy, USA/USSR.* Ed. Charles W. Kegley Jr. and Pat McGowan. Beverly Hills: Sage, 1982.

Kaldor, Mary. *The Imaginary War: Understanding the East-West Conflict.* Cambridge: Basil Blackwell, 1990.

Kaplan, Alice Yaeger. *Reproductions of Banality: Fascism, Literature, and French Intellectual Life.* Minneapolis: U of Minnesota P, 1986.

Kenner, Hugh. *The Pound Era.* Berkeley: U of California P, 1971.

Keulen, Margarete. *Radical Imagination: Feminist Conceptions of the Future in Ursula Le Guin, Marge Piercy, and Sally Miller Gearhart.* New York: P. Lang, 1991.

Kimbrell, Andrew. *The Masculine Mystique: The Politics of Masculinity.* New York: Ballantine, 1995.

Kimmel, Michael S., and Thomas E. Mosmiller. *Against the Tide: Pro-Feminist Men in the United States, 1776–1990: A Documentary History.* Boston: Beacon, 1992.

Kirkham, Pat, and Janet Thumim. *You Tarzan: Masculinity, Movies, and Men.* New York: St. Martin's, 1993.

Konrad, George. *Antipolitics.* Trans. Richard E. Allen. San Diego: Harcourt, 1984.

Krieger, Murray. *The New Apologists for Poetry.* Minneapolis: U of Minnesota P, 1956.

———. *The Tragic Vision: Variations on a Theme in Literary Interpretation.* Chicago: U of Chicago P, 1960.

Kristeva, Julia. *Black Sun.* Trans. Leon Roudiez. New York: Columbia UP, 1989.

———. "On Women's Time." Trans. Alice Jardine and Harry Blake. *The Kristeva Reader.* Ed. Toril Moi. New York: Columbia UP, 1986.

———. *Powers of Horror: An Essay on Abjection.* Trans. Leon S. Roudiez. New York: Columbia UP, 1984.

———. *Revolution in Poetic Language.* Trans. Margaret Waller. New York: Columbia UP, 1984.

———. *Strangers to Ourselves.* Trans. Leon S. Roudiez. New York: Columbia UP, 1991.

———. "The True-Real." Trans. Sean Hand. *The Kristeva Reader.* Ed. Toril Moi. New York: Columbia UP, 1986. 214–37.

Kroeber, Theodora. *Alfred Kroeber: A Personal Configuration.* Berkeley: U of California P, 1970.

———. *The Inland Whale.* Fwd. Oliver La Farge. Bloomington: Indiana UP, 1959.

———. *Ishi in Two Worlds: A Biography of the Last Wild Indian in North America.* Berkeley: U of California P, 1971.

Krupat, Arnold. "Scholarship and Native American Studies: A Response to Daniel Littlefield, Jr." *American Studies* 34.2 (1993): 81–100.

Krupnick, Mark. *Lionel Trilling and the Fate of Cultural Criticism.* Evanston: Northwestern UP, 1986.

Krutnik, Frank. *In a Lonely Street: Film Noir, Genre, Masculinity.* New York: Routledge, 1998.

Lacan, Jacques. "The Mirror Stage as Formative of the Function of the I as Revealed in Psychoanalytic Experience." *Ecrits.* Trans. Alan Sheridan. New York: Norton, 1977. 1–7.

Lauter, Paul. *Canons and Contexts.* New York: Oxford UP, 1991.

Lears, Jackson. "A Matter of Taste." *Recasting America: Culture and Politics in the Age of the Cold War.* Ed. Lary May. Chicago: U of Chicago P, 1989. 38–57.

Le Guin, Magnolia Wynn. *A Home-Concealed Woman: The Diaries of Magnolia Wynn Le Guin, 1901–1913.* Ed. Charles A. Le Guin. Fwd. Ursula K. Le Guin. Athens: U of Georgia P, 1990.

Le Guin, Ursula. *Buffalo Gals and Other Animal Presences.* Santa Barbara: Capra, 1987.

———. *The Compass Rose: Short Stories.* New York: Harper, 1982.

———. *Dancing at the Edge of the World: Thoughts on Words, Women, Places.* New York: Grove, 1989.

———. *The Dispossessed.* 1974. New York: Avon, 1975.

———. *Dreams Must Explain Themselves.* San Bernardino: Borgo, 1983.

———. *Earthsea Revisioned.* Cambridge: Green Bay, 1993.

———. *The Farthest Shore.* New York: Atheneum, 1972.

———. *Four Ways to Forgiveness.* New York: HarperPrism, 1995.

———. *The Language of the Night: Essays on Fantasy and Science Fiction.* Ed. and introd. Susan Wood. New York: Putnam, 1979.

———. *The Left Hand of Darkness.* 1969. New York: Ace, 1976.

———. *Malafrena.* New York: Berkley, 1979.

———. *Orsinian Tales.* New York: Harper, 1976.

———. *Searoad: Chronicles of Klatsand.* New York: HarperCollins, 1991.

———. "The Stories We Agree to Tell." *New York Times Book Review* (12 Mar. 1995): 6.

———, trans. *Tao Te Ching: A Book about the Way and the Power of the Way.* By Lao Tzu. Boston: Shambala, 1997.

———. *Tehanu: The Last Book of Earthsea.* New York: Atheneum, 1990.

———. *Three Hainish Novels. Rocannon's World Planet of Exile City of Illusions.* 1967. Garden City: Doubleday, 1978.

———. *The Tombs of Atuan.* New York: Atheneum, 1971.

———. *Unlocking the Air and Other Stories.* New York: HarperCollins, 1996.

———. *The Wind's Twelve Quarters: Short Stories.* New York: Harper, 1975.

———. *A Wizard of Earthsea.* Oakland: Parnassus. 1968.

———. *The Word for World Is Forest.* New York: Berkley, 1972.

Le Guin, Ursula, and Brian Attebery, eds. *The Norton Book of Science Fiction: North American Science Fiction, 1960–1990*. New York: Norton, 1993.

Le Guin, Ursula, and Roger Dorband. *Blue Moon over Thurman Street*. Portland: NewSage, 1993.

Lewis, R. W. B. *The American Adam: Innocence, Tragedy, and Tradition in the Nineteenth Century*. Chicago: U of Chicago P, 1955.

Lewis, Robert W., Jr. *Hemingway on Love*. Austin: U of Texas P, 1965.

———. "'Long Time Ago Good, Now No Good:' Hemingway's Indian Stories." *New Critical Approaches to the Short Stories of Ernest Hemingway*. Ed. Jackson J. Benson. Durham: Duke UP, 1990. 200–212.

Limerick, Patricia. *The Legacy of Conquest: The Unbroken Past of the American West*. New York: Norton, 1987.

Littlefield, Daniel F., Jr. "American Indians, American Scholars, and the American Literary Canon." *American Studies* 33.2 (1992): 95–109.

Love, Glen. "Hemingway's Indian Virtues: An Ecological Reconsideration." *Western American Literature* 22.3 (1987): 201–13.

Lupton, Marylyn A. "The Seduction of Jim Gilmore." *Hemingway Review* 15.1 (1995): 1–9.

Lutts, Ralph H. *Nature Fakers: Wildlife, Science & Sentiment*. Golden: Fulcrum, 1990.

Lynn, Kenneth. *Hemingway*. New York: Simon & Schuster, 1987.

Lyotard, Jean-François. *The Postmodern Condition: A Report on Knowledge*. Trans. Geoff Bennington and Brian Massumi. Minneapolis: U of Minnesota P, 1984.

Macdonald, Dwight. "A Theory of Mass Culture." *Mass Culture: The Popular Arts in America*. Ed. Bernard Rosenberg and David Manning White. Glencoe: Free Press, 1957. 59–73.

MacInnes, John. *The End of Masculinity: The Confusion of Sexual Genesis and Sexual Difference in Modern Society*. Philadelphia: Open University P, 1998.

Malamud, Bernard. *The Assistant*. New York: Farrar, 1957.

———. *Dubin's Lives*. New York: Farrar, 1979.

———. *The Fixer*. New York: Farrar, 1966.

———. *God's Grace*. New York: Farrar, 1982.

———. *Idiots First*. New York: Farrar, 1963.

———. Introduction and Reading: Corvallis, Oregon, 1967. Malamud Collection. Valley Library. Oregon State U, Corvallis.

———. *Long Work, Short Life*. Chapbook of lecture at Bennington, Oct. 30, 1984. Bennington: Bennington College, 1985.

———. *The Magic Barrel*. New York: Farrar, Straus, and Cudahy, 1958.

———. *The Natural*. New York: Harcourt, Brace, 1952.

———. *A New Life*. New York: Farrar, Straus, Giroux, 1961.

———. *The People and Uncollected Stories*. Farrar, Straus, Giroux, 1989.

———. *Pictures of Fidelman*. New York: Farrar, Straus, Giroux, 1969.

———. *Rembrandt's Hat*. New York: Farrar, Straus, Giroux, 1973.

———. *The Tenants*. New York: Farrar, Straus, Giroux, 1971.

May, Elaine Tyler. *Homeward Bound: American Families in the Cold War Era*. New York: Basic, 1988.

May, Larry. *Masculinity and Morality.* Ithaca: Cornell UP, 1998.

———. *Recasting America: Culture and Politics in the Age of Cold War.* Chicago: U of Chicago P, 1989.

May, Larry, Robert A. Strikwerda, and Patrick D. Hopkins. *Rethinking Masculinity: Philosophical Explorations in Light of Feminism.* Lanham: Littlefield Adams, 1992.

McCarthy, Mary. *The Groves of Academe.* New York: Harcourt, 1952.

McCullough, David. *Mornings on Horseback.* New York: Simon, 1981.

McLauchlan, Gregory, and Gregory Hooks. "Last of the Dinosaurs: Big Weapons, Big Science, and the American State from Hiroshima to the End of the Cold War." *Sociological Quarterly* 36 (1995): 749–76.

McNickle, D'Arcy. *The Indian Tribes of the United States: Ethnic and Cultural Survival.* New York: Oxford UP, 1962.

———. *They Came Here First: The Epic of the American Indian.* 1949. Rev. ed. New York: Harper, 1975.

Meyers, Jeffrey. *Hemingway: The Critical Heritage.* London: Routledge, 1982.

Michaels, Walter Benn. *Our America: Nativism, Modernism, and Pluralism.* Durham: Duke UP, 1995.

Michener, James. Introd. *The Dangerous Summer.* By Ernest Hemingway. New York: Scribner's, 1985.

Middleton, Peter. *The Inward Gaze: Masculinity and Subjectivity in Modern Culture.* New York: Routledge, 1992.

Mitchell, Greg. *The Campaign of the Century: Upton Sinclair's Race for Governor of California and the Birth of Media Politics.* New York: Random, 1992.

Mitgang, Herbert. *Dangerous Dossiers: Exposing the Secret War Against America's Greatest Authors.* New York: Donald I. Fine, 1988.

Morrison, Toni. *Playing in the Dark: Whiteness and the Literary Imagination.* Cambridge: Harvard UP, 1992.

Morse, Wayne. Speech in the United States Senate. *Congressional Record.* March 3, 1949, recorded in the appendix A1821–27.

Mosse, George L. *The Image of Man: The Creation of Modern Masculinity.* New York: Oxford, 1996.

———. *Nationalism and Sexuality: Middle-Class Morality and Sexual Norms in Modern Europe.* Madison: U of Wisconsin P, 1985.

Mullen, R. D., and Darko Suvin. *Science-Fiction Studies: Selected Articles on Science Fiction, 1973–1975.* Boston: Gregg, 1976.

Murphy, Peter Francis. *Fictions of Masculinity: Crossing Cultures, Crossing Sexualities.* New York: New York UP, 1994.

Nadel, Alan. *Containment Culture.* Durham: Duke UP, 1995.

Nelson, Cary. "Hemingway, the American Left, and the Soviet Union: Some Forgotten Episodes." *Hemingway Review* 14.1 (1994): 36–45.

———. *Repression and Recovery: Modern American Poetry and the Politics Of Cultural Memory, 1910–1945.* Madison: U of Wisconsin P, 1989.

Nietzsche, Friedrick. *The Birth of Tragedy and the Genealogy of Morals.* Trans. Francis Golffing. 1956. New York: Anchor, 1990.

Nixon, Richard. *In the Arena: A Memoir of Victory, Defeat, and Renewal.* New York: Simon, 1990.

————. *Six Crises*. Garden City: Doubleday, 1962.

North, Michael. *The Dialect of Modernism: Race, Language, and Twentieth Century Literature*. New York: Oxford UP, 1994.

Oates, Joyce Carol. *(Woman) Writer: Occasions and Opportunites*. New York: Dutton, 1988.

O'Hara, Daniel T. *Lionel Trilling: The Work of Liberation*. Madison: U of Wisconsin P, 1988.

————. "The Reality of Theory." *Criticism Without Boundaries: Directions and Crosscurrents in Postmodern Critical Theory*. Ed. Joseph A. Buttigieg. Notre Dame: U of Notre Dame P, 1987: 177–201.

Olander, Joseph D., and Martin Harry Greenberg. *Ursula K. Le Guin*. New York: Taplinger, 1979.

Oliver, Gary J. *Masculinity at the Crossroads*. Chicago: Moody, 1993.

Orvell, Miles. *The Real Thing*. Chapel Hill: U of North Carolina P, 1989.

Parker, Andrew, Mary Russo, Doris Sommer, and Patricia Yaeger, eds. *Nationalisms and Sexualities*. New York: Routledge, 1992.

Pattee, Fred Lewis. *The Feminine Fifties*. New York: Appleton-Century, 1940.

Pauling, Linus. Letter to Milton Burton. 28 Feb. 1949. Ava and Linus Pauling Papers. Valley Library. Oregon State U, Corvallis.

————. Letter to Ralph Spitzer. 26 Sept. 1945. Ava and Linus Pauling Papers. Valley Library. Oregon State U, Corvallis.

Payne, Darwin. *Owen Wister: Chronicler of the West, Gentleman of the East*. Dallas: Southern Methodist UP, 1985.

Pease, Donald. "National Identities, Postmodern Artifacts, and Postnational Narratives." *boundary 2* 19.1 (1992): 1–13.

————. "New Americanists: Revisionist Interventions into the Canon." *boundary 2* 17.1 (Spring 1990): 1–37.

————. *Visionary Compacts: American Renaissance Writings in Cultural Context*. Madison: U of Wisconsin P, 1987.

Pells, Richard. *The Liberal Mind in a Conservative Age: American Intellectuals in the 1940s and 1950s*. New York: Harper, 1985.

Pinsker, Sanford. *Jewish-American Fiction, 1917–1987*. New York: Twayne, 1992.

Pittman, Frank S. *Man Enough: Fathers, Sons, and the Search for Masculinity*. New York: Putnam, 1993.

Postema, Jim. "Crazy Horse Protest." 14 Apr. 1995. Online posting. "Crazy Horse, Oglala." Native American Literature list. <http://kuhttp.cc.ukans.edu/~marc/natlit/crazyhor.html>. 13 June 1995.

Pound, Ezra. *ABC of Reading*. 1934. New York: New Directions, 1960.

Rabinowitz, Paula. *Labor & Desire: Women's Revolutionary Fiction in Depression America*. Chapel Hill: U of North Carolina P, 1991.

Radway, Janice. "The Book-of-the-Month Club and the General Reader: The Uses of 'Serious' Fiction." *Reading in America*. Ed. Cathy N. Davidson. Baltimore: Johns Hopkins UP, 1989. 259–84.

————. "Mail-Order Culture and Its Critics." *Cultural Studies*. Ed. Lawrence Grossberg, Cary Nelson, and Paula Treichler. New York: Routledge, 1992. 512–30.

Raeburn, John. *Fame Became of Him: Hemingway as Public Writer*. Bloomington: Indiana UP, 1984.

Reginald, R., and George Edgar Slusser. *Zephyr and Boreas: Winds of Change in the Fiction of Ursula K. Le Guin.* San Bernardino: Borgo, 1996.

Reising, Russell. *The Unusable Past: Theory and the Study of American Literature.* New York: Methuen, 1986.

Reynolds, Michael. *Hemingway's Reading, 1910–1940.* Princeton: Princeton UP, 1981.

———. *Hemingway, the Paris Years.* Oxford: Blackwell, 1989.

———. *The Young Hemingway.* New York: Blackwell, 1986.

Rippey, Barbara. "Toward a New Paradigm: Mari Sandoz's Study of Red and White Myth in *Cheyenne Autumn.*" *Women and Western American Literature.* Ed. Helen Winter Stauffer and Susan J. Rosowski. Troy: Whitston, 1982. 247–66.

Robertson, Nora. "Hills like White Elephants." Unpublished manuscript. Eugene, Oregon, 1996.

Rogin, Michael Paul. *The Intellectuals and McCarthy: The Radical Specter.* Cambridge: MIT Press, 1967.

———. *Ronald Reagan, the Movie, and Other Episodes in Political Demonology.* Berkeley: U of California P, 1987.

Roosevelt, Theodore. *On Race—Riots—Reds—Crime.* Comp. Archibald B. Roosevelt. Metairie: Sons of Liberty Press, 1968.

———. *Ranch Life and the Hunting Trail.* Illus. Frederic Remington. New York: Century, 1920.

Rosaldo, Renato. *Culture and Truth: The Remaking of Social Analysis.* Boston: Beacon, 1989.

Rosen, David. *The Changing Fictions of Masculinity.* Urbana: U of Illinois P, 1993.

Rosteck, Thomas. *"See It Now" Confronts McCarthyism: Television Documentary and the Politics of Representation.* Tuscaloosa: U of Alabama P, 1994.

Rotundo, E. Anthony. *American Manhood: Transformations in Masculinity from the Revolution to the Modern Era.* New York: Basic, 1993.

Russo, Vito. *The Celluloid Closet: Homosexuality in the Movies.* Rev. ed. New York: Harper, 1987.

Said, Edward. *Culture and Imperialism.* New York: Knopf, 1993.

Sale, Maggie Montesinos. *The Slumbering Volcano: American Slave Ship Revolts and the Production of Rebellious Masculinity.* Durham: Duke UP, 1997.

Sandgren, Nelson. Personal Interview. 28 May 1988. Corvallis, Oregon.

Sandgren, Nelson, and Warren Hovland. Panel Discussion. Malamud Conference. Oregon State University, Corvallis. 26 May 1996.

Sandoz, Mari. *Cheyenne Autumn.* 1953. New York: Avon, 1964.

———. *Crazy Horse: The Strange Man of the Oglalas.* 1942. Lincoln: U of Nebraska P, 1961.

———. *Letters of Mari Sandoz.* Ed. and introd. Helen Winter Stauffer. Lincoln: U of Nebraska P, 1992.

———. *Love Song to the Plains.* New York: Harper, 1961.

———. *Old Jules.* 1935. Lincoln: U of Nebraska P, 1985.

———. *Son of the Gamblin' Man: The Youth of an Artist.* New York: Clarkson N. Potter, 1960.

———. *The Tom-Walker.* New York: Dial, 1947.

Savran, David. *Communists, Cowboys, and Queers: The Politics of Masculinity in the Work of Arthur Miller and Tennessee Williams.* Minneapolis: U of Minnesota P, 1992.

———. *Taking It Like a Man: White Masculinity, Masochism, and Contemporary American Culture.* Princeton: Princeton UP, 1998.

Scarry, Elaine. *The Body in Pain: The Making and Unmaking of the World.* New York: Oxford UP, 1985.

Schaub, Thomas. *American Fiction in the Cold War.* Madison: U of Wisconsin P, 1991.

Schoenberg, B. Mark. *Growing Up Male: The Psychology of Masculinity.* Westport: Bergin & Garvey, 1993.

Scholes, Robert. "Is There a Fish in This Text?" *Textual Power: Literary Theory and the Teaching of English.* New Haven: Yale UP, 1985.

Schrecker, Ellen. "Academic Freedom: The Historical View." *Regulating the Intellectuals.* Ed. Craig Kaplan and Ellen Schrecker. New York: Praeger, 1983. 25–44.

———. *The Age of McCarthyism: A Brief History with Documents.* Boston: Bedford, 1994.

———. *Many Are the Crimes: McCarthyism in America.* Boston: Little, 1998.

Schwenger, Peter. *Letter Bomb: Nuclear Holocaust and the Exploding Word.* Baltimore: Johns Hopkins UP, 1992.

———. *Phallic Critiques: Masculinity and Twentieth-Century Literature.* Boston: Routledge, 1984.

Scott, Bonnie Kime. *The Gender of Modernism.* Bloomington: Indiana UP, 1990.

———. *Refiguring Modernism.* Bloomington: Indiana UP, 1995.

Seidler, Victor J. *Unreasonable Men: Masculinity and Social Theory.* New York: Routledge, 1994.

Selinger, Bernard. *Le Guin and Identity in Contemporary Fiction.* Ann Arbor: UMI Research, 1988.

Sheridan, Diana. "Ecofeminist Strategies of Peacemaking." Diss. U of Oregon. 1990.

Shklovsky, Victor. "Art as Technique." *Critical Theory since Plato.* Ed. Hazard Adams. New York: Harcourt, 1992. 728–34.

Shumway, David. *Creating American Civilization: A Genealogy of American Literature as an Academic Discipline.* Minneapolis: U of Minnesota P, 1994.

Siebers, Tobin. *Cold War Criticism and the Politics of Skepticism.* New York: Oxford UP, 1993.

Silverman, Kaja. *Male Subjectivity at the Margins.* New York: Routledge, 1992.

Slotkin, Richard. *Gunfighter Nation: The Myth of the Frontier in Twentieth-Century America.* New York: Atheneum, 1992.

Slusser, George Edgar. *Between Two Worlds: The Literary Dilemma of Ursula K. Le Guin.* San Bernardino: Borgo, 1996.

Smith, Philip. "Unbuilding Walls: Human Nature and the Nature of Evolutionary and Political Theory in *The Dispossessed.*" *Ursula K. Le Guin.* Ed. Joseph D. Olander and Martin H. Greenberg. New York: Taplinger, 1979. 77–96.

Solotaroff, Theodore. "Bernard Malamud's Fiction: The Old Life and the New." *Commentary.* Copy. Malamud Papers. Library of Congress.

Spanier, Sandra. "Catherine Barkley and the Hemingway Code: Ritual and Survival in a Great War." *New Essays on "A Farewell to Arms."* Ed. Scott Donaldson. New York: Cambridge UP, 1990. 75–108.

———. "Hemingway's Unknown Soldier: Catherine Barkley, the Critics, and the Farewell to Arms." *Modern Critical Interpretations: "A Farewell to Arms."* Ed. Harold Bloom. New Haven: Chelsea House, 1987. 131–48.

Spitzer, Ralph. Letter. *Chemical and Engineering News.* 27.5 (1949): 306–7.

———. Letters to Linus Pauling. 22 Apr. 1945, 9 Feb. 1949. Ava and Linus Pauling Papers. Valley Library. Oregon State U, Corvallis.

———. Testimony. "Hearings Before the Subcommittee to Investigate the Administration of the Internal Security Act and Other Internal Security Laws of the Committee on the Judiciary, United States Senate, Eighty-Third Congress". Part 12. 8, 9, and 11 June 1953. Washington, D.C., United States Printing Office, 1953.

Spivack, Charlotte. *Ursula K. Le Guin.* Boston: Twayne, 1984.

Spivak, Gayatri Chakravorty. *In Other Worlds: Essays in Cultural Politics.* New York: Methuen, 1987.

—— ——. *Outside in the Teaching Machine.* New York: Routledge, 1993.

Stauffer, Helen. *Mari Sandoz. Story Catcher of the Plains.* Lincoln: U of Nebraska P, 1982.

Stephens, Robert O., ed. *Ernest Hemingway: The Critical Reception.* New York: Burt Franklin, 1977.

Strand, August L. The LaVallee and Spitzer Case, 1949–1952: Correspondence, 1949–1952. President's Office Records, Reel 84. University Archives. Oregon State U, Corvallis.

Studlar, Gaylyn. *This Mad Masquerade: Stardom and Masculinity in the Jazz Age.* New York: Columbia UP, 1996.

Teller, James David. *Louis Agassiz, Scientist and Teacher.* Columbus: Ohio State UP, 1947.

Tenney, Senator Jack B. *Cry Brotherhood! Condensed from the Tenney Reports on World Zionism.* Sacramento: Standard, 1965.

———. *Zion's Fifth Column.* Tujunga. Standard, 1953.

Tharp, Louise Hall. *Adventurous Alliance: The Story of the Agassiz Family of Boston.* Boston: Little, 1959.

Theoharis, Athan G., ed. *Beyond the Hiss Case: The FBI, Congress, and the Cold War.* Philadelphia: Temple UP, 1982.

Theweleit, Klaus. "The Bomb's Womb." *Gendering War Talk.* Ed. Miriam Cooke and Angela Woollacott. Princeton: Princeton UP, 1993.

———. *Male Fantasies.* Vol. 1. *Women Floods Bodies History.* Vol. 2. *Male Bodies: Psychoanalyzing the White Terror.* Minneapolis: U Minnesota P, 1987–89.

Thomas, Calvin. *Male Matters: Masculinity, Anxiety, and the Male Body on the Line.* Urbana: U of Illinois P, 1996.

Thompson, E. P. *Exterminism and the Cold War.* New Left Books, 1982.

Tompkins, Jane. *West of Everything.* New York: Oxford UP, 1992.

Townsend, Kim. *Manhood at Harvard: William James and Others.* New York: Norton, 1996.

Trilling, Lionel. *The Middle of the Journey.* New York: Viking, 1947.

———. "On the Modern Element in Modern Literature." *The Partisan Review Anthology.* Ed. William Phillips and Philip Rahv. New York: Holt, 1962. 263–79.

Tyler, Lisa. "Ernest Hemingway's Date Rape Story: Sexual Trauma in 'Up in Michigan.'" *Hemingway Review* 13.2 (1994): 1–11.

Vizenor, Gerald, ed. *Narrative Chance: Postmodern Discourse on Native American Indian Literatures*. Albuquerque: U of New Mexico P, 1989.

———. *The Trickster of Liberty: Tribal Heirs to a Wild Baronage*. Minneapolis: U of Minnesota P, 1988.

Wagner-Martin, Linda, ed. *Ernest Hemingway: Five Decades of Criticism*. East Lansing: Michigan State UP, 1974.

———. *Ernest Hemingway: Six Decades of Criticism*. East Lansing: Michigan State UP, 1987.

Wald, Alan. *The New York Intellectuals: The Rise and Decline of the Anti-Stalinist Left from the 1930s to the 1980s*. Chapel Hill: U of North Carolina P, 1987.

Wald, Priscilla. "Terms of Assimilation: Legislating Subjectivity in the Emerging Nation." *Cultures of United States Imperialism*. Durham: Duke UP, 1993. 59–84.

Warner, Marina. *Alone of All Her Sex: The Myth and the Cult of the Virgin Mary*. London: Weidenfeld, 1976.

Wayne, Katherine Ross. "Redefining Moral Education: Life, Le Guin, and Language." Diss. U of Oregon, 1993.

Webb, Walter Prescott. *The Great Plains*. New York: Grosset, 1931.

Weber, Ronald. *Hemingway's Art of Non-Fiction*. London: Macmillan, 1990.

Welch, James. *Killing Custer: The Battle of the Little Bighorn and the Fate of the Plains Indians*. New York: Norton, 1994.

White, Donna R. *Dancing with Dragons: Ursula K. Le Guin and the Critics*. Columbia: Camden, 1998.

White, G. Edward. *The Eastern Establishment and the Western Experience*. New Haven: Yale UP, 1968.

Whitfield, Stephen J. *The Culture of the Cold War*. Baltimore: Johns Hopkins UP, 1991.

Whitlow, Roger. *Cassandra's Daughters: The Women in Hemingway*. Westport: Greenwood, 1984.

Wicks, Stephen. *Warriors and Wildmen: Men, Masculinity, and Gender*. Westport: Bergin, 1996.

Wilford, Hugh. *The New York Intellectuals: From Vanguard to Institution*. New York: Manchester UP, 1995.

Williams, William Appleman. *American-Russian Relations, 1781–1947*. New York: Rinehart, 1952.

Williams, William Carlos. *The Embodiment of Knowledge*. Ed. and introd. Ron Loewinsohn. New York: New Directions, 1974.

Wills, Garry. *John Wayne's America: The Politics of Celebrity*. New York: Simon, 1997.

———. "John Wayne's Body." *New Yorker* (19 Aug. 1996): 39–49.

Wimsatt, W. K. *The Verbal Icon: Studies in the Meaning of Poetry*. Lexington: UP of Kentucky, 1954.

Wister, Owen. *The Virginian: A Horseman of the Plains*. 1902. Boston: Houghton, 1968.

Young, Philip. *Ernest Hemingway*. New York: Rinehart, 1952.

———. "Hemingway: The Writer in Decline." *Hemingway: A Revaluation*. Ed. Donald R. Noble. Troy: Whitston, 1983. 225–39.

Young-Bruehl, Elizabeth. *Hannah Arendt: For Love of the World*. New Haven: Yale UP, 1982.

Index

abjection, 7, 26; and fascism, 38; in "long telegram," 24–26, in *Old Jules*, 139–40, 141

Abraham Lincoln Brigade, 65, 85, 93

Adorno, Theodor, 43, 99, 177

aesthetic, 32, 33, 84–85, 136, 172

African-Americans, 12, 38, 49, 52

Agassiz, Louis, 34, 73–76, 85, 86

Alcott, Louisa May, 191

Aldridge, John, 61

alienation, 33, 43, 46, 48, 182

Althusser, Louis, 49

American Association of University Professors (AAUP), 115–16, 121, 126; on academic freedom, 110, 118

American Chemical Society, 120

American Civil Liberties Union (ACLU), 123

anarchy, 139, 190, 192–93; and communism, 189; and revolution, 174–75

anticommunism, 22, 44, 45, 98, 108, 129; and anti-Semitism, 7, 51; as banality, 99; coalition of, 5, 28, 48, 119; and fascism, 8, 112; scapegoating logic of, 1, 9–10, 50–51, 53, 122

antihero, 9, 15, 102

anti-Semitism, 7, 49, 51, 102, 129

Arendt, Hannah, 37, 51, 99

Armstrong, Nancy, 224n.19

Austin, Mary, 150

Autry, Gene, 7

Baker, Carlos, 64

banality, 30, 51, 99, 108, 110, 124

Barlowe, Jamie, 84

Barr, Marleen S., 199

Bateson, Mary Catherine, 200

Baym, Nina: "Melodramas of Beset Manhood," 11–13, 21, 66

Bederman, Gail, 69, 212–13n.11

Bellow, Saul, 101

beloved community, 190–91

Benjamin, Walter: on art and class struggle, 99–100; the storyteller, 44, 97, 173

Bercovitch, Sacvan, 185

Berkman, Alexander, 28

Bhabha, Homi K., 133; and mimicry, 150; and postcolonial hybridity, 17, 149, 170; and subjectivity, 49; and time, 151, 224n.13

Bierstadt, Albert, 40

body, 26–28, 198; organizations as, 24–25

Book of the Month Club (BOMC), 30, 98, 164, 165–66

Booth, Wayne, 187

Brininstool, E. A., 166

Brooks, Cleanth, 3, 34, 54, 108

Brown, Don: and the International Longshore and Warehouse Union (ILWU), 115

Bryant, Louise, 175

Burroughs, John, 75

Bush, Vannevar: and the "endless frontier," 19, 203

Butler, Judith, 2, 26, 198, 211n.1

Caldicott, Helen, 187

Cambridge History of American Literature, 52

Carver, Raymond, 201

Cather, Willa, 32, 38, 165

censorship, 53, 90, 93, 204; of the Left,

Suzanne Clark is a professor of English at the University of Oregon, where she teaches modern literature, literary theory, and rhetoric. She is the author of *Sentimental Modernism: Women Writers and the Revolution of the Word* and of articles and essays on feminist rhetoric, the sentimental, Julia Kristeva, Kay Boyle, Edna St. Vincent Millay, Hart Crane, Ernest Hemingway, Bernard Malamud, and others.

BAKER & TAYLOR